POSTCOLONIAL CRITICISM AND
BIBLICAL INTERPRETATION

POSTCOLONIAL CRITICISM AND BIBLICAL INTERPRETATION

R. S. Sugirtharajah

OXFORD
UNIVERSITY PRESS

This book has been printed digitally and produced in a standard specification
in order to ensure its continuing availability

OXFORD
UNIVERSITY PRESS

Great Clarendon Street, Oxford OX2 6DP

Oxford University Press is a department of the University of Oxford.
It furthers the University's objective of excellence in research, scholarship,
and education by publishing worldwide in

Oxford New York

Auckland Cape Town Dar es Salaam Hong Kong Karachi
Kuala Lumpur Madrid Melbourne Mexico City Nairobi
New Delhi Shanghai Taipei Toronto
With offices in
Argentina Austria Brazil Chile Czech Republic France Greece
Guatemala Hungary Italy Japan South Korea Poland Portugal
Singapore Switzerland Thailand Turkey Ukraine Vietnam

Oxford is a registered trade mark of Oxford University Press
in the UK and in certain other countries

Published in the United States
by Oxford University Press Inc., New York

© R. S. Sugirtharajah 2002

The moral rights of the author have been asserted

Database right Oxford University Press (maker)

Reprinted 2009

ISBN 978-0-19-875269-1

ACKNOWLEDGEMENTS

Many people have helped me in writing this book.

I would like to thank all those at the Oxford University Press. Angela Griffin who first supported the idea of this book, and Fiona Kinnear, Jo Stanbridge, Matthew Cotton, and Sarah Hyland, who expertly steered it through the different stages of its production; Lynn Childres for copy-editing the manuscript with assiduity and humour; Heung Soon Park for photocopying kilos of articles; the staff of the Orchard Learning Centre— Michael Gale, Deborah Drury, Jane Saunders, Pauline Hartley, Rachel Hayhow, Julie Farruggia, Dianne McCann, Celia Evans, and Judith Davies for their ever friendly and helpful service; Cecil Hargreaves for his invaluable help with the sixth chapter; and Markus Vinzent, the head of the Department, for his encouragement and support.

Besides the people mentioned above, there is a coterie of people who have become part of my publishing project and have over the years shown deep interest in all that I do. Dan O'Connor, with whom I have discussed many aspects of the book and who has not only embellished the script but also has saved it from many errors and infelicities. Ralph Broadbent has always been at hand whenever I ran into computing problems. Lorraine Smith went through some parts of the book with her usual diligence.

Finally to my wife Sharada without whose intellectual support and care nothing would have been possible.

R.S.S.

CONTENTS

INTRODUCTION   1

PART I: POSTCOLONIAL CONSTRUALS

1. CHARTING THE AFTERMATH: A REVIEW OF
   POSTCOLONIAL CRITICISM   11
   The arrival of postcolonial criticism   14
   Creative literature   18
   The contours of postcolonial criticism   21
   Clarification of the lexicon   24
   Postcolonialism and biblical studies   25
   Empire and theological reflections   26
   Postcolonial criticism and cognate disciplines—feminism   28
   Global intentions and postcolonial concerns   30
   Is the United States postcolonial?   33
   Concerns, temptations, conclusions   36

2. REDRESS, REGENERATION, REDEMPTION: A
   SURVEY OF BIBLICAL INTERPRETATION   43
   Dissident readings   44
   Resistant readings   52
   Heritagist readings   55
   Nationalistic readings   63
   Liberationist readings   65
   Dissentient readings   67
   Concluding remarks   70

3. CODING AND DECODING: POSTCOLONIAL
   CRITICISM AND BIBLICAL INTERPRETATION   74
   Orientalist tendencies   75
   Decoding texts   79
   Jesus and the colonial context   86

Colonial trauma and madness: The case of the Gerasene
Demoniac   91
Transcending the text, visualizing the reality   94
Propagandist literature or confessional writings   97

4. CONVERGENT TRAJECTORIES? LIBERATION
   HERMENEUTICS AND POSTCOLONIAL BIBLICAL
   CRITICISM   103
   Marks of classic liberation hermeneutics   104
   Gutiérrez's Job   107
   Tamez's Paul   110
   Liberation hermeneutics and its entanglements   112
   Religion and liberation   115
   Postcolonialism and liberation hermeneutics as companions
   in struggle   117

PART II: POSTCOLONIAL PREOCCUPATIONS

5. THE VERSION ON WHICH THE SUN NEVER SETS:
   THE ENGLISH BIBLE AND ITS AUTHORIZING
   TENDENCIES   127
   The context of the English Bible   129
   The rise of the English Bible   131
   The Englishness of the Bible   134
   Simple people and the simplicity of the Scripture: The
   Geneva Bible   139
   A text for the empire: A post-imperial footnote   144
   Colonial parallels   145
   Concluding remarks   150

6. BLOTTING THE MASTER'S COPY: LOCATING BIBLE
   TRANSLATIONS   155
   Confusing and confused tongues   156
   Dismissing and embracing   161
   Translations and their preoccupations   164

A postcolonial gaze at the New Revised Standard Version
(NRSV)   168
Some notes on postcolonial biblical translation   171

7. HERMENEUTICS IN TRANSIT: DIASPORA AND
    INTERPRETATION   179
    Defining diaspora   180
    Postcolonialism and diaspora   183
    Uprootings of text and persons: Diaspora and biblical
    interpretation   185
    Diasporic hermeneutics: Some markers   190
    Some concluding remarks   195

    Afterword   200
    References   208
    Index of biblical references   225
    Index of names and subjects   227

INTRODUCTION

The trouble with texts, especially if they are ancient and sacred, is that they can be summoned and assigned meanings to prove or legitimize any cause, theory, or perspective. Interpretative history is littered with such examples. When European colonialism was at its peak, biblical texts were taken out of context to prove biblical sanction for such a venture. Let me extract a gem from colonial history. When, for instance, Britain gradually gained power and expanded its territorial control in the north, south, east, and west, such an expansion was seen as the fulfilment of biblical expectation. New Foundland, Britain's first colony in the West, was acquired in 1583. Territorial gains were made in the East in the sixteenth century. The most northerly of Britain's possessions, Canada, was added in the eighteenth century and its southern dominions—Australia, New Zealand, and South Africa—were colonized in the early nineteenth century. Such a territorial acquisition was perceived by Bernard Bateson as Britain fulfilling the prediction of Gen. 28: 14: 'Thou shalt spread abroad to the west, and to the east, and to the north, and to the south' (Bateson 1947: 63). What this volume attempts to do is to go beyond such a facile reading of texts and to look deeply at the way colonialism interconnects with texts and interpretation.

Besides postmodernism, postcolonial studies have been rapidly gaining attention as notoriously argumentative critical categories of our time.[1] As a critical theory, they have been able to magnify and draw attention to the importance and presence of minority and subjugated voices which have been lost, overlooked, or suppressed in histories and narratives. In disciplines like English, History, Anthropology, Cultural Studies, postcolonial critical categories have already forged productive, and at times uneasy alliances, and have come to assume such a significance that they are in danger of becoming mainstream. Recently medievalists, too, have been subjecting the positioning of race, class, nation, Europe, and Christianity in the narratives of the Middle Ages, to postcolonial theories (J. Cohen 2000). Biblical studies has been a reluctant entrant to the arena. The world of biblical interpretation is a calm and sedate world. To a great extent biblical interpretation is about taking refuge in the study of the biblical past, and occasionally it is about reassuring the faithful when their faith is rattled by new moral questions. Although there is a reluctance to admit it, the liberal interpretation is largely confessional and pastoral in its tone and direction. The world of postcolonialism, by contrast, is about change and struggle. It is about being conjectural, hesitant, and interventionist. This book is a modest attempt to bridge the gap between these two discourses.

Next, let me rectify some misconceptions. At the outset I must make it clear that postcolonialism has no fixed starting date. Unfortunately, the term 'postcolonialism' purports a perfect rupture between the earlier period of colonization and the present period of decolonization. Certainly, postcolonialism did not dawn when the last bugle of the empire had been sounded, or on the morning after India got its independence, or when Ghana gained a new national airline. One cannot date or periodize the shift between the two any more than one can specify the progression from feudalism to modernity, or from modernity to postmodernity.

The first use of the term, according to the *Oxford English Dictionary*, occurred in 1959 when the British newspaper, *Daily Telegraph*, used it in reference to India which gained its independence in 1947.[2] Since then it has been fairly common to term the former colonized countries of Asia and Africa, the Caribbean and the Pacific as postcolonial as they become self-governing states. Recently there has been a development and shift in the meaning of the term. It has moved from a fairly common understanding as a linear chronological sequence to a much more catholic and more diverse sense, as an index of historical and cultural changes. Despite the formal withdrawal of European nations, the term 'postcolonial' is thought to be an appropriate one because of the persistence of newer forms of economic and cultural colonialism which keep a number of newly independent states in check and constrain their freedom. The term, as it is now used, whether referring to textual practices, or psychological conditions, or historical processes, depends on who uses it and what purpose it serves.

It is worth reiterating that postcolonial discourse did not start out with that appellation. Its roots go back to the historical legacy of European colonialism. It manifested itself in different forms before it assumed its current position and significance. There is a fairly general acknowledgement that it was the European expansion and its cultural and psychological impact that resulted in a hive of literary activity which evolved into different genres. Sometimes the interaction came about through creative literature, and sometimes through resistance political discourse. How these two genres, the result of the meeting and interacting of two or more cultures, gradually metamorphosed into and came to be baptized under the new nomenclature 'postcolonialism', is a long and protracted process which I will explicate elsewhere in this volume.

In this book, I continue to use the term 'Third World' which is a troubling one for many. I have sufficiently explained elsewhere the reason for retaining it. Without rehearsing the whole argument, the term is used not in a negative or geographical sense but in a rehabilitated sense, as a semantic metaphor to convey the power of imbalance between those who are politically, culturally, and economically strong, and those who are weak. It is a hermeneutical contrivance to capture the mood of a particular way of existence and experience:

It is about a people who have been left out and do not have the power to shape their future. It describes a relationship marked, in the past, by power and mediated through old colonial ties and, currently, through the cultural and economic presence of neocolonialism. Such iniquitous relationships exist both globally and locally. In this sense, there is already a Third World in the First World, just as there is a First World in the Third World—the world of the economic and political elite who are in collusion with the world powers. Ultimately, what is important is not the nomenclature but the idea it conveys and the analysis it provides. (Fabella and Sugirtharajah 2000: p. xxii)

It is too simplistic to assume that colonialism was confined to European nations. There were other forms of colonialism before and after the European expansion and withdrawal. There is also internal colonialism within countries which were once under colonial rule, where indigenous people, women, and their histories and cultures have been annexed and annihilated, this time not by the outside invader but by local elites. The dangers and temptations of these colonialisms need a closer look and entail a different exercise, a task to be undertaken in the future. The focus of this volume is on European colonialism and its indelible impact on the peoples of Asia, Africa, Latin America, the Caribbean, and the Pacific.

About this volume

The book has two parts. Part I 'Postcolonial construals' opens with a chapter 'Charting the aftermath: A review of postcolonial criticism', which provides an overview of postcolonial discourse, a definition of terms, a historical background to its arrival on the hermeneutical scene, and its earlier incarnations as resistance literature and creative writing before it became a diagnostic tool in the hands of academics. It also gives an overview of current practitioners of the discourse and their procedures. It brings to the fore often overlooked works in postcolonial discourse such as that of the Sri Lankan cultural theoretician, Ananda Coomarswamy, and the Ugandan novelist, Akiki Nyabongo. The chapter also discusses postcolonialism's relation to two significant critical movements of our time, feminism and globalization. There is also an examination of the vexed question of the status of the United States of America in postcolonial discourse, making a case for its inclusion because of the genocidal policies of the United States both in the past and the present, and its current position as a superpower. A central aspect of the chapter is its scrutinizing of a rare critique of colonialism from a theological perspective. Acknowledging the unwieldiness of the subject, the chapter focuses only on issues relevant to biblical studies.

Chapter 2, 'Redress, regeneration, redemption: A survey of biblical interpretation', traces the different modes of biblical interpretation. Deviating from the customary fashion of placing biblical interpretation within the modernistic project and categorizing it as 'historical', 'literary', and 'contextual', I link it with colonialism and demonstrate how interpretations from different continents are intertwined with colonialism and how this colonial connection manifests itself in their various appropriations of the Bible. The chapter identifies varied readings—dissident, resistant, heritagist, liberationist, nationalist, and dissentient—as responses to colonialism and to the after effects, neocolonialism. What is noticeable from these readings is how different stages of colonialism, or its aftermath, produced varying relationships to the Bible—from appropriation to subversion.

Although these six readings do not necessarily follow a straightforward or linear historical development, they nicely set the scene for postcolonial biblical interpretation.

Chapter 3 'Coding and decoding: Postcolonial criticism and biblical interpretation', tries to put into practice and demonstrate how postcolonial criticism works with biblical texts. The first part of the chapter uses Stuart Hall's categorization, 'hegemonic', 'professional', 'negotiated', and 'oppositional' as a way of identifying ideological overtones entrenched in biblical texts. It examines Jesus's attitude to the colonial presence of his day, and also looks at the Markan account of the Gerasene Demoniac as an example of a narrative prompted and permeated by colonial intentions and terminology. It also provides contours for postcolonial biblical criticism. The overbearing thrust of this chapter is that postcolonial biblical criticism as such does not render meanings or answers but provides the ground rules for arriving at potential meanings. The chapter also contains self-help exercises for those who wish to pursue postcolonial biblical criticism further.

The last chapter in this part, 'Convergent trajectories? Liberation hermeneutics and postcolonial biblical criticism', looks at the relationship between two of the most energizing critical categories to take up the cause of Third World people, liberation hermeneutics and postcolonialism. The chapter draws attention to the enslavement of liberation hermeneutics to some of the negative aspects of modernism and how this restricts its influence and thwarts its further development. It points out how, in spite of differences, both disclosures can cooperate for the greater benefit of the people they represent and serve.

Part II 'Postcolonial preoccupations' starts with a chapter entitled 'The version on which the sun never sets: The English Bible and its authorizing tendencies'. It looks at the English Bible and examines the cultural, political, and religious background to the emergence of the vernacular Bible in English, and the final triumph of the King James Version as the Bible of the English people and its eventual ascendancy as the book of the empire. The chapter ends with a glimpse at how the standard bearer of the empire and the conveyer of God's word was strangely dislocated and its authorizing tendencies punctured. 'The Book' finally ends up as a book among books. The next two chapters take up two important postcolonial concerns—translation and diaspora.

Chapter 6, 'Blotting the master's copy: Locating Bible translations', investigates the connection between colonialism and Bible translation. It examines how Bible translation was undertaken in a missionary context where imbalances among the languages were visible, and how missionaries perceived and made use of these 'vulgar tongues' to convey God's word. As an exercise in how modern translations fare when subjected to postcolonial scrutiny, the chapter investigates the New Revised Standard Version (NRSV) and brings to the fore some of the colonial intentions embedded in a translation which is in other respects superior to the others currently available. It concludes with some markers for postcolonial translation.

The last chapter, 'Hermeneutics in transit: Diaspora and interpretation', begins with a summary of how the term 'diaspora' has changed over the years from being a religious term in the Jewish-Christian context to being reconfigured as secular in postcolonial discourse. The chapter also evaluates the proposals and practices of the nascent but rapidly emerging sub-discipline, diasporic biblical hermeneutics. The chapter ends with a proposal for a hybridized form of textual interpretation.

The volume contains material reflecting patriarchal, gender, religious, and racial bias in language. These are mainly found in quotations which come from an era where discriminatory language was absent and its insensitivity not widely recognized. The easiest thing would be to sanitize them of their biases and make them look pretty and palatable. But they all have been retained as an index of the remarkable change in our thinking over the years. The biblical quotations come from different versions of the Bible, indicating that there is no one supreme version, and none which can be definitive, and that each version in its own way elucidates the word.

Those who are in the business of interpretation know that reading is a complicated matter. There is an ongoing tension between a single, authoritarian reading and multiple and emancipatory readings of a text. This volume argues against a single dominant meaning and draws attention to the fact that both texts and interpreters have multiple contexts. Let me end with an Indian parable which encapsulates both potential and predicament, excitement and frustration, the simple and the complicated nature of interpretation which this volume hopes to convey:

A man who had seen a chameleon under a tree returned and said, 'I have seen a beautiful red chameleon under the tree.' Another said, 'I was there before you.

The chameleon was not red, but green. I have seen it with my own eyes.'A third said, 'I too know it well. I saw it before either of you, and it was neither red nor green, but—and I saw with my own eyes—it was blue.' Others declared it was yellow, or grey, and so on. Soon they began to quarrel among themselves as to who was correct. A man passing by asked what the trouble was. When he was told he said, 'I live under the very tree, and I know the chameleon well. All of you are right, everyone. The chameleon is sometimes green, sometimes blue, it is all colours by turn, and sometimes it is absolutely colourless.[3]

NOTES

1. For a vigorous debate among those from within and outside the field, see *Interventions: International Journal of Postcolonial Studies*, 1/1 (1998/9), 4–53 and 1/2 (1999), 255–90.
2. See *A Supplement to the Oxford English Dictionary*, iii (Oxford: Oxford University Press, 1982), 691.
3. Cited in Partha Chatterji's *The Nation and its Fragments: Colonial and Postcolonial Histories* (Delhi: Oxford University Press, 1995), 44.

PART I

POSTCOLONIAL CONSTRUALS

1

CHARTING THE AFTERMATH:
A REVIEW OF
POSTCOLONIAL CRITICISM

The colonialist likes neither theory nor theorists.

(Albert Memmi 1990: 136)

We are surrounded by theories. They grow as thick as trees around us, everyday new saplings sprout up among the hoary old veterans.

(In the Garden Secretly and Other Stories, Arasanayagam 2000: 87)

Postcolonial studies emerged as a way of engaging with the textual, historical, and cultural articulations of societies disturbed and transformed by the historical reality of colonial presence.[1] In this respect, in its earlier incarnation, postcolonialism was never conceived as a grand theory, but as creative literature and as a resistance discourse emerging in the former colonies of the Western empires. Postcolonialism as a methodological category and as a critical practice followed later. There were two aspects: first, to analyse the diverse strategies by which the colonizers constructed images of the colonized; and second, to study how the colonized themselves made use of and went beyond many of those strategies in order to articulate their identity, self-worth, and empowerment. Postcolonialism has been taking a long historical look at both old and new forms of domination. Its insight lies in understanding how the past informs the present.

As a field of enquiry, postcolonialism is not monolithic but rather a field which provides and caters to a variety of concerns, oppositional stances, and even contradictory positions. Nonetheless, it generates a noticeable theoretical strength. It provides valuable resources for thinking about those social, cultural, political, and historical contexts in which domestication takes place. As a style of inquiry, it emerged more or less simultaneously in a variety of disciplines including Anthropology, Geography, International Studies, History, English, Music, and Medieval Studies. When used in conjunction with 'theory' or 'criticism', the term 'postcolonialism' signifies a distinct methodological category and acts as a discursive force. In its reconsideration of colonialism and its aftermath, it draws on poststructuralism, Marxism, cultural studies, linguistics, and literary studies. In its application, postcolonial criticism differs not only from location to location but also from discipline to discipline. In his essay 'The Scramble for Post-Colonialism' Stephen Slemon remarks:

'Postcolonialism', as it is now used in its various fields, de-scribes a remarkably heterogenous set of subject positions, professional fields, and critical enterprises. It has been used as a way of ordering a critique of totalising forms of Western historicism; as a portmanteau term for a retooled notion of 'class'; as a subset of both postmodernism and post-structuralism (and conversely, as the condition from which those two structures of cultural logic and cultural critique themselves are seen to emerge); as the name for a condition of nativist longing in post-independence national groupings; as a cultural marker of non-residency for a Third World intellectual cadre; as the inevitable underside of a fractured and ambivalent discourse of colonialist power; as an oppositional form of 'reading practice'; and . . . as the name for a category of 'literary' activity which sprang from a new and welcome political energy going on within what used to be called 'Commonwealth' literary studies. (Slemon 1994: 16–17)

Postcolonialism is a discipline in which everything is contested, everything is contestable, from the use of terms to the defining of chronological boundaries. Postcolonialism, as one would expect, is a much disputed term. Inevitably it has chronological dimensions attached to it. In popular perception, postcolonialism is seen as a period which began in the 1960s after the demise of formal European colonialism following the struggle for independence waged by the colonized people. The term as used at present is ineluctably tied to modern European imperialism. It does not allow an understanding of colonialism outside modern European colonialism. It is seen as a condition of no longer being what one was, a colony but as finding a space in the world as a newly independent nation state, and its citizens referred to as postcolonials. In postcolonial discursive practice, several critics contend and recognize that, when it is used with a hyphen, 'post-colonial', the term is seen as indicating the historical period aftermath of colonialism, and without the hyphen, 'postcolonial', as signifying a reactive resistance discourse of the colonized who critically interrogate dominant knowledge systems in order to recover the past from the Western slander and misinformation of the colonial period, and who also continue to interrogate neo-colonizing tendencies after the declaration of independence. It is in this latter sense that the term will be employed in this volume. Homi Bhabha sums up what postcolonial criticism is about:

Postcolonial criticism bears witness to the unequal and uneven forces of cultural representation involved in the contest for political and social authority within the modern world order. Postcolonial perspectives emerge from the colonial testimony of Third World countries, and the discourses of 'minorities' within the geopolitical divisions of East and West, North and South. They intervene in those ideological discourses of modernity that attempt to give a hegemonic 'normality' to the uneven development and the differential, often disadvantaged, histories, of nations, races, communities, people. (Bhabha 1994: 171)

As with the case of the other critical category, postmodernism, which is no longer seen as implying a linear progression from modernism, but as a continuum, postcolonialism too is no longer perceived as a chronological progression from colonialism but as a perpetual set of critical possibilities which were already available with the formal advent of modern colonialism. It is an instrument or method of analysing situations where one social group dominated another.

One of the vexing questions which bedevils the debate is whether to treat postcolonialism as theory or as criticism. If one applies the Foucaultian parameter that theory is 'the deduction, on the basis of a number of axioms, of an abstract model applicable to an indefinite number of empirical descriptions',[2] then postcolonialism will not fit. Postcolonialism is essentially a style of enquiry, an insight or a perspective, a catalyst, a new way of life. As an enquiry, it instigates and creates possibilities, and provides a platform for the widest possible convergence of critical forces, of multi-ethnic, multi-religious, and multicultural voices, to assert their denied rights and rattle the centre. It is an assemblage of interests and attitudes and is remarkably productive because it offers a perspective complementing and in some ways transcending the

Enlightenment's modernizing project. As postcolonialism is not a theory in the strict sense of the term, but a collection of critical and conceptual attitudes, an apt description would be to term it criticism. Criticism is not an exact science, but an undertaking of social and political commitment which should not be reduced to or solidified into a dogma. It is always oppositional. Edward Said sees criticism 'as life-enhancing and constitutively opposed to every form of tyranny, domination, and abuse, its social goals are noncoercive knowledge produced in the interests of human freedom' (Said 1991: 29). Put at its simplest, criticism is always contextual; it is paradoxical, secular, and always open to its own contradictions and shortcomings. And, to cite Said again: 'I take criticism so seriously as to believe that, even in the very midst of a battle in which one is unmistakably on one side against another, there should be criticism, because there must be critical consciousness if there are to be issues, problems, values, even lives to be fought for' (Said 1991: 28). It is in this sense that 'postcolonial' is used in this volume.

The arrival of postcolonial criticism

Theorizing, contrary to popular perception, is not necessarily a Western phenomenon. Writers from the Third World have used abstract logic in narrative forms to intellectualize and analyse art, literature, and theatre. Indians and Chinese have evolved sophisticated and sustained analyses of how meaning is constructed in texts. For instance, Indians have a well-developed system of *śāstra paddhati*, 'which employs different interpretative instruments, including philosophy, grammar, etymology, logical reasoning, theory of meaning and metarules' (Kapoor 1998: 15).[3] Similarly, Barbara Christian has noted, people of colour have developed their own theorizing, using their experiences of the struggle of everyday life, distinct from the abstract theoretical fashion practised in the West. Her implication is that theories can arise not only in intellectual and academic institutions: 'I am inclined to say that our theorizing (and I intentionally use the verb rather than the noun) is often in narrative forms, in the stories we create, in riddles and proverbs, in the play with language, since dynamic rather than fixed ideas seem more to our liking' (Christian 1995: 457). The crucial question is not where theories originate or who owns them but whether they have diagnostic capabilities to promote the cause of the marginalized.

The considerable presence and recognition of postcolonial thinking in Western academia is due to the favourable intellectual environment for the rise of resistance theories in the 1980s. The arrival and acceptance of post-colonialism, especially in the United States, is noticeably different from that of any other minority discourse such as African-American, Chicano, gender, even though these interventionary disciplines share some common political preoccupations and theoretical presuppositions. Ethnic-minority studies were introduced into the US academy as a result of student demon-strations against white institutions which excluded minority cultures from college syllabi and racial minorities from the faculty and student bodies. Postcolonialism, on the other hand, according to Jenny Sharpe, 'constitutes an institutional reform from "within"' (Sharpe 2000: 108). The text which paved the way was Edward Said's *Orientalism*, published in 1978. Said defined 'Orientalism' as a Western way of 'dominating, restructuring, and having authority over the Orient' (Said 1985: 3). What was noticeably dif-ferent about Said's work was that it was able to establish the connection between the production of academic knowledge and colonialism, which earlier interpreters of the history of ideas failed to acknowledge and expose. The key to power is knowledge, and true power is held with the conviction that the ruler knows better than the ruled, and must convince the ruled that whatever the colonial master does is for the benefit of the ruled. The assumption undergirding this thinking is the belief that 'know-ledge of subject races or Orientals is what makes their management easy and profitable; knowledge gives power, more power requires more know-ledge, and so on in an increasingly profitable dialectic of information and control' (Said 1985: 36).

There are other factors, too, that promoted the arrival of postcolonial-ism. The 1980s saw the emergence of theorizing and literary analysis gain-ing a fresh lease in the academy. At a time when the socialist experiment advocated by the Soviet bureaucracy failed to produce the expected results, the fortunes of Marxist criticism took a deep dive, and, with the arrival of Reaganism and Thatcherism, a new form of literary analysis arrived on the scene. Reflecting the multicultural mood of the period, these literary analyses and theorizings were irredeemably eclectic, hybridized, and cross-disciplinary in character and in execution. They borrowed critically and fused imaginatively from a variety of disciplines ranging from philosophy, psychology, politics, anthropology, to linguistics (McLeod 2000: 23–4).

Though postcolonial criticism was not minted in the academy, the imprimatur accorded by the guild raised its status and authority. In the current theoretical foundry, the names of Edward Said, Homi Bhabha, and Gayatri Spivak, occupy an important place, and they are generally spoken of as being influential in fomenting the theory. The trouble with such a notion is that none of these writers, however indispensable they are to the theoretical cause, ever set out to be postcolonial in their writings. It was only after postcolonial analysis had reached its momentum that Said, Spivak, and Bhabha were identified and hailed as instigators. The other difficulty with such a narrowing of the list of personalities is that it overlooks anti-colonial liberationist writings which emerged outside the academy long before they were accorded academic appreciation. They were considered lacking in academic pedigree. These discourses were spearheaded by Amilcar Cabral, Frantz Fanon, C. L. R. James, Aimé Césaire, Albert Memmi, and Ananda Coomarswamy, who were openly anti-colonial in their writings and praxis. Each in his own way tried to articulate the psychological, cultural, and political damage that European colonialism had inflicted on millions of people. Recently, there is a move to bring others into the postcolonial framework, figures like the African-American W. E. B. Du Bois, and the Cuban José Marti, both intellectuals with socialist leanings, who in their literary and political activities engaged in national emancipation for African-Americans and Cubans, and denounced the global imperial policies of the United States (Cooppan 2000: 1–35).

The articulations of these earlier writers are too extensive to be dealt with here in a way that would do justice to their work. More importantly, they have been analysed perceptively elsewhere.[4] But to give a flavour, let me briefly look at the works of two writers, one pre-eminent, the other less so. Frantz Fanon was born in Martinique. He was a psychiatrist and activist who involved himself in the Algerian War of Independence. In his writings, Fanon argued that colonialism instilled deep in the minds of the native population that before its advent their history was dominated by savagery and internecine tribal warfare, and that if the colonialists were to leave they would fall back into 'barbarism, degradation and bestiality' (Fanon 1990: 169).[5] The trick of colonialism, according to Fanon, was to project itself as a mother, but not as a gentle and loving mother who sheltered and steered her child from situations surrounded with hostility, but rather as a mother who reigned over and restrained her wayward child from practising evil deeds. To put it bluntly, what the colonial mother did was to 'protect the child from itself, from its ego, and from its physiology, its biology and its own unhappiness which is its very essence' (Fanon 1990: 170). In other words, for colonialism, it was not merely sufficient for the colonizer to manage the present and the future of the native population, their past also must be rewritten, creating a cultural vacuum:

[C]olonialism is not simply content to impose its rule upon the present and the future of a dominated country. Colonialism is not satisfied merely with holding a people in its grip and emptying the native's brain of all form and content. By a kind of a perverted logic, it turns to the past of the oppressed people, and distorts, disfigures and destroys it. (Fanon 1990: 169)

For colonialism the vast continent of Africa was a 'haunt of savages', replete with 'superstitions and fanaticisms', and was held in contempt and cursed by God. Fanon's answer was to urge Africans to recover their history and reassert their identity and culture. Fanon advocated the reclamation of aspects of the past culture conscious of the fact that an idealized past can be problematic. For him there was no point in reviving 'mummified fragments' of the past because, when people are involved in a struggle against colonialism, the significance of the past changes. The aim was not to replace colonial European culture with an uncomplicated, celebratory, and uncritical negro culture (his word). For Fanon, culture and nation are not isolated entities but are at the core of every national and cultural consciousness which develops into an international cosmopolitan consciousness. His work provides tools for the former colonized to conceptualize and take control of their identities and rectify the falsification and harm done by colonial misrepresentation.

In a list riddled with African personalities, the work that is often overlooked in postcolonial critical thinking is that of a Sri Lankan, Ananda Coomaraswamy. His essays on nationalism were published in 1909, at the height of classical colonialism. He recognized that what was needed more than political and economic freedom was cultural liberation. Anticipating Ngũgĩ wa Thiong'o, Coomaraswamy called for an active decolonizing of the mind:

For this struggle is much more than a political conflict. It is a struggle for spiritual and mental freedom from the domination of an alien ideal. In such a conflict, political and economic victory are but half the battle; for an India, 'free in name, but subdued by Europe in her inmost soul' would ill justify the price of freedom. It is not so much the material, as the moral and spiritual subjugation of Indian civilisation that in the end impoverishes humanity. (Coomaraswamy 1909: p.i)

For Coomaraswamy, the regeneration of India had to be expressed in art and spirituality. He spoke about nationalism too, but he saw it as a service and a duty to be undertaken by the subjugated people.

These brief descriptions of Fanon and Coomaraswamy are little more than caricatures, but they point to the significant contribution of their work.

Creative literature

Unlike metropolitan practitioners of theory who concentrate on representation of the other in colonial history and literature, the liberationist writings of Fanon, Memmi, C. L. R. James, and others like them, were concerned with studying how decolonization destabilized the exotic images fixed within the Western imagination. It is crucial to acknowledge these writers as intellectual antecedents of postcolonial studies, though they cannot be pressed into the service of a simple and single reading of colonialism because, before academic institutions became infatuated with their work and bestowed recognition, their concerns and constituencies were varied and specific.

Along with resistant discourse, creative literature also, which emerged from Commonwealth countries, played a critical role as a precursor to the current postcolonial thinking. Current studies of postcolonial work focus largely on the writings of Chinua Achebe, Ngũgĩ wa Thiong'o, Wole Soyinka, and V. S. Naipaul. One novel which has been overlooked in postcolonial discussion and is relevant to our purpose, is Akiki Nyabongo's *Africa Answers Back* (Nyabongo 1936).[6] Its importance lies in the fact that it contains a heady mixture of colonialism and the Bible. The author, a descendant of the Toro kings, was born in Uganda. The novel is autobiographical, and mixes both fact and fabrication, chronicle and memoirs. The story is set in Buganda at the turn of the nineteenth century and spans fifty years. As the title indicates, it a subversive African tale which talks back to colonial discourse by rupturing and remoulding it. The novel reverses a seemingly successful missionary story into a narrative of the empowerment and emancipation of the missionized. The novel is about the hero, Abala Stanley Mujungu, and his journey of self-discovery as he tries to straddle both the ancient culture his parents want to maintain, and the modern Western culture introduced by the missionary, Hubert, and how the latter transformed Mujungu from being an exemplary mission-school student into an African rebel.

The interesting aspect of the novel, for us, takes place in part III, where the text introduced by the missionary—the Bible, which symbolizes and legitimizes Western culture—comes under a heavy hermeneutical bombardment. Curiously, the Bible, the Englishman's book, loses its authority at the beginning of the novel, when Stanley, the first missionary to Buganda, reads the story of the Israelites crossing the Red Sea to the King. The King's response is, 'Hm, that's just like our story, because when the Gods came from the north they reached the River Kira and the waters stopped flowing, so that they could get across. Isn't it strange that his story and ours should be the same' (Nyabongo 1936: 10). Instead of confronting and dislodging the heathen world, now the 'White man's mythology' as the King called it, has a parallel story, to vie with the 'heathen' version, for attention and authority. At school, besides the Bible, Mujungu is introduced to other monumental texts of Western literary supremacy, Gibbon's *Rise and Fall of the Roman Empire* and the works of William Shakespeare. But it is over the Bible that hermeneutical contestations take place. Mujungu, who has acquired the modernist habit of writing and reading, and, more importantly, rational thinking, at a school run by the missionary Hubert, refuses to succumb to interpretations imposed by him, thereby challenging monopoly of the interpretative authority enjoyed by the missionary. The Bible's legitimizing power melts away on two particular occasions.

One such is when Hubert tries to introduce biblical stories to the class, with the condescending attitude that his students will not 'grasp the full significance of the White Man's Bible' (Nyabongo 1936: 223). Whatever the story, Jonah, Adam and Eve, or the Virgin Birth, Mujungu continues to question it. He disputes the Jonah story by asking 'how could a whale swallow a man whole?' And wonders 'how could a man go through so

small a throat unharmed?' (Nyabongo 1936: 224). He questions the story of
the Creation in Genesis by pointing out that 'no woman came from a
man's rib'. His biggest suspicion is reserved for the story of the Virgin
Birth. For him it is a fairy-tale, since it was recorded only by two of the
evangelists and in any case it was a biologically impossible feat: 'Sir, how
could the seed of a man get into the womb of a woman without intercourse?' (Nyabongo 1936: 226). When Hubert tries to get out of the difficulty by saying that Mary had two husbands, God and Joseph, Mujungu's
immediate riposte is: 'You won't baptize the children of men with two
wives, yet John baptized Jesus' (Nyabongo 1936: 226), an obvious reference
to the missionary practice of not baptizing Africans engaged in
polygamous relationships.

The second occasion is when Mujungu is on holiday, and he reads aloud
from the Hebrew Scripture about King Solomon and his seven hundred
wives and three hundred concubines, in order to prove to his parents that
he has acquired the new skill of reading. Ati, his father and his wives are
astonished to find that the practice of polygamy, the very practice condemned elsewhere in the Englishman's book, is approved of here. The
book and the missionary are as they see it now exposed for their double
standards. After hearing the story read, one of the wives of Ati exclaims:
'Ha, ha, your son will find him out. He can read his books, too! The
Reverend Mr. Hubert can't tell us lies any more' (Nyabongo 1936: 207).

The final straw is when Mujungu, deprived of his holidays as a punishment for asking impertinent questions, accompanies the missionary as his
interpreter on his visits to different churches. Mujungu uses his experience
in the mission school and his knowledge of the Bible to warn his listeners
that Hubert's intentions to teach people 'the new ways' will result in dis-
respect to their elders and their culture. Handicapped by not being able to
speak the native language, the missionary accepted defeat and announces
that further evangelizing mission activities are over (Nyabongo 1936: 234).[7]

Arguing from what he regarded as a commonsensical and rational point
of view, Mujungu, undermines, if only temporarily, God's word, the
English book. Hubert, instead of engaging in dialogue with Mujungu,
dismisses him as jeopardizing evangelization and retreats into the safety of
authoritative dogma and the missionary homiletical practice of denunci-
ation: 'There is no hope for you. You are dangerous to the faith of the rest
of the class. I shall pray for you' (Nyabongo 1936: 228). Hubert found that

Mujungu had read 'too much' and the only way to stop him from further 'misreadings' is to ask him to withdraw from the class. It was only by refusing to dialogue with Mujungu, that Hubert managed to maintain his own authority and pre-empted any further question: 'I will not tolerate your talking back to me, as you have just done. I am the master of the school' (Nyabongo 1936: 218–19). The superiority of the Christian text is established through Hubert's assertion of his power as headmaster of the school rather than by cogently presenting its case. Hubert's desire to produce spiritually Christian Africans, even though, as he saw it, they looked like heathens, ends with his decision to make no further converts.

It was the resistant discourse of political activists and imaginative literature by novelists such as Nyabongo which sowed the seeds of the current postcolonial thinking.

The contours of postcolonial criticism

What postcolonialism did was to introduce power and politics into the world of literary criticism in such a way as to expose how some literature, art, and drama were implicitly linked to European colonialism. As indicated earlier, the text which initiated this kind of thinking was Edward Said's *Orientalism* (Said 1985).[8] Though not always consistent, the core proposal of the book was to expose the connection between imperial power and the production of literary and historical traditions. According to John McLeod, this literary analysis manifested itself in three ways (McLeod 2000: 17–29).

First, there was a rereading of Western canonical texts to detect conscious or dormant colonial elements in them. This involved scouring texts, some of which were set in a colonial context, as in the case of Conrad's *Heart of Darkness*, or which, as in the case of Jane Austen's *Mansfield Park*, apparently had nothing to do with colonialism but unwittingly espoused colonialist intentions.

Secondly, literary analysis encouraged critics to search not just literary but other texts such as historical discourses, official documents, missionary reports, to see how the colonized were represented and how they resisted or accepted colonial values. It was the post-structuralist thought of Jacques Derrida, Michel Foucault, and Jacques Lacan which provided the theoretical impulse here. The critics who were at the forefront were Homi Bhabha, Gayatri Spivak, and the historians who belonged to the 'Subaltern studies' group. Bhabha argued that hybridity and mimicry were strategies forged by the colonized as ways of responding to colonial rule. Hybridity is an 'in-between space' in which the colonialized translate or undo the binaries imposed by the colonial project: 'From the perspective of the "in-between", claims to cultural authenticity and sovereignty—supremacy, autonomy, hierarchy—are less significant 'values' than an awareness of the hybrid conditions of inter-cultural exchange' (Bhabha 2000: 139). For Bhabha, the significant characters in Naipaul's novels are those who, in spite of their defeat and degradation, transgress the conformity enforced by colonialism through mimicry and fusion. Spivak, in her oft-quoted essay, 'Can the Subaltern Speak?' problematizes the difficulties of recovering the voices constructed in colonial texts, especially those of the women, and reads them as potentially insurrectionary (Spivak 1993: 66–111). This unnecessarily complicated essay has to be read in conjunction with the interview with the author in *The Spivak Reader* to get a fuller picture. Her concern is that speaking should not be taken literally as talk. Women did speak, but the problem was with the constrictions placed on translating their speech through the accepted conceptual mindset: 'The actual fact of giving utterance is not what I was concerned about. What I was concerned about was that even when one uttered, one was constructed, by a certain kind of psychobiography, so that the utterance itself—this is another side of the argument—would have to be interpreted in the way in which we historically interpret anything' (Landry and Maclean 1996: 291). In other words, the marginalized can make themselves known only in relation to metropolitan conceptual practices. The central aim of those scholars who are involved in the Subaltern Studies project is to rectify the disproportionate space accorded to the interests of the elite in the writings of South Asian history. They redefine subaltern as the non-elite, rural section of Indian society, ranging from destitutes to the upper ranks of the peasantry, and see their task as amplifying the contribution made by 'the people *on their own,* that is, *independently of the élite* to the making and development of this nationalism' (Guha 1988: 39; italics in original).

Thirdly, there was literary analysis of literature which emerged from the colonies, as a way of writing back to the centre, questioning and challenging colonialist discourses, and in the process producing a new form of representation. The work which pioneered such an analysis was *The Empire Writes Back* (Ashcroft, Griffiths, and Tiffin 1989). It opened up the debate surrounding the explosion of powerful and diverse writings especially those emerging from the former Commonwealth countries, their interrelatedness, their politicization, and their use of language as subversion. Ashcroft, Griffiths, and Tiffin identify four modes of 'writing back'— national or regional (reflecting and emphasizing the country's culture), black writing (by Africans in diaspora), comparative (literatures of the past and present Commonwealth countries which emerge out of shared history), and hybridized or syncretic (eclectic use of theories, histories, forms, and concepts) (Ashcroft, Griffiths, and Tiffin 1989: 15–37). Despite their different emphases, and variant needs, what binds these literatures together is their recognition and challenge of the notion of the ruler and the ruled, and the dominating and dominated.[9]

The advent of postcolonial theory in the late 1980s, nearly two decades after the formal ending of territorial colonialism, is indicative of the fact that postcolonial thinking was not a direct critique of colonial devastation. The delay suggests that postcolonialism was an 'intellectual symptom' a reaction against the failure of the newly independent nation states to initiate pluralistic democratic structures and environmentally balanced development, to bridge the gap between rich and poor, and meet the needs of indigenous peoples. Postcolonial studies are not simply about what went wrong during colonial days and what went wrong in the anticolonial struggle where gender and class went unnoticed or were subsumed under the nationalist cause, but has also to do with the non-materialization after the euphoria of freedom of greater democracy, justice for indigenous people, and minorities like Dalits and *burakumins*, gender equality and the end of poverty and hunger. The Subaltern Studies initiative is a salient example of this newer approach.

To conclude this section: postcolonial criticism, like the hybridity it celebrates, is itself a product of hybridity. It is an inevitable growth of an interaction between colonizing countries and the colonized. It owes its origin neither to the First nor the Third World, but is a product of the contentious reciprocation between the two.

Clarification of the lexicon

In postcolonial writing, terms such as 'imperialism' and 'colonialism' are often lumped together, and tend to be used interchangeably. Edward Said has returned to the standard distinction between the two. In this usage, 'the term "imperialism" means the practice, the theory, and the attitudes of a dominating metropolitan centre ruling a distant territory; "colonialism", which is almost always a consequence of imperialism, is the implanting of settlements on distant territory' (Said 1993: 8). Put differently, imperialism is often taken to mean literally 'of empire' and indicates the control exercised by one nation state over another and its inhabitants to exploit and develop the resources of the land, for the benefit of the imperial government. It is often accompanied by an imperial propaganda in the form of ceremonies, coronations, parades, pageants, and military supremacy. Colonialism, on the other hand, implies settlement, but also necessitates controlling and 'civilizing' indigenous people. The predatory nature of imperialism, namely acquiring distant territories for economic and political reasons only became unambiguous in the later nineteenth century. Prior to that, empire was seen as a humanitarian enterprise where an amiable form of civilization was pressed upon the hapless and ignoble races. The revival of the Roman empire as a model helped to provide an articulation of the aims of high imperialism. The ideology of the Roman empire consolidated the notion that superior races are entitled to power over savage races because the natives are unruly and incapable of ruling themselves.

The other term which has a high purchase in postcolonial discourse is neo-colonialism. Its first usage was attributed to the first president of Ghana, Kwame Nkrumah. 'The essence of neo-colonialism', he wrote, 'is that the state which is subject to it is, in theory, independent and has all the outward trappings of international sovereignty. In reality its economic system and thus its political policy is directed from outside' (Nkrumah 1965: p.ix). In his view, this was a new form of economic hegemony exercised by former colonizers through international banks and multinational corporations, after territorial freedom had been gained by newly independent countries. Unlike the earlier colonialism, which was visible, the new form of indirect control was much more subtle and less visible. Recently, with the former colonial European countries losing their hold on the international political scene, the term has been transferred to indicate principally the influence and intervention of the United States in the economic and political affairs of the world. In essence, what neo-colonialism means is the inability of the Third World countries to work out an economic policy and strategy without the interference of Western powers, although Nkrumah went on to warn that neo-colonialism was injurious not only to the dominated but also to the dominating countries: 'Neo-colonialism is a mill-stone around the necks of the developed countries which practise it. Unless they can rid themselves of it, it will drown them' (Nkrumah 1965: p.xvi).

Postcolonialism and biblical studies

The greatest single aim of postcolonial biblical criticism is to situate colonialism at the centre of the Bible and biblical interpretation. What we find in both the historical and the hermeneutical literature of biblical scholarship over the last four hundred years is the impact of the Reformation or the Counter-reformation, or the effects of the Enlightenment in defining and shaping the discipline by rationalistic thinking or its offshoot, historical criticism. But there has been a remarkable unwillingness to mention imperialism as shaping the contours of biblical scholarship. What postcolonial biblical criticism does is to focus on the whole issue of expansion, domination, and imperialism as central forces in defining both the biblical narratives and biblical interpretation.

Postcolonial criticism opens up potential areas for biblical studies to work in tandem with other disciplines. Biblical scholars have in other ways been open to trends from elsewhere and have used insights from other disciplines with profit. Postcolonialism's ongoing battle for emancipation, and continuing attempt to dismantle imperial institutions and dominating structures offers a valuable field for collaboration. The overlapping areas in which biblical scholars can cooperate with the postcolonial agenda include: race, nation, translation, mission, textuality, spirituality, representation. It can also explore plurality, hybridity, and postnationalism, the hallmarks of the postcolonial condition. Related identity categories are undergoing vigorous rethinking, including: slaves, sex-workers, the homosexual/heterosexual divide, people of mixed race. Each of these topics deserves attention, although in this volume, we will confine ourselves to a few of the issues which are critical to biblical interpretation, such as textuality, translation, and diasporic hermeneutics.

Another area where biblical studies could benefit from postcolonial discourse is the place and function of criticism in the contemporary world. What Said says of the American literary scene is equally true of biblical studies. Biblical studies, as in the case of literary studies, is enmeshed in the labyrinth of textuality, and obsessed with professionalism and specialization: 'As it is practised in the American academy today, literary theory has for the most part isolated textuality from the circumstances, the events, the physical senses, that made it possible and render it intelligible as the result of human work' (Said 1991: 4). There are two greater dangers within the field. One is an uncritical acceptance of the principal tenets of the discipline, and the other, its failure to relate it to the society in which its work is done. Biblical studies is still seduced by the modernistic notion of using the rational as a key to open up texts and fails to accept intuition, sentiment, and emotion as a way into the text. By and large, the world of biblical interpretation is detached from the problems of the contemporary world and has become ineffectual because it has failed to challenge the status quo or work for any sort of social change. Recently, feminist and liberation hermeneutics have reacted with increasing impatience to the way mainstream biblical scholarship has detached itself from real social and political issues.

Empire and theological reflections

Scholars of biblical studies, or, for that matter, scholars working in the field of theological studies have yet to address the relation between European expansionism and the rise of their own discipline. More importantly, there is yet to be a theological critique of the empire, especially among English theologians. Precisely in the 1960s when the process of decolonization was taking place, Western theologians spent their creative energies addressing issues such as secularization and its impact on Christian faith. They were eloquent in their silence when it came to assessing the role of the West in the colonial domination, the one exception being the British theologian and missiologist, M. A. C. Warren. In his 1955 Reinecker Lectures at the

Virginia Theological Seminary, *Caesar the Beloved Enemy*, he acknowledged the link between colonialism and mission, at that time an unusual
admission: 'Christianity in Asia and Africa is associated with the past
political, economic and cultural "aggression" of the West' (Warren 1955:
12). Warren's contention in the lectures was that the attack on imperialism
had been largely misconceived, and one 'cannot just dismiss it as "an
organized selfishness" or "something minted in hell"' (Warren 1955: 28).
His thesis was that to gain a true knowledge about colonialism one had to
look at and appreciate the concrete examples of benefits it brought to the
natives, rather than treat imperialism as an abstract notion, which Warren
thought was an illegitimate way to study the subject. For him imperialism
had to be evaluated theologically, in terms of God's purpose in history,
which, among other things was 'to bring mankind to a true knowledge of
Himself who is Love, Power and Justice' (Warren 1955: 24).[10] In his view,
imperialism could 'be the vehicle of great good to a subject people' (Warren 1955: 36), and functioned as a 'diffusion of good life' (Warren 1955: 21),
and more importantly as 'a *preparatio* for God's good will for the world'
(Warren 1955: 28). The imperium was set as the providence of God to
establish law and order and to forge unity among people driven by
anarchy, by enlarging the idea of neighbourhood for all those who came
under the wings of the empire. Instead of being a citizen of a tribe, what
colonial rule offered was a chance to be a citizen of the world and share in
a common culture. He reminded his audience that African culture with its
practice of witchcraft, ritual murder, and tribal warfare would not have
prepared Africans to face the modern world. To justify his claim biblically,
Warren cited examples from the Hebrew Scripture as evidence of God
operating in and through the great concentrations of power exercised by
the empires of the ancient world. He also summoned the exegetical comments of Edward Selwyn on 1 Peter 2: 14 about the authority of the
emperor and the state. But this concentration of power, in Warren's view,
was positively a better alternative than the unruliness which prevailed in
the colonies before the introduction of the Roman orderliness. The control and consolidation of power was an instrument to do justice. The role
of the empire was teleological. Warren claimed: 'It can, I think, be fairly
argued that successive imperialisms have made a significant contribution
to the realization of the vision of the time when "the earth shall be filled
with the knowledge of God as the water covers the sea"' (Warren 1955: 27).

Under colonial rule, 'love, power and justice have been seen to take shape redeeming some tragic situation' (Warren 1955: 31). Then he went on to claim that 'at least, up till today, no other method has been devised for so successfully keeping the peace and making progress possible' (Warren 1955: 28). If there were any fault in the imperial enterprise it was because 'imperialism is an activity of fallen humanity' (Warren 1955: 40). Quoting Paul Tillich, Warren also went on to remind the American audience of America's 'vocational consciousness', the American dream, 'namely to establish the earthly form of the kingdom of God by a new beginning' which was meant first for America alone but now 'is meant explicitly for one-half of the world and implicitly for the whole world' (Warren 1955: 30).

Warren echoes the views of those who saw the empire with touching fondness, as the personification of grandeur and as the instigator of civilizing values. It is these facets of imperial glory that Warren wanted to rescue from the clutches of postcolonial revisionism. I have taken time over the work of Warren to reiterate two points. One, that in spite of all atrocities, which he calls aberrations, the empire was a good thing and the other, the notable absence of the empire in English theological reflections. Warren's main thesis is that, despite the involvement of Christian mission with colonialism, its praiseworthy achievements speak for themselves. This view is still prevalent among many who look at missionary activities with nostalgia (Coote 2000: 100). I will come back to this point and try to offer a response in the concluding section. Western theologians have yet to offer a sustained theological analysis of the impact of colonialism. Colonialism has not received anything like as much attention as the Holocaust in recent theological reflection in the West. There is no admission of the place of colonialism in the shaping of English theology.[11]

Postcolonial criticism and cognate disciplines—feminism

Some of the critical undertakings pursued by postcolonialism coincide with such liberative movements as feminism. What unites feminist and postcolonial critique is their mutual resistance to any form of oppression—be it patriarchy or colonialism. In their strategies of resistance, both feminist and postcolonial critics are of one accord. They seek to uncover the subjugation of both men and women in colonial texts, and the modes of resistance of the subjugated, and expose the use of gender in both colonial discourse and social reality. In spite of their cordial collaboration, however, there is an in-house debate within the field, which manifests itself in three forms. First, there is a concern among feminists, of both the First and Third Worlds that in building up the larger picture of colonialism, male-centred postcolonial work tends to overlook and under-play gender differences, women's concerns, and their role in emancipatory struggles. Secondly, Third World feminist scholars are of the view that, notwithstanding their solidarity, First World biblical scholars still work within and often replicate male colonial tendencies. Thirdly, recently, post-colonial feminist biblical scholars have joined in the criticism of the First World feminist biblical scholars, in pointing out that in the noble aim of feminist construction of biblical narratives, they often compromise and overlook the colonial context of these texts, and their exegetical conclu-sions are often arrived at without problematizing the colonial agenda embedded in the biblical narratives.[12]

While conceding that, just as there are many forms of patriarchy, there are many forms of colonialism. First World feminists tend to conflate them. Third World feminist scholars, on the other hand, make it clear that they are not identical. Though women are doubly victimized by patriarchy and colonialism, the former is seen as male domination of the female, whereas the latter is defined as nation states which include both men and women who subjugate and control men and women of other nation states. Third World feminists complain that collapsing them into one category, fails to acknowledge different strategies of subjugation. Third World fem-inists criticize First World feminists for homogenizing Third World women in their works and portraying them as perpetual and hapless vic-tims, or in some cases, failing to recognize the contribution Third World women have made in different fields.

Third World feminists have acted as a necessary corrective to main-stream postcolonial thinking. They have extended their work to include issues overlooked by the dominant postcolonial thinking. Rajeswari Sun-der Rajan and You-me Park have outlined the following as the postcolonial feminist agenda: the retrieval and investigation of the role of women in independence movements, social roles of women, motherhood, and relations among women of different castes, class, and religious communities. They also include how these were reformulated under modernity and the colonial state's reformist legislation, women's role and contribution in economic development, the interface between the emancipatory goals of feminism and the agendas of nationalism, religious fundamentalism, communalism, the rights of immigrant women in metropolitan centres when they are pitched against modern, secular values, and the virulent nationalism of the host countries (Sunder Rajan and Park 2000: 53–71). To this one could add the link between race and gender in colonial expansion.

Though there is a potential tension between feminism and postcolonialism, feminism should not be seen as an adjunct to postcolonialism. Notwithstanding tensions within the field, feminist critical work should be seen as integral to postcolonial thinking.

Global intentions and postcolonial concerns

The current globalization is not something that happened suddenly. Its roots go back to colonial history and it is a legacy of European colonialism and modernity. Syed Ahmed Khan, the Indian reformer, about whom we will hear more in the next chapter, was able to detect how the combined efforts of colonialism and the inventions of modernity were able to transform and shrink the world: 'Railways, Steam Vessels and the Electric Telegraph, are rapidly uniting all the nations of the earth: the more they are brought together, the more certain does the conclusion become, that all have the same wants, the same anxieties, the same hopes, and the same fears, and therefore the same nature and the same origin' (Ahmed Khan 1873: 55). Globalization is not something new. It has been going on for ages. There is a world legacy of interchange and interaction. The influences have gone in different directions. Recently, the flow has been mainly from the West to the rest of the world. Previously it was the other way round. It was Europe which was assimilating Arabic science and technology and Indian mathematics, and consuming goods from China. Like most of the cultural forces of our time, globalization manifests itself in a variety of ways—economically, politically, and culturally—and all of these evolved over several centuries of European imperialism. In some ways, what the present globalization does, following the demise of the old colonialism, is to intensify the power relations in a more acute manner. The crucial difference between the old colonialism and the current globalization is the unrivalled grip of the United States on the world economy through military and foreign policies, its financial and mercantile corporations, and its hold on world culture through its massive media outputs—television, film, and publishing.

There is also another key difference between modernity's old universalizing tendencies and the current globalization. Zygmunt Bauman is of the view that universalization and globalization represent more than a shift in vocabulary. He sees a distinction between the two—one religiously espousing emancipation, rationality, and the autonomy of the individual, the other an experience which people unwittingly comply with because of its overpowering presence and its relentless impingement on their lives:

Modernity once deemed itself *universal*. It now thinks of itself instead as *global*. Behind the change of terms hides a watershed in the history of modern self-awareness and self-confidence. Universal was to be the rule of reason—the order of things that would replace slavery to passions with the autonomy of rational beings, superstition and ignorance with truth, tribulations of the drifting plankton with self-made and thoroughly monitored history-by-design. 'Globality' in contrast, means merely that everyone everywhere may feed on McDonald's burgers and watch the latest made-for-TV docudrama. Universality was a proud project, a herculean mission to perform. Globality in contrast, is a meek acquiescence to what is happening 'out there'; . . . Universality was a feather in philosophers' caps. Globality, exiles the philosophers, naked, back into the wilderness from which universality promised to emancipate them. (Bauman 1995: 24; italics in original)

Though Bauman's distinction between the missionizing project of the Enlightenment and current popular cultural practices may be contrived, his claim that both are culturally controlled by the West is important. One also needs to differentiate, as Arjun Appadurai has pointed out, between cultural imperialism and the globalization of culture. In his view, the former stands for uniformity in the global spread of Western consumer culture, whereas the latter demonstrates how Western commodities are transformed into indigenous hybridized forms by local cultures (Appadurai 1990: 1–21).

There are two varieties of globalization: élite and grassroots. It is the latter which is of special interest to postcolonialism. The singular aim of elite globalization is to maximize profits for international corporations. It is this form of globalization which compels Third World countries to deregulate their markets and open up national economies to multinational companies, advocates drastic cutbacks in social welfare programmes, promulgates laws against trade union rights, and preaches the virtues of privatization of state-owned utilities. It speaks the vocabulary of efficiency, profit, and competition. Its organizing principle is the market, and everything and everyone must be subject to its forces. But there is another form of globalization which operates on different values. It focuses on the quality of human life, sustaining the environment, upholding human rights, and safeguarding the cultures of indigenous people. This grassroots globalization consists of people from both First and Third Worlds. It is composed of expert scientists, officials of international agencies, activists of non-governmental organizations, environmentalists, farmers and consumers, and members of people movements.[13] It is they who agitate for fair trade and fight to protect ecological balance and conserve the forests. What these different campaigns and movements are trying to do is, to use Naomi Klein's phrase, to 'reclaim the commons', such communal spaces as 'town squares, streets, schools, farms and plants' (Klein 2001: 82). They are working against forces which are bent on privatizing every aspect of life—health, education, and natural resources—into commodities. The issue is not whether poor countries should be economically developed or benefit from trade. They are already in the process of development. The issue is also not whether such developments would change the character of these countries. The changes are already afoot. The issue is about the terms on which change takes place and who will benefit as a result. It is here that postcolonialism can a play a positive role in exposing the exploitative policies of donor countries and organizations which force the under-developed nations to adopt measures which would make them conducive to the investment of multinational corporations.

A postcolonial approach is useful in dealing with the issues generated by globalization. The strategies for transformation used in postcolonial responses to colonial discourse, such as representation, exposure of the link between power and knowledge, resistance, can become useful tools in the hands of local communities who engage with the forces of globalization. The earlier paradigms of how subjugated people under colonialism achieved agency, can provide models for local cultures and communities to compete and reassert and reclaim their agency under the pressures of global hegemony.

Is the United States postcolonial?

Postcolonial studies have been largely seen as concerned with former colonies of Europe and generated by the hermeneutical efforts of a Commonwealth-led literary activity. The canon is in the main populated with literature from Africa and Asia, and spiced up with articulations of thinkers who were actively engaged in anti-colonial struggles, such as Fanon, Cabral, and James referred to above. Such accepted notions tend to keep the United States of America, the present imperialist giant, outside the discursive loop. There is an uneasiness in associating the United States with postcoloniality.[14] Curiously enough, in their watershed book, *The Empire Writes Back*, Bill Ashcroft, Gareth Griffiths, and Helen Tiffin advanced the notion that the United States was 'the first post-colonial society to produce a "national" literature' and, to the great annoyance of other critics, the trio went on to claim the United States as an exemplar of postcolonial literary activity: 'In many ways the American experience and its attempt to produce a new kind of literature can be seen to be the model for all later post-colonial writing' (Ashcroft, Griffiths, and Tiffin 1989: 16). In spite of advancing this proposition, Ashcroft, Griffiths, and Tiffin, did not, in their book, look at American literature or its role in the global cultural landscape. The question then is, does the United States become postcolonial simply because it broke its connection with England in the eighteenth century, and does this count for more than its neo-colonial position as an unrivalled financial, military, and political power in the world which has no equal competitors. However, there is a crucial difference between US and European colonialism. Malini Johar Schueller, who has studied the nineteenth-century American discourses, points out that for England and France the narrative of the empire needed to be undergirded by 'firm national character', but in the United States the imperialism was constructed much more benevolently as a teleological project:

Since the 'discovery' of the Americas by Columbus was popularly transmitted as the outcome of a vision to reach the Orient, contemporary arguments about seizing Oriental trade or civilizing Orientals through missionary activity were accompanied by visionary statements about completing Columbus's original mission. Tropes of expansion and control over various specific Orients were thus mystified as 'natural' through the complex genealogy of the country's intimate associations with the search for the Orient.   (Schueller 1998: 9)[15]

Paul Tillich, whom Warren quoted enthusiastically, saw American expansion as a vocational consciousness which expressed itself in laws which embody love and justice. He also foresaw it as one of the great powers emerging as a 'world centre, ruling the other nations through liberal methods and in democratic forms!' (Tillich 1954: 105).[16]

The question as to whether the United States is postcolonial or not depends more on how one defines postcolonialism than on the status of the United States. There is an attempt among some American scholars working in the field to extend the term 'postcolonial' to cover not only the traditional catchment area of Europe and its colonies but also the United States. The strategy here is to redefine and advance notions of postcolonialism as a more processual, fluid, and dynamic concept. With such a reconfiguration in mind, Karen Piper defines postcolonialism as 'after the imprint of colonialism'. She goes on to claim: 'The US, then, is postcolonial in the sense that its fundamental identity is wrapped in a colonizing project—whether settler or indigenous, the inhabitants of the US have been impacted by the colonial ideal of resource "development" or exploitation' (Piper 1999: 19). The tendency is to disregard 'post' in the term 'postcolonial' as an evaluative term denoting 'after colonialism', and appropriate it as a descriptive one and as a legacy which continues to survive as an existential reality for many Americans. Two such legacies, according to Karen Piper, are 'internal extermination', where the United States is engaged in displacing people, and the other is 'successive waves of immigration', which still continues (Piper 1999: 14–28).

Another marker of colonialism which helps to redefine America as postcolonial is the marginalization faced by American ethnic minorities. If postcolonial discursive practices emerge from the experience of colonial dominance, then, according to Deborah Madsen, Native American, Chicano American, African American, and Asian American writers face precisely a similar kind of 'marginalization and cultural erasure' to that which writers from Africa, India, and other settler colonies face. In Deborah Madsen's view, the US minorities are left out of the current discussion because of an obsolete concept of American literature as 'originating in Massachusetts with the Winthrop and Bradford settlements and developing through the American resistance of the 1850s to a twentieth-century Modernist-Postmodernist literature' (Madsen 1999: 4). Since a sense of commonality runs through the writings of the Third World and American minority writers, based on experience of 'imperial domination, cultural catastrophe, genocide, and erasure' (Madsen 1999: 11), there is no justification for excluding their texts:

In comparison with the post-colonial expression of Australian Aboriginal writers, Canadian First Nations writers, New Zealand Maori writers, indigenous African writers, the work of American Indian writers assumes a new set of significances that is derived from a matrix of indigenous experience, and not from the stifling paradigm of sophisticated metropolitan centre versus primitive post-colonial margin. This is important, because the values assigned to literary expression in native cultures may share more in common with each other than with the values of Western literary representation. (Madsen 1999: 11)

The scenario is similar to the one the Ecumenical Association of Third World Theologians (EATWOT) faced in its formative years. The vexing question which tormented the original founders, who came from Asia and Africa and Latin America, was whether to include African Americans and Native Americans in their newly formed group. Their decision to allow them to be part of EATWOT was eventually decided on the basis of their marginality.

According a marginal status to American minority writers is not without problems. While concurring with, and at the same time not discounting the value of marginal status in the prevailing models of postcolonial studies, Jenny Sharpe observes that such a reduction of the field to discussions surrounding marginality and oppression in the texts of the past and present diasporic experience of African slaves, and diverse experiences of immigrants from the Third World to industrialized nations, offers explanations of past history but not of the present state of the United States as a neo-colonial power. Her proposal is that postcolonialism as a critical category should move beyond these accepted notions and be seen as the study of differential power and transnationalism: 'I want to propose that the postcolonial be theorized as the point at which internal social relations intersect with global capitalism and the international division of labour. In other words, I want us to define the "after" to colonialism as the neocolonial relations into which the United States entered with decolonized nations' (Sharpe 2000: 106). Richard King, in a volume of essays which maps out and clarifies the applicability of postcolonialty to America, states: 'Indeed, framing the United States as postcolonial, as emergent through its changing relations both with European imperialism and with its own imperial endeavours, directs attention to its production as an imperial nation-state' (King 2000: 5). Associating the United States with postcoloniality, captures many of the complicated experiences of contemporary American life.

Concerns, temptations, conclusions

Those engaged in postcolonial discourse are, among other things, constantly confronted with two questions. One, whether one should rake up the past and blame earlier generations and make their present successors feel guilty for the misdeeds of their forebears. The other side of this is to make all victims innocent and virtuous. The issue is not that one is at fault, and the other is blameless. The issue is how one makes use of the past and who benefits from it. If one is in the business of glorifying the past, and making use of stereotypical images from a bygone era to decide policies which affect the housing, education, and health of ethnic minorities, then one should recognize the ambivalence of past achievements. If the empire is portrayed as a magnificent achievement, then one should be reminded of the atrocities, ranging from the slave trade to planned genocide and forced resettlement, which were committed in the name of the empire. These heinous events should not be airbrushed out of the record because they make unpleasant reading but should be highlighted as integral to the achievement. If history books rhapsodize Victorian achievements, then it is reasonable also to recount colonial genocides which resulted in the killing of sixty million Asians, Latin Americans, and Africans, which Mike Davies calls the 'Victorian Holocaust'.[17] If Winston Churchill is portrayed as typifying the British bulldog spirit, then reverential accounts of his life should also refer to his part in perpetuating the famine in Bengal which killed nearly three million people because of his uncompromising stance on sending relief to help the victims. In order to further reveal his xenophobic nature, it would not be a bad idea to recall his extraordinary proposal that Gandhi should be bound hand and foot and trampled by viceregal elephants (Raychaudhuri 1999: pp.x, xi). History books which highlight the wonderful achievements of the East India Company and its clerk Lord Clive should also point out the rapacious nature of their enterprise and his criminal deeds. Similarly, if Indian nationalists stress the Jalianwala Bagh incident of 1918, where innocent protesters were massacred by British troops under the command of General Dyer, it would also be right to recall that four years later 1,200 Gujarati tribals, more than three times the number killed in the Amritsar incident, were gunned down by the local landowners with the help of the British simply because they were demanding a lower levy by the landowners.

The second question which is often raised by apologists for colonialism is what is wrong in regenerating, renovating, and civilizing a people who were 'living in darkness'. This kind of argument was advocated by Warren, as we saw earlier. The supporters of this claim often point to the benefits bestowed by the Western powers upon people who were deemed to be uncivilized. One often hears about the British abolishing *sati* in India, polygamy in Africa, human sacrifice in the Pacific, and how European clothes and Western knowledge were introduced. Or as Warren claimed: 'Would a Nkrumah on the Gold Coast have sprung like an African Athene "full-armed" from the bush?' (Warren 1955: 28). Tzvetan Todorov, who studied Western colonial atrocities in the Americas, provides an apt answer to such queries:

A civilization may have features we can say are superior or inferior; but this does not justify their being imposed on others. Even more, to impose one's will on others implies that one does not concede to that other the same humanity one grants to oneself, an implication which precisely characterises a lower civilization. No one asked the Indians if they wanted the wheel, or looms, or forges; they were obliged to accept them. Here is where the violence resides, and it does not depend on the possible utility of these objects. (Todorov 1992: 179)

The current postcolonial discourse places a high emphasis on the nineteenth century and along with it the British empire and its achievements.

The trouble with such a preoccupation is that it gives a distorted version of Britain, and is, to use Linda Colley's phrase, 'over-flattering to the West' (Colley 2000: 19). True, Britain was at the zenith of its power in the nineteenth century, but it was from this highly advantageous position that the previous centuries of British history were interpreted. Postcolonial criticism often works on the premiss that, because of the scale of European dominance in the nineteenth century, the West was able to map out its responses to the Orient and to Islam from a towering position of might, belligerence, and military superiority. It was not the case, as Linda Colley has pointed out:

British knowledge and preconceptions about Islam were not and could not be translated into durable colonizing ventures as far as the Ottomans or the North African powers were concerned before 1800. Until the mid-1700s at least, Ottoman Turkey was a more formidable and in many ways a more sophisticated state than Britain, while the North African powers not only remained independent of Europe but also preyed effectively on Western commerce and seized large numbers of European captives.   (Colley 2000: 18)

Postcolonial criticism should abandon its obsession with the nineteenth century and widen its net to include other forms of colonialism and other influences before and since the nineteenth century. Nayantara Sahgal expressed aptly at the Silver Jubilee conference of the Association of the Commonwealth Literature and Language Studies:

So is 'colonial' the new Anno Domini from which events are to be everlastingly measured? My own awareness as a writer reaches back to x-thousand B.C., at the very end of which measureless timeless time the British came, and stayed, and left. And now they're gone, and their residue is simply one more layer added to the layer upon layer of Indian consciousness. Just one more.   (Sahgal 1992: 30)

There is, further, a tendency among postcolonial critics to homogenize colonial experience. The sheer diversity of colonial encounters from settler to imperial projects is too complicated and complex to see as a single pattern. Often a certain colonial experience is highlighted and it is from this prism that the rest of colonial encounters are read. For instance, Fanon's *Wretched of the Earth*, has become a paradigmatic text to judge and evaluate other colonialisms, often forgetting that it was tied to a particular locale. It was written in 1961 as a response to a specific Algerian context. It came out of and was addressed to a very specific group of people in French-speaking West Africa, the native intellectuals and the middle-class who were yet to be emancipated. Despite the different manifestations of colonialism with their different codes of practice and different styles of assimilation and different modes of power relations, there is a tendency to see all these experiences as a single, undifferentiated whole.

One of the most challenging and exciting aspects of postcolonial criticism has been its rereading of ancient documents and literary texts. Its application has produced unexpected results to those not familiar with this literature. It has brought to the fore some of the often neglected and even in some cases unrecognized aspects of well-known texts. Now it has become impossible to read texts such as Joseph Conrad's *Heart of Darkness*, or E. M. Forster's *A Passage to India* or Jane Austen's *Mansfield Park* without noticing colonial allusions to, for example, slavery, sugar plantations, racial tensions, and the scramble for Africa, embedded in these novels. Such a preoccupation with tracking down ideologies in the plots and characterization has resulted in two things. One, it has re-emphasized and re-empowered the role of the critic. The critic is now invested with power and knowledge and acts as a broker between literature and the lay reader. Secondly, however, such an exercise can become an esoteric and an escapist activity. It might encourage the notion that deconstructing a narrative is the ultimate form of liberation, and lead to complacency and overlook continuing structural inequalities that are staring at us. Unless there is a serious effort to connect the interrogations of these narratives with the concerns of people, such as housing, education, health, human rights, and asylum, postcolonial criticism will lose its potency and credibility.

Postcolonialism has enabled those of us who were part of the former empires to see ourselves differently. It has helped us to go beyond thinking in contrastive pairs 'us' and 'them', 'East' and 'West'. Such a duality reduces everyone to an undifferentiated entity. What postcolonialism does is to help us to free ourselves from such neatly drawn confines. At least it seems possible to throw off the victim syndrome. Positively, what postcolonial criticism does is to prevent interpretation from becoming too nativistic or nationalistic. One is freed from the cultural compulsion to assert one's own heritage and self-consciously interpret everything as an Indian or Sri Lankan or whatever. It also enables Western countries to recognize the extent to which European culture and knowledge were involved in and contributed to older and continuing forms of deprivation, exploitation, and colonization. Negatively, too much theory-chasing and too much enchantment with it, and a hope that modern theory will make up for the lack of imaginative hermeneutics, will not take us far. Its specific usefulness lies in its capacity to detect oppression, expose misrepresentation, and to promote a fairer world rather than in its sophistry, precision, and its erudite qualities as a critical tool. Postcolonial criticism will enhance its value if it can foster a greater interchange between theoretical fine-tuning in the academy and the wider world.

NOTES

1. There are a number of readers and introductions which deal with the history, theory, practice, and debates about postcolonialism. For history, see Bill Ashcroft, Gareth Griffiths, and Helen Tiffin, *The Empire Writes Back: Theory and Practice in Post-Colonial Literatures* (London: Routledge, 1989) and Robert J. C. Young, *Postcolonialism: An Historical Introduction* (Oxford: Blackwell Publishers, 2001); for explanation of terms, see Bill Ashcroft, Gareth Griffiths, and Helen Tiffin, *Key Concepts in Post-Colonial Studies* (London: Routledge, 1998); for various issues related to postcolonialism, see Henry Schwarz and Sangeetha Ray (eds.), *A Companion to Postcolonial Studies* (Oxford: Blackwell Publishers, 2000) and Bill Ashcroft, *Post-Colonial Transformation* (London: Routledge, 2001); for an introduction and some of the debates surrounding postcolonialism, see Ania Loomba, *Colonialism/Postcolonialism* (London: Routledge, 1998), Peter Childs and Patrick Williams, *An Introduction to Post-Colonial Theory* (London: Prentice-Hall, 1997), Ato Quayson, *Postcolonialism: Theory, Practice or Process?* (Cambridge: Polity Press, 2000), Leela Gandhi, *Postcolonial Theory: A Critical Introduction* (Edinburgh: Edinburgh University Press, 1998), and John McLeod, *Beginning Postcolonialism* (Manchester: Manchester University Press, 2000); for anthologies, see Padmini Mongia (ed.), *Contemporary Postcolonial Theory: A Reader* (London: Arnold, 1996) and Bill Ashcroft, Gareth Griffiths, and Helen Tiffin, *The Post-Colonial Studies Reader* (London: Routledge, 1995). The journals which deal with postcolonial issues are: *Interventions: International Journal of Postcolonial Studies* and *Postcolonial Studies: Culture, Politics, Economy*.

2. I found this quotation in Robert J. C. Young, *Postcolonialism: An Historical Introduction* (Oxford: Blackwell Publishers, 2001), 64.

3. For other Indian theorizing, see V. K. Chari, *Sanskrit Criticism* (Delhi: Motilal Banarsidass Publishers, 1990) and K. Satchidanandan, *Indian Literature: Positions and Propositions* (Delhi: Pencraft International, 1999).

4. For an incisive introduction and critique, see Grant Farred (ed.), *Rethinking C. L. R. James* (Oxford: Blackwell Publishers, 1996) and Lewis R. D. Gordon, Dean T. Sharpley-Whiting, and Renée T. White (eds.), *Fanon: A Critical Reader* (Oxford: Blackwell Publishers, 1996).

5. Frantz Fanon's other writings include: *A Dying Colonialism*, trans. H. Chevalier (Harmondsworth: Penguin Books, 1970) and *Black Skin, White Masks*, trans. C. L. Markmann (London: Pluto Press, 1986).

6. For essays on biblical themes on justice and liberation in the writings of Latin American and African novelists, see Susan VanZanten Gallagher, *Postcolonial Literature and the Biblical Call for Justice* (Jackson: University Press of Mississippi, 1994). For the use of the Bible in Ngũgĩ wa Thiong'o's novels, see Peter Wamulungwe Mwikisa, 'The Limits of Difference: Ngũgĩ wa Thiong'o's Redeployment of Biblical Signifiers in *A Grain of Wheat* and *I will marry when I want*', in G. O. West and M. W. Dube (eds.), *The Bible in Africa: Transactions, Trajectories, Trends* (Leiden: Brill, 2000), 163–83.

7. For further examples of profuse use of the Bible in novels which deal with colonialism and newly independent nations in the Pacific, see Epeli Hau'ofa, *Tales of the Tikongs* (Honolulu: University of Hawaii Press, 1983). Also see Leñero's reworking of St Luke's gospel from a Mexican perspective, which also falls within the larger context of postcolonial literature and biblical interpretation, Vicente Leñero, *The Gospel of Lucan Gavilán*, trans. R. Mowry (Lanham, Md.: University Press of America, 1991). For a critique of Leñero's work, see Hector Avalos, '*The Gospel of Lucan Gavilán* as Postcolonial Biblical Exegesis', *Semeia: An Experimental Journal for Biblical Criticism*, 75 (1996), 87–105.

8. Said's work concentrates mainly on the Middle East. For a similar treatment of Latin America, see Tzvetan Todorov, *The Conquest of America: The Question of the Other*, trans. R. Howard (New York: Harper Perennial, 1992); and for Africa, see Walter Rodney, *How Europe Underdeveloped Africa* (Harare: Zimbabwe Publishing House, 1972).

9. For a succinct critique of the Ashcroft, Griffiths, and Tiffin model, see McLeod, *Beginning Postcolonialism*, 27–8. Since the publication of the *Empire Writes Back*, there has been a proliferation of literature which builds on and goes beyond issues related to literatures of the Third World. For a convenient entry into the subject, see Bruce King, *New National and Post-colonial Literatures: An Introduction* (Oxford: Clarendon Press, 1996).

10. This kind of view, acknowledging the grandeur of British achievement in India notwithstanding its failures, was held by some Indian Christians also. For instance, soon after Indian Independence, the renowned Indian theologian M. M. Thomas wrote that under God's providence, British imperialism in India was laying the foundation for political unity and social progress. Echoing Karl Marx's double vision of the British in India—one destructive and the other regenerative—Thomas wrote that God used British imperialism 'to judge and correct traditional Indian life and put India on the path of progress' ('Indian Nationalism: A Christian Interpretation', *Religion and Society*, 6/2 (1959), 7). Interestingly, in his private correspondence with Warren, Thomas agreed with his main proposal but castigated Warren for his narrow understanding of theology which centred on creation but failed to take note of the fall, judgement, and redemption (ibid. 1617). For a trenchant critique of Warren's thesis by R. L. Hsu, the Chinese theologian, see ibid. 1924.

11. For the English Churches' attitude over the last four decades to race, immigration, nationality, and asylum, which are all interconnected with British colonialism, see Kenneth Leech, 'From Chaplaincy towards Prophecy: Racism and Christian Theology over Four Decades', *Race and Class*, 41/1–2 (1999), 131–42.

12. For a vigorous critique of First World feminist biblical scholars by Third World feminist interpreters, see Musa W. Dube, *Postcolonial Feminist Interpretation of the Bible* (St Louis:

Chalice Press, 2000) and Laura E. Donaldson, 'Postcolonialism and Biblical Reading: Introduction', *Semeia: An Experimental Journal for Biblical Criticism*, 75 (1996), 114.

13. For the possibilities and dangers of such alliances, see Alan Thomas, 'Modernisation Versus the Environment? Shifting Objectives of Progress', in T. Skelton and T. Allen (eds.), *Culture and Global Change* (London: Routledge, 1999), 4557.

14. For a neat summary and critique of the debate and the personalities involved, see Jon Stratton, 'The Beast of the Apocalypse: The Postcolonial Experience of the United States', in C. R. King (ed.), *Post-Colonial America* (Urbana: University of Illinois Press, 2000), 2164, esp. 51–61; Karen Piper, 'Post-Colonialism in the United States: Diversity or Hybridity', in D. L. Madsen (ed.), *Post-Colonial Literatures: Expanding the Canon* (London: Pluto Press, 1999), 20; and C. Richard King, 'Introduction: Dislocating Postcoloniality, Relocating American Empire', in C. Richard King (ed.), *Post-Colonial America* (Urbana: University of Illinois Press, 2000), 35.

15. For the absence of the American empire in American studies, see Amy Kaplan and Donald E. Pease (eds.), *Cultures of United States Imperialism* (Durham, NC: Duke University Press, 1993).

16. To be fair to Tillich, he also warned that there would be a threat to the centre of power, first from within and openly 'driving towards separation from or towards radical transformation of the whole. They may develop a vocational consciousness of their own' (Paul Tillich, *Love, Power and Justice: Ontological Analyses and Ethical Applications* (London: Oxford University Press, 1954), 106). The current anti-capitalist movement may be a sign of this disruption and dissension which Tillich predicted.

17. From the review of Mike Davis's book, *Late Victorian Holocausts: El niño Famines and the Making of the Third World* (London: Verso, 2001), by Michael Watts, 'Black Acts', *New Left Review*, 9 (2001), 125–40.

2

REDRESS, REGENERATION, REDEMPTION: A SURVEY OF BIBLICAL INTERPRETATION

The French corrupt the natives with useless frivolity, the English—
the greatest hypocrites—sell rum and rifles with the Bible.

(A Dutch cartoon of 1897)

'We have no desire to impose our characteristic institutions on you;
our function is only to remind you of the forgotten Man, our
Common Man, whose name you take in vain when you come to us
with the Bible in one hand and laissez faire in the other.

(Ananda Coomaraswamy 1983: 25–6)

Before we explore how the alliance between postcolonial criticism and
biblical studies might open up new possibilities, let me recall briefly the
present status of biblical studies. When Western biblical scholars map out
the history of interpretation, they register a range of trajectories, but they
invariably begin with the Enlightenment and modernity, and their impact
on biblical studies, and especially the growth and development of
historical-critical methods and offshoots. I, too, start with modernity, not
with its noble agenda but with its contemptible manifestation—
colonialism—and how its legacy generated and influenced the development of biblical interpretation. At the risk of oversimplification, I identify
different stages of biblical interpretation as it interfaced with the varying
contours of colonialism. Though these stages seem gradual and linear,
what is crucial is that they demonstrate characteristic emphases, and the
impact and aftermath of colonialism as it proceeded.

Modern colonialism and Western expansion started in the fifteenth and sixteenth centuries with the Renaissance Iberian empires in the 'age of discovery', and were followed in the seventeenth and eighteenth centuries by the seaborne empires of Holland, France, and England in the 'age of mercantile capitalism'. Colonial settlement as a way of both consolidating colonial possession and dealing with European excess population began at this time and continued to the mid-twentieth century; the last and decisive wave, which is known as the 'era of high imperialism', occurred between 1870 and 1914 in a highly charged international competitive climate where virtually the whole of Africa, South-East Asia, and the South Pacific were brought under British, French, German, Dutch, Danish, Portuguese, Belgian, Spanish, or American occupation. Britain had the largest share, ruling over one-fourth of the world's land area and one-fifth of humanity (S. Cook 1996: 2). Our purpose is not to explore the frenzy of colonizing nor the motives and methods of the colonizers but to address the question of hermeneutics and to investigate how the Christian Bible fared in the experiences of both the colonizer and the colonized.

Dissident readings

Looking at the period, one can discern various types of reading. One is dissident, a form of oppositional discursive practice undertaken by some colonialists. Although located within and co-opted by the colonial system, what the discourse of dissidence did was to subvert it from within. It did this by indicating the awful things that colonialism had done or was capable of doing to those who were under its control. Prompted by both pangs of guilt and humanitarian motives, the intention of dissident discourse was to ameliorate colonialism and temper its predatory intentions. As a discursive practice, it could never hope to dismantle the whole edifice of imperialism, but in its own innocuous way it caused unsettlement, dislocation, and placed a question mark over territorial and cultural expansion. Both dissident reading and the resistant readings which we will look at later are interrogative discourses which recognize and work within the staple ingredients of imperial narrative.

One of the earliest examples of the discourse of dissidence was the work of Bartolomé de Las Casas (1487–1566), a Dominican friar, who was himself part of the colonial enterprise and witnessed at first hand the atrocities of Spanish colonialism in the Americas: 'We cut people savagely to pieces. We spare no one for their sex, their dignity, their age. We tear sucklings from the teats of their mothers and brain them on rocks. We fill straw-roofed log huts with men, women, children, babies, mothers of many or pregnant mothers, we set fire to the huts, burn them alive' (Las Casas 1992a: 149). Stephen Neill, who wrote a history of mission in which he raised the whole enterprise to near-heroic status, described Las Casas as a 'gentleman cleric' who lived much as the other colonialists lived (Neill 1964: 171). Like them, he profited from the colonial system. He was a beneficiary of a system known as *encomienda* (lit. recommendations). This allowed for Indians to be placed under a Spaniard with the right to extract tribute or labour, and in return the indigenous population were offered protection and instruction in Christian faith. There was no prospect of manumission. As a result of the atrocities he witnessed, Las Casas soon found himself caught up in the plight of the conquered victims, and this led him gradually to plead their cause and for the abolition of *encomienda*. In this pursuit, the Bible played a vital role. First, it was instrumental in modifying his thinking. Second, it provided him with sufficient ammunition to challenge the dominant views of the age in his theological debates at Valladolid (1550–1551) with Juan Ginés de Sepúlveda, a formidable philosopher and theologian of the time. The event which prompted a change in Las Casas's thinking was the 1513 Caonao massacre in Cuba. This contributed to his growing awareness of the inhumanity of the Spanish presence in the Americas, and moved Las Casas to write that 'everything perpetrated upon the Indians in these Indies was unjust and tyrannical'.[1] The scriptural illumination occurred when he was preparing a sermon for Pentecost in 1514. Interestingly, unlike the current liberation theologians, who are stirred either by the prophetic critique or by the liberative message of Jesus, it was the words of a Jewish sage which moved Las Casas. It was the powerful sayings of Ben Sirach, which seemed to resonate with what was happening in the Americas, that brought home the enormity of the wickedness in which Las Casas found himself entrapped and compromised. The telling verse was:

> Tainted his gifts who offers in sacrifice ill-gotten goods!
> Mock-presents from the lawless win not God's favor.

The Most High approves not the gifts of the godless.
[Not for their many sacrifices does he forgive their sins.]
Like the man who slays a son in his father's presence
is he who offers sacrifice from the possessions of the poor.
The bread of charity is life itself for the needy,
he who withholds it is a person of blood.
He slays his neighbor who deprives him of his living;
he shed his blood who denies the laborer his wages.

(Ecclus. 34: 18–22)[2]

The illumination was far from dramatic and sudden, but it gradually led Las Casas to call for a reform of the colonial system and an end to abuses, cruelty, and the genocide of the indigenous population.

The next phase in which the Bible played a critical role was at the Valladolid meeting. This was convened by the Emperor Charles V to consider the justification or otherwise of Spain's waging war in the Americas. The debate, which was often convoluted and protracted, need not detain us here.[3] Both contenders, Sepúlveda and Las Casas, endorsed the view of the Christendom of the time, that the natives of the Americas were pagans and must be converted to the true faith, and that their territory should come under Spanish jurisdiction. Where these venerable priests differed was in the methods they proposed to achieve this. One advocated an all-out war, the other went for gentle persuasion. Basically, what Sepúlveda, a Cardinal Ratzinger of his time, did was to argue on the basis of the Aristotelian principle that anyone who was not superior to a civilized European male was inferior and therefore it was justifiable to hunt them down as one would animals. Sepúlveda mobilized the Bible to put across his argument. He cited Deuteronomy 7 and the Book of Joshua as scriptural examples of God destroying the seven nations which dwelt in the Promised Land because of the crimes they had committed, as providing justification for waging war against the indigenous population. The indigenous population, too, like the idolaters who lived in the Promised Land, committed evil deeds. They oppressed innocent people, killed in order to engage in human sacrifice, and ate human flesh.

Las Casas's answer was that anyone who followed the teaching of Aristotle was 'not a Christian, a son of Satan, not of God; a plunderer, not a shepherd; a person who is led by the spirit of the devil, not heaven' (Las

Casas 1992*b*: 40). Dismissing Aristotle as irrelevant to the issue at hand, Las Casas went on to say: 'Good-bye, Aristotle! From Christ, the eternal truth, we have the command "You must love your neighbor as yourself" (Matt. 22. 40). And again Paul says "Love is not selfish" (1 Cor. 13. 5)' (Las Casas 1992*b*: 40). For him, missionaries accompanied with armed force did not enhance the image of the Catholic Church. He asked: 'What does the herald of the gospel have to do with firearms? What does the herald of the gospel have to do with armed thieves? (Las Casas 1992*b*: 173). Exhibiting an early instance of orientalism, Las Casas claimed that preaching the faith by force, massacre, and terror was an Islamic practice, and must not be emulated by the followers of Christ. Moreover, the Indians of the Americas were 'not that barbaric, nor are they dull-witted or stupid, but they are easy to teach and very talented in learning all the liberal arts, and very ready to accept, honor, and observe the Christian religion and correct their sins (as experience has taught) once priests have introduced them to the sacred mysteries and taught them the word of God' (Las Casas 1992*b*: 43–4). In opposition to colonial cruelty, his method was to approach the Indians of the Americas, 'gently, mildly, quietly, humanely, and in a Christian manner' (Las Casas 1992*b*: 40). He wrote: 'One way, one way only, of teaching a living faith, to everyone, everywhere, always, set by Divine Providence: the way that wins the mind with reasons, that wins the will with gentleness, with invitation. It has to fit all people on earth, no distinction made for sect, for error, even for evil' (Las Casas 1992*a*: 68). The Indians of the Americas have to be invited to the faith of Christ by both preaching the word of God and by the example of a good life. His method was the method of peaceful persuasion, to be preached 'in a spirit of brotherly love' (Las Casas 1992*a*: 96). His message to his compatriots was to imitate Jesus: 'Learn from me, I am meek and humble of heart.' (Matt.11: 29), 'I have given you an example. As I have done, so you also should do' (John 13: 5).

In Las Casas's view, Sepúlveda had neither examined the Scriptures thoroughly, nor understood its nuances sufficiently to apply them to the present context. When Sepúlveda cited God's command to destroy the Egyptians, and the Canaanites as a scriptural warrant to support the annihilation of the Indians, Las Casas's response was that 'not all of God's judgements are example for us' (Las Casas 1992*b*: 121). In his view, 'the examples of the Old Testament are to be admired but not always imitated' (Las Casas 1992*b*: 195). The prophet Elisha cursed the forty-two boys who mocked him, calling him a 'bald head'. 'If we were to imitate them, undoubtedly we would commit a vast number of most unjust and serious sins and thousands of absurdities would follow' (Las Casas 1992*b*: 121). The annihilation of the people settled in the Promised Land had a 'special cause' and it was never meant to be used as a general rule. In Las Casas's view, Sepúlveda was trying to hold on to 'the rigid precepts of the Old Law' which were given for special circumstances. The application of such laws would 'open up the way for tyrants and plunderers to cruel invasion, oppression, spoilation, and harsh enslavement of harmless nations' (Las Casas 1992*b*: 110). The present, however, was the era of grace and mercy. Since the coming of Christ, 'the Lord has distributed the treasures of his mercy throughout the entire earth and every nation. That is why this time is called the time of grace, the time of love, the year of the propitiation, the day of salvation, and the freely sent and good messenger of joy' (Las Casas 1992*b*: 110). Similarly the saying in the parable—'force them to come in'— another text which Sepúlveda latched on to, was not about compelling unbelievers to Christian faith. Citing Augustine and the Council of Toledo, Las Casas established that the verse was about compelling heretics who had left the body of Christ due to their heretical views to return to the Catholic Church.

In a way, anticipating the popular critical claim of today that a text has 'a reservoir of meanings', Las Casas argued that the richness of divine Scripture is so great 'that each word has many literal and pious meanings' (Las Casas 1992*b*: 304). His opponents, in Las Casas's view, instead of presenting the truth of the gospel and the example of the apostles, were offering 'adulterated passages of the Scriptures', lies, and empty dreams (Las Casas 1992*b*: 279).

Though the Bible played a critical role in the dialogue between Las Casas and Sepúlveda, the ordinary people of the Americas were left out of the debate. In the first place, they did not possess a text in their own language, and the Bible remained untranslated at this time. It would be another two hundred years before the Indians possessed a version of their own. The earliest date the Bible was available in Mexican Indian languages was in 1759, and even then only a few selections were printed. St Luke's gospel was published in Mexican, or Aztec, in 1833 (Kilgour 1939: 162–3). The Bible that Las Casas and Sepúlveda used in their erudite debate was the Latin Vulgate, an inaccessible book to the people. Like most colonial debates, the issues pertaining to the lives of the 'natives' were discussed without any meaningful participation from the local people or their making any significant contribution to the conversation. The Book and the debate remained remote from the Indians of the Americas.

There were several missionary figures who engaged in oppositional discursive practice against their own system. Among them, two important ones were John Colenso (1814–1883)[4] and James Long (1814–1887), whose missionary careers coincided. The former was a missionary of the Society for the Propagation of the Gospel (SPG) in South Africa, the latter was of the Church Missionary Society (CMS) in India. Both were favourably disposed towards the indigenous people, and engaged in controversial political campaigns, the cause of the Zulus in the case of Colenso and the struggles of Bengali indigo growers in the case of Long. What is significant to our purpose is their use of the Bible. John Colenso, employing the then emerging historical criticism, which landed him in trouble with his Church authorities, not only exposed the contradictions and paradoxes within the text, but also marshalled the same tools to rectify the uncharitable portrayals of the Zulus painted by the colonial administration. He also challenged the denunciatory preaching of the missionaries, which condemned the unrepentant heathen to hell, as intrinsic to the teaching of the Bible. Armed with his first-hand knowledge of the Zulus, Colenso was able to discern parallels between the customs of the contemporary 'savages' and the cultured biblical Jews. In translating the Bible with his Zulu helpers, it dawned on Colenso that their 'mode of life and habits, and even the nature of their country, so nearly correspond to those of the ancient Israelites, that the very same scenes are brought continually, as it were, before our eyes, and *vividly realised in a practical point of view*, in a way in which an English student would scarcely think of looking at them' (Colenso 1862: p. xxi; italics in original). At a time when missionaries were trying to equate ancient Graeco-Roman religions with African religious practices as idolatrous and superstitious, Colenso distanced himself from such perceptions. For the missionaries of the period, Paul's description of the pagan world in Romans 1: 18–32 seemed similar to the one they saw in foreign fields. David Jonathan East, in the 1840s produced a significant account of Africa based on travellers' tales. In this, he registered African slavery, drunkenness, immorality, and lack of commercial probity, and immediately cited Romans 1: 18–32 as an application of Paul's diatribe to African

paganism: 'What an awful comment upon this affecting portion of the
Holy Writ are the humiliating facts which these and the preceding chapters
record.'[5] In Colenso's rereading of Romans, which he produced before his
imposing work on the Pentateuch, he was able to demonstrate that Paul's
critique was directed only at some of the heathen of his own time, and that
he was not 'speaking of all heathens indiscriminately' (Colenso 1861: 54).

Unlike Colenso, who benefited from the historical-critical method and
applied it relentlessly to ascertain the facts of the biblical narrative, Long,
working in a different continent and with different people, felt that 'dwelling on the mere facts of the Bible' was 'of little profit'. To him, the Bible's
abstract dogmas, and 'ethical platitudes fell dull' on Eastern ears. The way
to make the Christian Scriptures 'interesting and intelligible' to oriental
people was to clothe them 'with the beautiful drapery of emblem, metaphor, proverb' (Long 1874: 2). Hence, Long resorted to and advocated a
literary mode of interpretation. Even before Deissmann claimed that the
Bible was an Eastern book (Deissmann 1910: 1), Long with his experience
of Eastern sensibilities was able to label it an oriental book: 'But the great
point is—the charter of our salvation, the Bible, is an *oriental* book, thoroughly Eastern, cast in a mould that no Saxon could have shaped' (Long
1874: 1; italics in original). He saw it as a book which was much easier for
Indians to understand than the English, 'as the poetry and imagery, being
oriental, came home to them. Hence the Psalms of David, as being cast in
the oriental mould, are much more acceptable to the Indian mind than the
English Prayer-Book, fashioned after the Teutonic or Latin rite' (Long 1874:
2). He went on to say that when India had its own independent native
Church, it should model it on Chrysostom and not Cranmer. In keeping
with the orientalist notion of India's preference for symbolic language,
Long tried to communicate biblical insights through parables and proverbs, which he reckoned would make the Bible 'impressive and interesting'
(Long 1874: 3). He often reminded his fellow missionaries that Jesus spoke
to ordinary people in parables and proverbs. With this in view, he assidu-
ously collected oriental proverbs and juxtaposed them with biblical ones.
By thus privileging the wisdom tradition, Long went against the current
notion of God's progressive self-disclosure through historical events which
culminated in the Incarnation, and brought to the fore the experience of
God through the realm of nature and in the mundane things of life. He
wrote: 'While the history and geography of the Bible require a certain

amount of education to be understood, parables, proverbs, and emblems, speak in a universal language, drawn from *God's book of nature*, open to all to read' (Long 1874: 2; emphasis added). In addition to advocating the introduction of Scripture through pictures and visual means, he encouraged the idea of learning passages by heart and chanting them, 'as intonation is a universal practice in the East'; he advanced this notion of teaching the Bible orally also because people had little time to acquaint themselves with the historical facts of the Scripture from the book itself. These, he argued, had 'to be given in the form of narrative without book, which is more accordant with the oriental mode, and decidedly more impressive' (Long 1874: 6). Unlike the British and Foreign Bible Society which was fervently trying to push the Protestant notion of private reading of the Bible, Long went against the grain of the time and promoted a non-logocentric approach which would win enthusiastic approval from those of today's practitioners who emphasize visual and oral representation.

Long's discourse, like that of Las Casas and Colenso, was essentially dissident. Aghast at the insulting tone of the British and the atrocities of British troops in India, Long advocated translating the Bible into the vernaculars. If the 'natives' were able to read for themselves, they would come to realize that the Christianity of the book was different from that practised by the English in India. In a letter, he wrote that 'the lives of many Europeans in India are so disgraceful to Christianity that unless the people have access to the *book* they can form no estimate of what Christianity is' (Oddie 1999: 44–5; italics in original). The dissident discourse of Las Casas, Colenso and Long, and others like them, was in a sense far ahead of its time. They recognized the fundamental elements of the imperial narrative and sought to dismantle it. Though they were highly critical of the imperial policy, they were firm advocates of a benevolent colonial rule, and believed in the providential nature of colonial expansion. But this did not prevent them from exposing the devious nature of colonial expansion, and they even went on to forecast punishment on their own countries. Las Casas and Colenso both prophesied judgement upon their own countries, Spain and England. To quote Las Casas: 'I think that God shall have to pour out His fury and anger on Spain for these damnable, rotten, infamous deeds done so unjustly, so tyrannically, so barbarously to those people, against those people' (Las Casas 1992a: 195). Colenso warned his people that if they continued to plunder the Zulus, mistreat their chief, ridicule

God's word, and failed to walk humbly before God, a 'great calamity' would befall them and that they would be overwhelmed by 'assegai, famine, or pestilence' (Colenso 1879: 23). Despite these harsh words, it was unavoidable that these dissident missionaries who were immersed in the imperial ideology had done nothing other than represent the natives in benevolent ways. Their inability to extricate themselves from imperial ideology within which these men lived complicated their work.

The hermeneutical issue posed by Las Casas, Colenso, and Long—how the 'cultured' or 'developed' behave towards an 'underdeveloped' people— is a particularly relevant one. These dissident missionaries were forerunners in accepting and acknowledging racial, religious, cultural, and linguistic pluralism, and realized that any intervention of 'advanced' societies in the affairs of the 'less' advanced had to take into account these multiple realities and had to be culturally sensitive. But in the end what they did was to impose and mediate a particular kind of Christianity and morality, which simultaneously challenged the then current perceptions but also compromised the gospel. Las Casas even had a quote from Colossians to support this kind of view: 'We who are strong have a duty to put up with the qualms of the weak without thinking of ourselves. Each of us should think of his neighbours and help them to become stronger Christians' (Col. 3: 17) (Las Casas 1992b: 39).

In essence, the dissident interpreters were products of the empire and believed that the best of European values and customs blended effortlessly with egalitarian religious concepts and robust indigenous social institutions. In their mind, the European rule was social reality, never a political imposition.

Resistant readings

Resistant reading, on the other hand, was undertaken by the colonized, the very people who felt the heavy hand of colonialism, suffocating under its rapacity. Basically, resistance reading did not repudiate Western rule, but made profitable use of a paradigm provided by the colonizer and tried successfully to turn it against him. What the discourse of resistance achieved was to make certain that the debate was not weighted towards the colonizer, and that the colonized too could talk back in their own voice, and disturb the dominant gaze. In the colonial context, the Bible became a convenient cultural weapon for both the colonizer and the colonized. While the missionaries saw it as a tool for civilizing and rescuing the degenerate heathen, some at least of the colonized employed it as a weapon of reprisal. Rather than seeing it as unsettling their way of life, the invaded turned it to their advantage. They learned to master it in order to survive or resist the new order which was sweeping across the world.

Olaudah Equiano, a native of West Africa, a freed slave, who lived in London and became an outspoken opponent of the slave trade, activated biblical texts in a purposeful way to unsettle the dominant views of the time. Mastering English while he was a slave, he acquired the most venerated cultural icon of the British culture of the time—the King James Version—and, though not a trained biblical scholar, employed it profusely in his *Interesting Narrative* (Equiano 1995). Using biblical allusions as his interpretative tool, Equiano was able to simultaneously prompt his readers to see the similarities and differences between his own life and the biblical narrative, and remind them of their Christian moral responsibility towards the vulnerable. As a freed slave, he reread Philemon, and argued that slavery went against the basic understanding of the doctrine of Atonement, which claimed that people were bought with the inestimable blood of Christ, and therefore should not end up 'as slaves and private property of their fellow-human beings' (Equiano 1995). Another resistant reader was William Apess (1798–1839), a Pequot. He used the Bible largely to reclaim an identity which was denied to his people. At a time when invading Europeans claimed racial superiority and postulated that God created separate races and placed the white children of Adam at the top of the order, denying his peoples' existence, as he pointed out, in official documents, Apess challenged this by tracing Native American lineage to the lost tribes of Israel. By invoking the lost tribes of Israel, and identifying Native Americans as the genuine heirs to the biblical tribes, Apess affirmed a common pedigree for all humanity, and equal status before God with others.[6]

One of the more trenchant resistant uses of the Bible was that of the eminent Indian Muslim reformer, Syed Ahmed Khan. He was born and brought up in the fading days of the Mughal empire, and was deeply concerned with, perturbed by, and implicated in the Indian rebellion of 1857. In his pamphlet, *The Causes of the Indian Revolt*, written soon after the terrible event, he sought to rectify the version popularized by the colonial administration, that the revolt was the result of a Muslim plot. He categorized the reasons for the revolt under five headings: ignorance on the part of the people—by which he meant misapprehension of the intentions of the government; passing of laws and regulations which were not only objectionable but were against the established practice and principles of India; ignorance on the part of the government to understand the condition of the people, their modes of thought, and life, and more importantly, their grievances; neglect on the part of the rulers of such points as were essential to good government; and the management and disaffection of the army (Ahmed Khan 1873: 15–16).

Under these headings, Ahmed Khan explicitly stated how the measures introduced by the British and the unmeasured language of missionary preaching and tracts, which increasingly marginalized a class of Indians and caused resentment among them, eventually led to the rebellion. While not discounting heavy assessment, interference in matters of religion, the abolition of village landowners' rights, the resumption of revenue from lands, the development of the property market, the provision accorded to bankers and moneylenders to use civil courts to oust the old landed families from their property, the chief reason for the revolt, according to Ahmed Khan, was political exclusion, the non-admission of Indians to the Legislative Council. This, in his view, was 'the origin of all the troubles that have befallen Hindustan' (Ahmed Khan 1873: 13). It was the negligence on the part of the rulers to offer a forum for the Indians to represent their grievances which led to their resentment: 'The people again having no voice in the government of the country could not well better their conditions, and if they did try to make themselves heard by means of petitions, these same petitions were seldom if ever attended to and sometimes never even heard.' Furthermore, he stated: 'The people were isolated, they had no champion to stand up for their rights and to see justice done to them and they were constrained to weep in silence' (Ahmed Khan 1873: 34).

In addition to refuting the mischievous propaganda of the colonial media of the time, an interesting aspect of the pamphlet was Ahmed Khan's employment of the Bible to expose the arrogance and insensitive behaviour of both petty and major British officials. He tellingly cites passages from the Bible to demonstrate how their treatment of Indians had failed to measure up to biblical standards, a standard by which they were claiming to adjudicate the moral codes and religious practice of Indians.

He countered the arrogant behaviour of the British by reminding them of the basic tenets of biblical teaching. What was expected of the government was friendship, social intercourse, and sympathy. He found these in the teaching of the New Testament. He quotes twice from 2 Peter 1: 7 'And to Godliness brotherly kindness; and to brotherly kindness charity.' He also cited the Pauline admonition: 'And the Lord make you to increase and abound in love one toward another, and toward all men, even as we do towards you' (1 Thess. 3: 12). His contention was that the British had 'not secured the affections of the people' (Ahmed Khan 1873: 41), and the only way to achieve this was to follow the precepts of Jesus, and show less arrogance and more gentleness and leniency to the people whom they governed. He reminded them it was the meek who would inherit the earth. In using these biblical passages, Ahmed Khan shifted the discussion by drawing attention to their civic utility. For him the Bible provided the blueprint and rationale for Christian civic duty towards one another.

It should be stressed that none of these resistant interpreters entertained any revolutionary intent or worked for the ending of the empire. They were astute observers of the time and were at the receiving end of the harsh realities of colonialism as it impacted on their lives and cultures. They often colluded with it, though not entirely mesmerized by its benefits. They did not reject the Bible. In it they found much-needed ammunition. They appropriated it, renegotiated its message, and created a discourse of resistant reading, and in the process sought to maintain their selfhood and dignity.

Heritagist readings

This mode of interpretation is an attempt by the colonized to find conceptual analogies in their high culture and textual traditions and philosophies, and also in their oral and visual art forms. It is an attempt to retrieve cultural memory from the amnesia caused by colonialism. This retrieval takes place sometimes in the form of reinterpretation of stories, myths, and legends as a remembered history of a region, class, caste, gender, or race, sometimes as intertextual interpolation of quotations, allusions, and references. This type of discursive practice was undertaken both during and after the colonial occupation. It operates differently in different continents.

In Asia, heritagist reading takes the form of identifying biblical ideas in Hindu, Buddhist, Confucian, Taoist, Shintoist traditions, and in the thought-worlds of indigenous peoples, as a way of explaining the basic elements of the Christian gospel, rather than solely relying on Semitic and Hellenistic terms to express them. In the initial stages, the heritagist mode of interpretation focused particularly on the textual tradition of Asia, as it was being unearthed by a group of benevolent European scholars known as 'Orientalists'. For the early high caste Indian converts of the nineteenth century, such a revisitation of their ancient texts provided a means to connect with their past and validate their 'noble' culture, and also enabled them to reconfigure their new identity as Indians and Christians. Such an exercise was not limited to nationals, or to India. Missionaries such as Jean Calmmette and W. H. Mill in India, Matteo Ricci in China, and Alexandre de Rhodes in Vietnam, played a critical role in utilizing profitably the high cultural and textual traditions of Asia.

Among Christian converts, an early exponent of heritagist hermeneutics in India was K. M. Banerjea, the Indian convert whose work I have discussed elsewhere.[7] A. S. Appasamy Pillai, (1848–1927) was another. His hermeneutical practice resembles closely that of Banerjea, but unlike Banerjea whose interpretive task was confined to texts, and especially *Vedic* texts, Appasamy Pillai's framework was far wider. He was familiar with not only Sanskrit texts but also Tamil sacred texts, but his hermeneutics was not confined to a textual mode but included a visual mode as well. The underlying principle for both men, however, was the same. Both found that Hindu sacred scriptures and Indian seers anticipated Christ. Appasamy Pillai claimed that 'long before Saint Thomas or any other Christian missionary came to India' (Appasamy Pillai 1924: 94), the Rishis had predicted the coming of Christ:

The Rishis of the *Rig Veda* sing of Hiranya Garbha, the golden egg, or "the golden child, who was born Lord of all." He created everything and asked the question *to whom shall I sacrifice?* In this verse is found the germ of two well known Christian doctrines: that of Christ the Logos who was before all things and from whom all things created were made: and the doctrine of atonement, or redemptive sacrifice, which is put forward by many Hindus as the stumbling block in the way of their acceptance of Christianity.   (Appasamy Pillai 1924: 93; italics in original)

Appasamy Pillai urged his fellow Christians to read the *Vedas* to see for themselves the anticipation of the old Indian sages: 'I should say study the old *Veda*, if you want to lay the foundation for the true or new *Veda*, which teaches us about an all-powerful God, the author of all things who is as rich in love and mercy as He is in power and majesty' (Appasamy Pillai 1924: 92).

Appasamy Pillai's interpretative efforts were not restricted to seeing intertextual connections between Hindu and Christian texts, one as faltering and the other as final, but he also made use of yoga techniques in his hermeneutics. By employing yoga practice in his prayer and meditation he was able see visions either of God as Light or of the heavenly Christ: 'I believe in God, in Jesus Christ, in the Trinity, in heaven and so forth not because I read about them in the Bible but because everyday I catch glimpses, gloriously and utterly real, of these divine realities' (Baago 1969: 110). What he saw in his visions was Christ appearing in his spiritual body, *sūksma sarīra*, of dazzling glory. It was in this spiritual body, Appasamy claimed, that Christ revealed himself to Abraham and Moses, led the children of Israel in the wilderness, appeared as the 'form of the fourth' when Nebuchadnezzar threw three young men into the furnace in the Book of Daniel (Dan. 3: 25), and appeared to the disciples at the Transfiguration. For Appasamy Pillai, visions were more than aids to meditation, they were manifestations of reality, and he claimed that they 'support and confirm my theological beliefs' (Baago 1969: 110). God's purpose for humankind was revealed through visions. In his view, the Hebrew prophets Daniel, Ezekiel, Isaiah, and the early apostles, Paul, and John, were seers—persons who saw the fullness of God's appearance. Appasamy Pillai appealed to and sought support not only in Jesus's words but also in his own experience: 'Our Lord declares, "Blessed are the pure in heart, for they shall see God.". In John 17: 1, our Lord Jesus himself lifted up His eyes unto heaven and showed the oneness of Himself with the Father, and oneness of Himself with His disciples so that three might be made perfect in one. Thus we derive our support for our position that this type of experience is vital from the experience of our Lord Himself' (Appasamy Pillai 1924: 113).

At a time when the British and Foreign Bible Society was full of stories of how the 'natives' were attracted to the gospel through practice of the Protestant principle of simple self-reading and study of the Bible, Appasamy Pillai's advocacy of visual hermeneutics went beyond such claims. Drawing on his Hindu understanding of the visual, the idea of God appearing to devotees, Appasamy Pillai was able to point out that the experience of the divine was not limited to history, or to text, but lay in one's capacity to see and be seen by God, to visualize and be in the presence of the divine. His advocacy of faith through vision was particularly important at a time when missionaries denigrated Hindu images of gods and goddesses. Appasamy Pillai claimed that visual vocabulary was not simply an extension of the oral or written word, but was another way of acquiring divine knowledge—through the eyes. Appasamy Pillai made use of the visual manifestation familiar to Hindus to reshape his understanding of Christ and biblical faith.

In Africa, the heritagist mode of interpretation acts out its role differently. Unlike some of the Asian interpreters who dared go beyond the biblical records to discern the presence of the divine in their own textual and experiential traditions, Africans tend to draw illumination from the religious phenomenology of the biblical world. The heritagist mode functions in two ways in African biblical hermeneutics. Sometimes it makes use of the cultural concepts and practices of Africa, and seeks for comparable echoes in the biblical tradition as a way of validating indigenous cultures and refining their deficiencies. The African cultural world is replete with spirits, ancestors, demons, and angels, kinship and indigenous healers, and with practices such as polygamy, libation, etc. These concepts and practices were seen as convenient prerequisites for entering the world of the Bible which was populated with similar notions and customs.[8] It was this that led Africans to claim that they had a special access to the texts denied to their counterparts in the West. Desmond Tutu, the celebrated opponent of apartheid, wrote: '[T]he biblical world view in many ways is far more congenial for the African than for Western man—the African is much more on the wave length of the Bible than Western man was originally' (Tutu 1972: 19). The other African vision of the heritagist mode draws upon the biblical heritage in order to highlight the presence of African people and place names in political, social, cultural, and religious life of the biblical world. Such an exercise involved unearthing African personalities like the Ethiopian Eunuch, Hagar, Ebedmelech, the Ethiopian who saved Jeremiah, Simon the Cyrene, Apollos of Alexandria, and also identifying countries located in the continent of Africa, such as Egypt, Cush, Put (Libya or Somalia), Lubim (Libya) and drawing attention to their substantial role in the biblical history. It also allowed Africans to rectify negative images of Africa, and by tracing the presence of Africans in the Bible, they reiterated the claim that Africans were part of salvation history even before Western missionaries introduced Christianity to the continent.

Referring to the ancient heritage is not confined to Asians or Africans. Latin Americans, too, have recently entered the scene. Latin American liberation theology, whose basic tenets were influenced and informed by Barthian and Marxian understandings which posited an unfavourable attitude towards religions and cultures, is now earnestly trying to turn its theological focus on its indigenous people and their religious precepts. One such attempt was undertaken by Elsa Tamez (Tamez 1993*b*: 33–56). She set out to reclaim an earlier form of Aztec religion where Quetzalcóatl of Nahuatl was venerated as the only God and remembered with affection as supreme God of compassion and peace. With the decline of theocracy, however, and the emergence of militarism, the God of life, Quetzalcóatl, had given way to Huitzilopochtli, the Sun God, who emerged as a warrior and conquistador God. In a changed context, the Aztecs erased the earlier beliefs about Quetzalcóatl and co-opted the warlike qualities of Huitzilopochtli. With several biblical texts as foundation (Ps. 19: 1–4; Luke 7: 1–10; Mark 7: 24–30), and citing profusely from Paul's letter to the Romans (1: 1 to 3: 20; 4: 17; 7: 18; 12), Tamez postulated that God had been made known to all humanity through divine power and work, thus drawing attention to the possibility of finding divine revelation in the native religions before the advent of the Europeans and their perceptions of the biblical God. She wrote: 'We can also speak of the God of life in Latin America before the invasion, and there are elements of Náhuatl culture that permit us to at least catch a glimpse of it' (Tamez 1993*b*: 36). Her argument, in line with those of Asians and Africans, was that the word of God cannot be limited, or confined to biblical revelation, but can also be experienced in other cultures. The key is the divine commitment to life, and this is the bridge to the God of the Bible.

Non-textual traditions, too, played a prominent part in heritagist reading. Here some of the popular folk tales, legends, riddles, plays, proverbs, and poems that are part of the common heritage of the people, are re-employed and placed vividly alongside biblical materials, in order to draw out their hermeneutical implications. The various versions of the Parable of the Prodigal Son in different cultures is a case in point. The parable of the Two Brothers, a popular story among the Sukuma people of Tanzania, has interesting parallels with the Lucan Prodigal Son. Both these stories have a father and two sons and in both the younger son is received back into the family and rewarded. Although in their plots and in their thematic emphasis they differ, the additional insights that the Sukuma parable provides, such as the values of community and unity, serve to enrich and complement the biblical story (Healy and Sybertz 1996: 104–106). Jyoti Sahi, the Indian artist and theologian, finds another dimension in the same parable, but this time from an environmental perspective. He reads concurrently the legend of the Uraons, the indigenous people of Central India who tell a similar story to that of the prodigal son. Compared to the biblical and to the African parable, both of which deal with inter-personal relationships, this legend is essentially about alienation from one's own environment. It is about a son finding fortune in an alien land. In this parable of the Uraons, the Karam tree, symbolizing the ancient tradition and which is the metonymy for the father in the gospel parable, is rejected and uprooted. The son goes through a long process of rediscovering his roots, and eventually finds peace and harmony with his environment (Sahi 1997: 181–3).

By its very nature, heritagist hermeneutics proved to be a corrective to cultural amnesia and offered a form of resistance to cultural imposition and silencing. European rulers introduced a system of education, which on the one hand, cleverly undervalued the indigenous history, culture and religions, and, on the other, made the events of European history and the illustrious figures of Western literature and culture more familiar to the emerging indigenous educated class than their own heritage. Listen to the words of Peter Phan, a Vietnamese, now an American who was taught to behave like a French boy and for whom the dead French heroes were more real than his own living Vietnamese compatriots:

There [at school] I not only had to use French as my mother tongue, but also to study French literature, history, geography, art, and way of life. The textbooks were the very same ones approved by the French Department of Education and used throughout France and its colonies. I memorized the names of all of

France's kings and queens, military victories and defeats, rivers and mountains and valleys that every French schoolchild must know. My native tongue was only the second 'foreign language' in the curriculum, after English. It was even taught in French! In the examinations we had to translate Vietnamese texts into French and comment on them in French as proof of our comprehension. (Phan 1999: 116)

Heritagist reading offered potentially a positive space for overcoming the trauma of colonialism and for regaining the lost indigenous cultural consciousness. Delving into their heritage not only helped the colonized to cope with colonialism and the missionary onslaught on their religious traditions, but it also helped them to nurture cultural pride. None of them envisaged political emancipation. Some of them even benefited from colonial rule. In Appasamy Pillai's case he was awarded a title in recognition of his loyalty to the British Raj. After the demise of European occupation, retreating into indigenous alternatives enabled Indian Christians to be part of the mainstream national life, thus avoiding being seen in their own countries as de-nationalized, de-racinated, and uprooted aliens.

It could be viewed as a limitation that the heritagist reading is apologetic in purpose and what it achieved with its clever and creative interweaving of ideas and intertextual readings was to bolster Christian orthodoxy. The desire is to vindicate and validate the traditional religious and cultural values of pre-Christian Latin America, Asia, and Africa, but the Bible and/or Christ is the index to measure, weigh, analyse, and explain common concerns and biblical themes embedded in the indigenous narratives. Recently, an Indian biblical scholar, Madanu Francis, has engaged in a comparative study of two men of legend textualized in the biblical Job and the puranic Harischandra as a way of probing the nature of human suffering. The story of Harischandra as a fighter for truth is familiar to most Indians. For his investigation, Francis used the fifteenth-century rework by a Telugu poet Gaurana, who based his version on two earlier works, *Markandeya Purna* and *Devi Bhagavata Purana*, the former compiled around fifth-century CE. Gaurana's embellishments come closer to the biblical version. Both these textual traditions have certain things in common: the narratives open with a divine assembly; raise the question whether a human being is truthful and righteous; as a test case a person is singled out; a wager is placed; protagonists lose their property and family but eventually regain everything they lost. The underlying aim of these legends is to portray their heroes as men of exemplary piety. Though Francis's enterprise is seen as an exercise in promoting better understanding between Hindus and Indian Christians, Francis makes clear his belief in the superiority of biblical faith when he postulates that the book of Job confronts the traditional teaching on retribution, whereas the Hindu text reinforces the doctrine of *Karma* which upholds the view that suffering is predetermined. He goes on to assert that the concern and love of God for the sufferer is explicit in biblical tradition: 'It is obvious that the God of the Bible is not far above, he is with the people, loving and caring for people. This concept is not clear in Harischandra' (M. Francis 1998: 76).

In Tamez's case, the Bible is utilized as a vehicle to establish the long-running continuity of indigenous identity by pointing to biblical passages which clearly acknowledge God's presence and power in other cultures and other times. The heritagist approach is also overtly Christocentric. In his call to retrieve the heritage, A. J. Appasamy, the son of Appasamy Pillai whom we encountered earlier, reminded his fellow Indian Christians of the need to emphasize the foreshadowing glimpses of Christ in the cultures of other people as a preparation for Christ as the apogee of revelation:

We Indian Christians have become denationalized. We have no knowledge of the culture of our country and are aliens in our own land. We must certainly see to it that this criticism is no longer true of us. Our witness to Christ will be far more effective if our links with the heritage of India are close. Our loyalty to Christ must not waver. He demands from us complete faith and full surrender. But He has come to fulfill and not to destroy. Whatever is noble, true and pure in the life of India must be dedicated to him.   (Appasamy 1992: 150–1)

Among the weaknesses of heritagist hermeneutics is that it gave Western audiences nicely finessed representations of the exotic. Another is that the glorification of native impulses, and their entrenchment in provincial contexts may continue to lead to insularity and isolation at a time when there is a lot of cross-over, interchange, and borrowing.

Nationalistic readings

Such interpretations emerged immediately after the colonized nations gained their territorial independence. These discourses are often character-ized by a mood of buoyancy and self-reliance. The prominent agenda, in the life of the newly emancipated nation states aimed not only to recapture the things which were profaned and degraded by colonialism and its ally modernism, but also to revitalize the nation's resources to build a prosper-ous and egalitarian society, and launch the nations firmly into the age of industrialization and the path of modernity. Whereas the heritagist read-ing focused on the cultural vandalism caused by colonialism, nationalistic reading gave its attention to the economic damage caused and tried to mark a complete break with it and repair its harmful effects. For the most part, what this discourse did was to harness the communal psyche of the Christian community and provide a biblical basis for the Christian Church's participation in building up the newly emancipated nation states.

Soon after Indian independence, Indian planners embarked upon an ambitious programme of development and initiated a series of Five Year Plans in which the alleviation of India's poverty and industrialization were the central themes. The statement issued by the Indian Churches' consult-ation on 'New Patterns of the Social Witness of the Church in India'[9] captured the mood of the time including the desire to emphasize national rather than communal, that is, in the Indian usage, religious community and identity: 'It is the Christian's duty to participate in building a new social and economic order in India, and thus to share in the creative action of God and to witness to the Lordship of Christ over human society. We Indian Christians are often preoccupied with our own needs. But we must resist the temptation to be communal, and must throw ourselves, whole heartedly into all truly nation building activities.'[10]

J. R. Chandran, who was one of the young theologians emerging at that time, welcomed as 'very commendable' the effort of the state to reduce economic inequalities, overcome unemployment and illiteracy, and increase the national wealth through agricultural and industrial output (Chandran 1953: 54), and encouraged the Indian Churches to join forces with the government planners. Rejecting both economic systems which benefit and promote individuals profiteering, and also totalitarian control which denies freedom of the masses, Chandran advocated responsible national planning and development. He identified in the Bible, the marks of social planning, which Indian economists could look for. In Leviticus chapters 19–25, he saw a blueprint for a well-ordered society 'not left to the whims and fancies of private enterprise' (Chandran 1953: 49). He appealed to the Leviticus code's insistence that land belonged to God, and 'the main principle was that the means of production were to be owned by the whole nation and not by any private individual or group' (Chandran 1953: 50). He wrote: 'The earliest expression of Christian community life, as seen in Acts was in terms of having all things in common, popularly known as the Primitive Christian Communism' (Chandran 1953: 50). Biblical faith was not motivated by the rational principle of economic life, and the underlying basis of primitive Christian communism was that all people belonged to God because Christ died for all. The distribution of wealth was the manifestation of the redeeming act of God in Christ. The experiment of early Christian movements, with their assertion that no person had absolute right over property and that the whole community was responsible for all its members, Chandran claimed, was not a transitory but an enduring paradigm worthy to be emulated. He appealed to James (2: 1–13; 5: 1–6), and 1 Corinthians (11: 17–22), as demonstrating the Christian Bible's concern for social and economic relationships. Ultimately for him, all social planning had to be evaluated in the light of the Christian gospel. He declared: 'Our faith is more fundamental than social planning' (Chandran 1953: 49), and went on to state that 'the Church has also the responsibility of placing every social and political activity of the people under the judgement of God', and the Christian Church 'always stands for the Word of God which judges and redeems the world' (Chandran 1953: 56).

The Indian Church's concern for justice was inspired, as all the Indian nationalistic readings affirm, by the continuous celebration of God in Christ, his incarnation and death, resurrection, and ascension. The characteristic aspect of the nationalist mode of interpretation was the power of the gospel to critique and reshape society. In the process, Indian Christian theologians revoked the orientalist notion of a cyclical view of history, and saw it as producing 'crippling social fatalism' (Chatterji 1967: 17), or saw Hinduism as a decadent religion which was in need of Western revitalization. What is new is that, instead of the colonialists, now it is the turn of some of the natives to cast aspersions on Hinduism and native customs.

Liberationist readings

This type of interpretation arose as a result of the failure of the development programmes inaugurated soon after independence. These came to be seen as a façade for a new colonialism practised by the developed countries of the West. They were regarded as a failure on two counts. First, they were achieved at the expense of the Third World people. Their beneficiaries were the investors and not the local people for whose welfare the programmes were initiated. Investment and production were oriented towards the needs of the markets outside Third World countries rather than towards the priorities of the Third World. In the Philippines, for example, rapid development and modernization led to the immiseration of the urban poor and the impoverishment of the rural population. Secondly, the programme of development was launched at the expense of the human rights of the local people. Industrialists with their eyes on profits were insisting on a climate conducive to investment. This could only be provided by a military takeover of the regions, especially Latin America. The local rulers, faced with economic crises, and allured by foreign investors, began the process of militarization. The Brazilian economic boom in the late 1960s proves this point: 'It is enough to remember that the harshest repression began simultaneously with the economic boom in 1968. . . . Behind repression there is not only inhumanity and ideology but a specific model of development' (Arias and Arias 1980: 57).[11] A similar story was played out in South Korea. Economic success began in South Korea at a time when it had ruthless military rule.

While left-leaning politicians and economists were working out in ideological and structural terms the way to move from dependence to liberation, theologians were looking at the issue from the perspective of ethics and were seeking for a liberation based on biblical foundations—a total liberation which was capable of creating a new person and a qualitatively different society. There was an awakening of collective consciousness among the disillusioned Latin American Christians who largely represented the presence of another world, a world which was conveniently forgotten by the rulers, many Church leaders, and the investors. The late archbishop Oscar Romero's words, though arising from a Latin American context, rang a bell for the rest of the Third World as well:

There we found peasants without land or steady work, without water or electricity in their poor dwellings, without medical assistance when women give birth, and without schools when the children begin to grow. There we found workers with no labour rights, workers who were fired when they demanded their rights, workers at the mercy of economy's cold calculations. There we found mothers and wives of the 'disappeared' and political prisoners. There we met the people who live in hovels where misery exceeds the imagination. (Romero 1982: 3)

The presence of this other world, and its 'irruption' to use the phrase made popular by Gutiérrez, brought out the worst in much of the Church's hierarchy as it hurried to distance itself from the Latin American social reality. The theme, nevertheless, that the new Latin American theologians found to offer assurance and hope to people who were confronted with suffering and misery was the biblical notion of liberation. The Church's central teaching—salvation—was seen as a way to happiness hereafter, as answering the old question of how to save unbelievers. The new question was how to transform the unjust world and how people can be saved from the effects of structural sin. The aim was to make the Church credible and the gospel meaningful. For such a task there was no dynamic message other than liberation. The liberation of the poor, the liberation theologians claimed, depended on hearing once again the word of God which was hidden in the pages of the Scriptures but tacitly suppressed and manipulated by the official Latin American Church. Thus began a very rigorous rereading of the Bible from a liberation perspective. Confronted with the socio-economic reality which provided no hope for the poor, and armed with the social analysis of this reality, Latin American liberation theologians delved into the Scriptures and unearthed a series of texts which were relevant to their context—the Exodus as a model for oppression and liberation, the prophetic writings as a critique of structural evil, the historic Jesus as an exemplar of liberative praxis, and the apologetic literature as a message of hope for the poor. Facing somewhat different contextual needs, Korean theologians came up with the theology of *minjung*, and the Filipinos with the Theology of Struggle, both finding much in the Bible to support and illuminate their concerns. An often-quoted work was the rereading of Mark's use of *ochlos* from the *minjung* perspective by Ahn Byung Mu. In this article, 'Jesus and the *Minjung* in the Gospel of Mark'

Ahn Byung Mu made a distinction between Mark's use of *laos* and *ochlos*. Utilizing the historical-critical method, Ahn Byung Mu established that the former connoted 'the elect', the 'chosen ones', whereas the latter connoted the ordinary people, the *minjung*. For Ahn Byung Mu, the identity of the *minjung* could be grasped with a 'theology of event' based on the relationship of Jesus to the *ochlos*, the *minjung*. Mark's preference for *ochlos* rather than *laos* was his way of an indicating a social class which had been marginalized and abandoned, namely the so-called 'sinners' and 'outcasts' befriended by Jesus (Ahn 1995: 85–104).[12]

Since I am dealing with liberation hermeneutics in a later chapter, let me offer a brief comment at this juncture. Liberation hermeneutics as an activity cuts across national and cultural boundaries, and such work is often addressed explicitly to the world at large rather than to a local audience. Hence its interpreters see themselves as part of an international community of interpreters. Although their subject matter may be region-specific, their audience, and their discursive style are Western. Though they try to provincialize the West in their work, there is an implicit acceptance of the Western mode of thinking. They are aware of the hegemonic and capitalist and predatory nature of the Western theory of discourse. Their mastery over methodology and scholarship allow them to interact with the West on its own terms.

Dissentient readings

These were undertaken by those who threw their lot in with the nationalists but whose concerns were not registered in the independence struggles, and now, after finding a political voice, challenge the national project in the name of class, gender, language, or ethnicity. They are characterized by a mood of disillusionment such as sometimes sets in after independence. Now, it was not against the missionaries or colonizers that they spoke but against their own interpreters, whose hermeneutics were seen as pollution-based or hierarchically, patriarchically, or communally influenced. While nationalist and liberationist readings were committed to economic development, holding to the view which held colonialism responsible for all inherited evils, dissentient reading attributed the blame to their own national planners for excluding them from the national scheme.

Essentially, this is a reading of internal dissent. These are discourses which emphasize the subjectivity of minorities—whether they are women,[13] Indian Dalits,[14] Japanese *burakumins*,[15] Tribals,[16] minority linguistic groups, and others who have been disenfranchised and cannot see themselves as part of the national mainstream. They are disenchanted with the narrative of the nation, and bitterly critical of nation-building and development projects which did not register the concerns of the minorities. As these newly freed nations have further degenerated into corruption, inefficiency, gender discrimination, and communal violence, these interpreters have identified with subnational or regional positions. Their critical identities were derived not from broader national movements and freedom struggles, but from ethnic or special-interest agitation based on caste, language, or gender. The most vibrant and creative among these dissenting voices have been women. They appropriated the Bible variously, some projecting biblical characters such as Miriam, Deborah, Orpah, or the daughters of Zelophehad as models for empowerment, others employing cultural anthropology and socio-political readings in order to reclaim the voices of women and recover their self-identity. Their methods, too, have varied, from dramatization to visualization, story-telling and creative performance.

To this discursive practice one could add the dissenting reading of the disenfranchised—people whose political freedom had been stifled or denied by newly independent nation states. The reading undertaken by the ordinary people of Malawi, at the time of the referendum about whether to move to a multi-party system is a notable case in point. A survey done among Christians during the Hastings Kamuzu Banda's regime found three texts were appropriate and spoke to the political choice faced by Malawians. The first came from the Wisdom tradition, the Book of Job: 'Let us discern for ourselves what is right; let us learn together what is good' (34: 4). The second was from the Book of Daniel whose enduring message was the intervention of God on behalf of the people who passively suffered persecution. The third was from the historical books— Judges to 2 Kings—whose message was that the fortune and misfortune of a nation was predicated upon the king's obeying and upholding the Law (Chingota 1996: 53). The Sunday sermons, too, were seen as vehicles for dissenting reading. One of the passages used was Genesis 2: 15 to 3: 13 which speaks of the freedom and responsibility of human beings, thereby urging Malawians to use God-given freedom to extricate themselves from the one-party state in which they found themselves (Chingota 1996: 47).[17]

The hermeneutical drama which was played out during and after the Nicaraguan political struggle was another example of a reading of internal dissent. The peasants of Nicaragua found support in biblical narrative for their fight against the neo-colonial lackey General Somoza, using both verbal and visual means to describe the oppression they confronted.[18] Now, however, the same Bible became a cultural-political tool in the hands of another group of ordinary people—the Miskitu Indians—to fight against the very nation state they helped to establish after the fall of Somoza. Their readings have roots in and derive their stimulus from historical and political schema of dissent outlined in the biblical narratives. The Sandinistas who supported various indigenous political organizations during their struggle against Somoza now, in government, found these groups and their new demands irksome. Initially they supported the indigenous language programme of the Miskitus and their bid for land rights, but when the Sandinistas realized that the indigenous political groups under MISURA-SATA (Miskitus, Sumus, Ramas, Sandinistas United Together) were claiming nearly 40 per cent of the land, they promptly jailed the leaders. When released, the leaders fled to Honduras, where they became the front for the American-backed Contras. Once again, the Bible played a key role, and the rebels relied on its pages to understand their world. They modelled themselves as the persecuted people of the Bible. The biblical story of oppression and glory was projected onto their own story of struggle. The Sandinistas who were once seen as the liberators were now perceived as oppressors. Various biblical images and personalities provided the Miskitu with ammunition to fight their opponents. The ruling Sandinistas were variously identified as Antiochus Epiphanes, the Egyptians, Babylon, and Rome. They were portrayed as the Canaanites and Philistines whom the Miskitus would drive out of the land. The Miskitus leaders who were championing the cause were the new Moses, Joshua, Gideon, and David.[19] Once again the biblical narrative served the needs of a minority community faced with oppression. The Bible was seen as the voice of God, providing instruction in their struggle against the enemy. Both the peasants of Nicaragua and the Miskitus employed a similar typology as the hermeneutical key. In the case of the former, the typology enabled them to face the common enemy, Somoza and his henchmen, but in the case of the latter, the same typology was used against their former comrades.

The interpretation of dissent seems at first glance to embody the kind of subversive character which promises to explode the hegemony of the heritagist and nationalist interpretation for ever. Yet when looked at more closely for the way in which it is constituted, it simply reassembles imperialist categories which it had seemed to deconstruct. Its attendant conceptual abstractions—race, ethnicity, class—when hived off into biblical interpretation, reveal the deeply compromised nature of its formation. The notion of the modern nation state and the discipline of theological reflection were mutually implicated from the start. What is surprising is that newer forms of hermeneutics which emerged in recent times especially excluded by the national narrative—those of women, Tribals, aborigines—were taking exactly the same discursive style. They were not only adopting a national focus but employing precisely this developmental evolutionary form that had been responsible for excluding them from the mainstream narrative.

Concluding remarks

In conclusion, a couple of points. One, it must be remembered that these groupings are not fixed. They are imprecise and overlap. They signify certain patterns and trends. This does not mean that everything has been made to fit within a particular framework. In selecting particular examples, my purpose is to highlight important key hermeneutical moods and moments. At best what this tries to achieve is to promote a discussion, and offer some markers, rather than to parcel out biblical interpretation into neat categories. There are many crossings-over and returns within these patterns and trends.

Two, we need to remind ourselves of the context in which the biblical interpretation with which we are concerned emerged and grew. The context was mission and colonialism, and it still continues to be so. In the West, where the present shape of biblical interpretation was transformed by the questions raised by the Enlightenment, by new archaeological and textual discoveries, and by new interpretative activities generated by historical-critical methods, the mission motif was never entirely forgotten.

Although in the West, especially in liberal academic circles, the mood has changed, and scholarship has been secularized, though with some of its totalizing tendencies usurped by postmodern concerns, the situation in the Third World remains the same and mission continues to exercise an influence in interpretation. Notwithstanding the sophistication of its method and the changed language, the target even of liberation hermeneutics, a hermeneutics which was hailed as a beacon of hope for the Third World, seems to be the same as in the old colonial era—that of evangelizing the poor. What postcolonial biblical criticism, on the other hand, tries to do is go beyond the Christendom model, and seek to place biblical scholarship in a non-missionary and less apologetical context.

NOTES

1. Cited in Gustavo Gutiérrez, *Las Casas: In Search of the Poor of Jesus Christ*, trans. R. Barr (Maryknoll, NY: Orbis Books, 1993), 47.

2. I have reproduced here the version used by Gutiérrez. For his textual comments on this verse, see ibid. 47, 484 n.

3. For a detailed examination of the debate, see Lewis Hanke, *All Mankind is One: A Study of the Disputation between Bartolome de Las Casas and Juan Gine de Sepulveda in 1550 on the Intellectual and Religious Capacity of the American Indians* (DeKalb: Northern Illinois University Press, 1974) and also Angel Losada, 'The Controversy between Sepúlveda and Las Casas in the Junta of Valladolid', in J. Friede and B. Keen (eds.), *Bartolomé de Las Casas in History: Toward an Understanding of the Man and his Work* (DeKalb: Northern Illinois University Press, 1971), 279–307.

4. I deal with Colenso's dissident reading at great length in my *The Bible and the Third World: Precolonial, Colonial and Postcolonial Encounters* (Cambridge: Cambridge University Press, 2000), ch. 4, 110–39.

5. Cited in Andrew F. Walls, *The Missionary Movement in Christian History: Studies in the Transformation of Faith* (Maryknoll, NY: Orbis Books, 1996), 62. In the same chapter, Walls also provides examples of how missionaries in the eighteenth and nineteenth centuries applied the Pauline passage to Asia and Africa.

6. For an extensive treatment of Equiano and Apess, see my *The Bible and the Third World*, ch. 3, 75–90.

7. See ibid., ch. 3, 90–7.

8. The literature surrounding these issues is too vast to be listed here. For a convenient introduction, see G. O. West and M. W. Dube, *The Bible in Africa: Transactions, Trajectories and Trends* (Leiden: Brill, 2000).

9. For the consultation report, see *Religion and Society*, 7/1 (1960), 42–72.

10. See 'Nasrapur Findings II Christian Participation in Economic Development', *Religion and Society*, 7/1 (1960), 46.

11. See also pages 40–58 for the negative aspects of development in the 1960s (Esther Arias and Mortimer Arias, *The Cry of My People: Out of Captivity in Latin America* (New York: Friendship Press, 1980)).

12. The original version appeared in *Minjung Theology: People as Subjects of History*, edited by the Commission for Theological Concerns of the Christian Conference of Asia (Maryknoll, NY: Orbis Books, 1981).

13. Literature on Third World feminist hermeneutics is too vast to be listed here. For a publication which covers the three continents, see 'Reading the Bible as Women: Perspectives from Africa, Asia, and Latin America', *Semeia: An Experimental Journal for Biblical Criticism*, 77 (1997). For a helpful survey, see Anne M. Clifford, *Introducing Feminist Theology* (Maryknoll, NY: Orbis Books, 2001), esp. the chapter entitled, 'Feminist Perspectives on the Bible', 46–91.

14. Dalit is the self-designated name for those who were formally known as untouchables in Indian society. Dalit is a Marathi word derived from '*dala*' which could mean either 'of soil or earth' or 'that which is rooted in the soil'. See Mini Krishnan's editorial note in Bama's *Karukku*, Macmillan's Dalit writings in translation (Krishnan 2000: p. v). For examples of Dalit biblical hermeneutics, see V. Devasahayam, *Outside the Camp: Bible Studies in Dalit Perspective* (Madras: Gurukul Lutheran Theological College and Research Institute, 1992); V. Devasahayam, *Doing Dalit Theology in Biblical Key* (Madras: Gurukul Lutheran Theological College and Research Institute, 1997); M. Gnanavaram, ' "Dalit Theology" and the Parable of the Good Samaritan', *Journal for the Study of the New Testament*, 50 (1993), 59–83; M. Arul Raja, 'Towards a Dalit Reading of the Bible: Some Hermeneutical Reflections', *Jeevadhara: A Journal of Christian Interpretation*, 26/151 (1996), 28–34; M. Arul Raja, 'Assertion of Periphery: Some Biblical Paradigms', *Jeevadhara: A Journal of Christian Interpretation*, 27/157 (1997), 25–35; M. Arul Raja, 'A Dialogue between Dalits and Bible: Certain Indicators for Interpretation', *Journal of Dharma*, 24/1 (1999), 40–50.

15. Japanese *burakumin*s are the people who are not part of the Japanese success story. They were the non-people who were settled in ghettos (*buraku*) because of the polluted nature of their work. For a biblical example, see Teruo Kuribayashi, 'Theology of Crowned with Thorns', in D. Carr (ed.), *God, Christ & God's People in Asia* (Hong Kong: CCA Theological Concerns, 1995), 93–114.

16. The term 'tribe' has caused conceptual as well as empirical problems. Now the term, which originated in colonial times as a convenient description, has been adopted by the Indian Tribals to mean dispossessed, deprived people of a region. See Virginius Xaxa, 'Tribes as Indigenous People of India', *Economic and Political Weekly*, 18/Dec. (1999), 3589–95. For examples of Tribal hermeneutics, see *Jeevadhara: A Journal of Christian Interpretation*, 24/140 (1994), a special volume entitled: 'Tribal Values in the Bible', and also Thanzauva and R. L. Hnuni, 'Ethnicity, Identity and Hermeneutics: An Indian Tribal Perspective', in M. G. Brett (ed.), *Ethnicity and the Bible* (Leiden: E. J. Brill, 1996), 343–57. For an Australian Aborigine reading of the Bible, see Anne Pattel-Gray, 'Dreaming: An Aboriginal Interpretation of the Bible', in D. Smith-Christopher (ed.), *Text & Experience: Towards a Cultural Exegesis of the Bible* (Sheffield: Sheffield Academic Press, 1995), 247–59, and for a Maori reading, see John H. Roberts, *Thinking Theologically in Aotearoa New Zealand* (Tui Gr Paihia: Colcom Press, 2000), esp. ch. 6 'Exodus through Canaanite Eyes', 34–42.

17. During the Malawian referendum debate, the use of the Bible was not a one-sided affair. Those who wished to maintain the status quo and who sided with the one-party rule

mobilized biblical passages to show that the present regime was ordained of God. It was the Markan text—'And a cloud overshadowed them, as a voice came out of the cloud, "This is my beloved Son, listen to him" ' (9: 7)—which was taken to establish the validity of Hasting Banda's rule. His supporters also cited texts to show that seeking a change against the anointed ruler went against the will of God (Ps. 2: 1–3), and therefore people should be obedient to the leadership appointed by God (Prov. 1: 1; Eccles. 4: 5, Rom. 13: 1, Titus 3: 1–2) (F. L. Chingota, 'The Use of the Bible in Social Transformation', in Kenneth R. Ross (ed.), *God, People and Power in Malawi: Democratization in Theological Perspective* (Blantyre: Christian Literature Association in Malawi, 1996), 49).

Institutional Churches such as Roman Catholic and Presbyterian played an important role in the referendum and produced pastoral letters and statements in which the Bible was used to critique the prevailing situation. I would like to call this dissentient reading from the top—reading undertaken on behalf of people rather than by people themselves. The Roman Catholic letter 'Choosing our Future: Pastoral Letter from the Roman Catholic Bishops 1993' and the Presbyterian document 'The Blantyre Synod Statement on the Transformation of Malawi 1993' both contain biblical passages which speak about God's justice, righteousness, and love as measures against which the government must be evaluated and judged. One of the texts cited by the Roman Catholic letter urging acceptance of plurality and of dissenting views was the saying of Jesus from Matthew: 'So always treat others as you would like them to treat you; that is the Law and the Prophet' (7: 12). The implication was that it was a patriotic duty as well as a biblical injunction to respect and be generous towards others who are different. The Pastoral letter of the Roman Catholic Church and the Presbyterian statement can be found in *Christianity in Malawi: A Source Book*, ed. Kenneth R. Ross (Gweru: Mambo Press, 1996), 203–35.

18. For the textualized form of their verbal commentaries, see Erneto Cardenal (ed.), *The Gospel in Solentiname*, trans. D. D. Walsh, vols. i-iv (Maryknoll, NY: Orbis Books, 1982), and for their visual representation, see Philip Scharper and Sally Scharper, *The Gospel in Art by the Peasants of Solentiname* (Maryknoll, NY: Orbis Books, 1980).

19. See Susan Hawley, 'Does God Speak Miskitu? The Bible and Ethnic Identity among Miskitu of Nicaragua', in M. G. Brett (ed.), *Ethnicity and the Bible* (Leiden: E. J. Brill, 1996), 315–42 and also Margaret D. Wilde, 'Faith and Endurance in Eastern Nicaragua', *Christian Century*, 1/Nov. (1989), 973–4.

3

CODING AND DECODING: POSTCOLONIAL CRITICISM AND BIBLICAL INTERPRETATION

> Today, Sacred Scripture is studied with the benevolent approval of *the pax imperialis*; no exegetical activity disturbs the tranquillity of the 'empire' for a single moment.
>
> (José Cárdenas Pallares 1986: 2)

> The Bible is at once our strongest weapon of conquest, and our most inoffensive method for constructive work.
>
> (*For the Healing of the Nations* 1916: 30)

> The basic question is not about scripture, but is about us.
>
> (Wilfred Cantwell Smith 1993: 242)

The singular aim of postcolonial biblical studies is to put colonialism at the centre of biblical scholarship. Both the historical and the hermeneutical literature of biblical interpretation over the last four hundred years has been defined by the needs of the Reformation and Counter-Reformation, and later by the Enlightenment and such attendant features as rationalism, or its offshoot historical criticism. There is a remarkable reluctance among biblical scholars to speak of imperialism as shaping the contours of biblical texts and their interpretation. What postcolonialism makes clear is that biblical studies can no longer be confined to the history of textual traditions, or to the doctrinal richness embedded in texts, but needs to extend its scope to include issues of domination, Western expansion, and its ideological manifestations, as central forces in defining biblical scholarship.

Postcolonial criticism has a variety of tools and it can be applied to biblical studies in a number of ways. As indicated earlier, it is a diverse field, but the two overriding interests which undergird it are pivotal to this discourse—text-based analysis and highly theoretically grounded textual reconstructions which derive their energy in the main from poststructuralism, but also from other resources in the range of critical theorizing such as semiotics. It is with the former, text-based analysis, that this chapter is concerned. Postcolonial criticism is at its best when it seeks to critique not only the interpretation of texts but also the texts themselves.[1] In this, postcolonial criticism is allied with most oppositional practices of our time, especially feminist.

Orientalist tendencies

Postcolonial criticism can do for biblical interpretation what the project initiated by Edward Said has been doing for the study of the literature, language, history, and documents which the West has produced and continues to produce about the Orient. His intervention has resulted in the introduction of a potent new critical marker—orientalism. Orientalism is a systematic way of conceptualizing the 'other' based on the 'ontological and epistemological difference between Eastern and Western economic (as well as religious) "mentalities"' (Said 1985: 259). Or, put at its simplest, it is a kind of narration which tends to misnarrate the 'other'. It is basically a hermeneutical manoeuvre and management of the colonial and neo-colonial world by the West, to make its representation of the 'other' liable to certain kinds of superintendence and manipulation. Orientalism operates in a number of ways. Its first mark is to stereotype the other as irrational, insincere, and unreliable, in contrast to Western rationality, sincerity, and reliability. For instance, Ernest Renan, in his *Life of Jesus*, expressed his doubts about the honesty and sincerity of Eastern people. Even the biblical writers themselves could not escape his negative portrayal:

But sincerity to one's self has not much meaning for Oriental peoples, little accustomed as they are to the subtleties of the critical spirit. Good faith and imposture are words which, in our rigid consciences, are opposed as two irreconcilable terms. In the East there are numberless ingenious loopholes of escape and circuitous paths from one to the other. Even highly exalted men, like the authors of apocryphal books, Daniel, for instance, and Enoch, committed, to aid their cause, and without the shadow of a scruple, acts which we should call frauds. Literal truth is of very little value to the Oriental; he sees everything through the medium of his ideas, his interests, and his passions. (Renan 1897: 159)

A commentary written during British colonial rule in India for the use of Indian theological students replicates this perception of the unreliability of Orientals. Commenting on the reference in Acts 21: 39 to 4,000 men, Walker notes: 'We know, in the East, how frequently numbers are exaggerated through the lack of mental accuracy' (Walker 1910: 472). A similar sentiment was expressed more recently after the Indian independence, by Elliott-Binns. He cautions that historical statements found within the texts have to be treated circumspectly because the authors are untrustworthy: 'But in listening to its voice, allowance had to be made for the very different methods of thought and utterance customary at that time and in the place of its origin. Even today, the mind of the Oriental works differently from that of the European, being careless of exact detail, and making statements which are not intended to be taken literally' (Elliott-Binns 1952: 58).

The second mark of orientalism is to project the 'other' as incapable of detached analysis. Godfrey Phillips, in his proposals for introducing the Old Testament to what he calls the 'younger churches', remarks that the 'lack of a sense of perspective and of historical knowledge' among Africans would 'make them find the prophets obscure and difficult' (Phillips 1942: 8). In view of their fondness for folklore, Phillips feared that 'simple African would be liable to miss the vital difference between fact and fiction, and to mingle together in his mind folklore tales and Bible stories, including those about Jesus' (Phillips 1942: 10). Africans, in Phillips's view, had 'not reached the stage of rationalizing their belief' (Phillips 1942: 8).

As recently as the 1980s, Friedrich Huber, teaching in an Indian theological school, found that the scientific sophistry of the historical-critical method was too much for the simple minds of Indian students. He found that the 'intellectual abilities of a BD [Bachelor of Divinity] student are limited' (Huber 1980: 136), and the 'critical method is too complex to be practised by them', and 'it would take them too much time to learn the method. At the end they would be completely exhausted' (Huber 1980: 140). His solution to the problem was to replicate the orientalist notion that Indians were only capable of an emotional response. His advice to Indian students was that they should develop a 'maximum ability to listen' and pose questions which would excite their emotions and sentiments such as: Was there anything in the text which surprised me? Was there anything which made me angry? What did I like especially? Is there anything which seems to be unacceptable? Which association came to my mind? Do I remember similar situations to those mentioned in the text? To support what Huber called practical-oriented exegesis, he brought in two sages, one modern and the other ancient. Abhishiktananda, a highly revered Frenchman who lived in twentieth-century India, advocated indigenization and adopted an Indian ashramic lifestyle. Standing within the long tradition of European orientalists who valorized a brahminical form of Hinduism, he constantly argued for the employment of the 'profound intuitions' found in the *Upanishads* as a way of doing Indian theology. Huber cited him as his authority: 'It remains true, however, that a purely rational and so-called scientific approach to any sacred Scripture will never succeed in penetrating its [i.e. the *Upanishads*] secret' (Huber 1980: 147). To clinch his argument, Huber also went on to cite a biblical authority in the person of an unknown Israelite sage: 'The fool takes no pleasure in understanding, but only in expressing his opinion' (Prov. 18: 2). What Huber failed to note is that India had a long-standing critical tradition and schools of interpretation and had developed over many centuries the science and systematic investigation of meaning (Manikkam 1982: 94–104; Chari 1990; Kapoor 1998).

This kind of orientalizing streak is not confined to Western interpreters. There are examples of Third World interpreters re-orientalizing stereotypical images constructed by the West. Indian biblical scholars often ventriloquize ideas popularized and propagated by orientalists. One such notion is that India has no understanding of history. Thus, in trying to establish parallels between the biblical Job and the puranic Harischandra, Madanu Francis falls in with the long-standing view that India lacks a sense of history: 'History is the one weak spot in Indian literature. It is in fact, non-existent. The total lack of historical sense is so characteristic, the whole source of Sanskritic literature is darkened by the shadow of this

defect, suffering as it does from an entire absence of exact chronology'
(Francis 1998: 37). The Indian historian, Romila Thapar has shown that the
Indian perception of history is different from the modern Western notion,
as also is the form in which it is maintained, namely in genealogies, myths,
and historical narratives (Thapar 1972: 1–22, 1992, and 2000). Another
example is in the construction of the notion of similarities between
ancient Israel and the present-day Third World situation, fixing both as
predictable and unchanging. Elements such as poverty, oppression,
religious authoritarianism, which were prevalent in biblical times, are seen
as resembling those in the current Third World situation. An Indian biblical scholar saw striking similarities between the prophet Amos's eighth-
century Israel and twentieth-century India, in cultic practices bereft of
social care and justice prevalent in public life (Koonthanam 1982: 112–13).
Similarly, Latin American liberation theologians have often, in their
enthusiasm to seek biblical warrant, identified the Roman-occupied
Palestinian setting with that of their own continent: 'The socio-political
situation in Jesus' day presents striking parallels to the situation that gave
rise to Liberation theology in Latin America' (Boff 1980: 103). In her
otherwise innovative study of St Mark's gospel from a Japanese feminist
perspective, Hisako Hinukawa, too, falls victim to internal orientalism
when she draws too-easy parallels between modern Japan and the
Palestine of old (Kinukawa 1994: 22). Such statements fail to note the
critical differences between exploitation in first-century Palestine and
the neo-colonial exploitation of Latin America today, or between ancient
Mediterranean cultures and modern Third World countries.

Pause and reflect

Galilee was the home of Jesus and played a key role in the gospel narratives.
It has become an important interpretative site in the search for the
historical Jesus, both past and present.

TASK ONE: Go through the gospel accounts and see how Galilee has been
portrayed there.

TASK TWO: Select a few commentaries written during and after colonialism
and see how these interpreters represent Galilee. Examine how ethnicity,
nationalism, and race inform and influence their exegetical explorations.

TASK THREE: Select biographies of Jesus written during the nineteenth-
century search for Jesus (David Frierich Strauss, A New Life of Jesus (1879);

Ernest Renan, *Life of Jesus* (1897)) and compare them with those written in the current search (E. P. Sanders, *The Historical Figure of Jesus* (1991); Sean Fryne, *Galilee and Gospel: Collected Essays* (2000)). How do they construct Galilee? What do they mean by Galilee? Is it a geographical location or a fabricated entity? What presuppositions lie behind their articulations? To what extent is their imaging of Galilee coloured by the social, cultural, and political position of these authors and their times.

As a helpful guide to the exercise read: Halvor Moxnes, 'The Construction of Galilee as a Place for the Historical Jesus', Part I and Part II, *Biblical Theology Bulletin: A Journal of Bible and Theology*, 31/2 and 3 (2001), 26–37 and 64–77.

Decoding texts

Anyone who engages with texts knows that they are not innocent and that they reflect the cultural, religious, political, and ideological interests and contexts out of which they emerge. What postcolonialism does is to high-light and scrutinize the ideologies these texts embody and that are entrenched in them as they relate to the fact of colonialism. Stuart Hall, the British cultural critic, analysing how televisual discourse operates, has identified four codes embodied in the narrative—hegemonic, professional, negotiated, and oppositional (Hall 1973: 16–18). The function of the hege-monic code, turned to our postcolonial purpose (Hall does not explicate this and other terms), is to legitimize, consolidate, and promote the dom-inant values and ideological interests of the ruling class. It tends to embrace colonial and monarchical models and patriarchal practices, and to praise, prescribe, and perpetuate them as sources of good governance. The professional code is concerned with preservation, centralization, and interpretation of laws, traditions, and customs. It promotes law and order, ideas of nationalism, religionism, and authority. The negotiated code is about how an event, action, or experience is interpreted or rearticulated to meet new theological or ideological situations. The oppositional code is the voice of the marginalized which finds its place in the discourse in spite of the fact that the text is produced by those who have vested interests. These categories can be easily discerned within the biblical narratives as well as in the current social texts, and provide a useful set of categories for a postcolonial reading.

Hegemonic code: A notable case in point is the throne-succession narrative which illustrates the successful assumption of power by David and his son Solomon, 2 Samuel 9–20 and 1 Kings 1–2. This textual segment must be one of the earliest written sources for these events, and by all accounts was produced by order of King Solomon and written possibly by one or several court scribes with the intention of producing an official history of the Davidic dynasty (Clévenot 1985: 13). The fact that in the list of the king's officers, a recorder and a secretary are mentioned, is an indication that literary activity was going on at the time (2 Sam. 20: 25, also 2 Sam. 8: 17). In any narrative it is the opening and the end which give clues as to the expectation and essential characteristics of the text. 2 Samuel 9: 1 begins with the question posed by David—Is there anyone left of the house of Saul?—and 1 Kings 2: 46 ends with the reassuring message that informal charismatic leadership has given way to the institution of kingship in the form of the Davidic dynasty: 'Thus Solomon's royal power was securely established.' In between the anxious question and the affirmative answer, the narrative contains a bewildering sequence of events. It deals with international politics (David's war against the Ammonites), exposes adultery and murder (David's illicit affair with Bathseba, and his killing of her husband Uriah), recounts family intrigues (rape, revenge, and rebellion involving Tamar and Amnon), records the consolidation of power by establishing Jerusalem as the capital, by appointing a class of powerful people (see 2 Sam. 20: 23–6 for the list of officers), and by creating royal tribunals to control the judiciary; it records family politics and the transition of palace power (the demise of David and rise of Solomon). What lies behind these adventure-like stories is how to gain and consolidate power by destroying the enemy. It is about offering security and stability to Solomon and, although he was not the older son, sanctioning his rule.

Another writing which reflects the view of the establishment is the Book of Ecclesiastes. It was written during the Hellenistic period when Palestine was under Ptolemaic control.[2] There emerged a new class of people—traders, crafts and business people who took advantage of imperial policies. The Preacher himself was one of those beneficiaries who built great houses, owned gardens and plantations, developed irrigation systems, gathered wealth, possessed herds, flocks, and slaves, and surrounded themselves with many concubines (2: 4–8). He was influenced by the ruling ideology which created a cultural milieu in which the creation of wealth and pursuit of money became increasingly important. His vocabulary was filled with commercial terminology—business, occupation, money, riches, success, ownership, financial bankruptcy. He not only advised his reader/hearers to be publicly loyal to the king and the powerful—'Even in your thought, do not curse the king, nor in your bedchamber curse the rich' (10: 20)—but also postulated the notion that 'money answers everything' (10: 19). His counsel to potential trouble-makers was not to interfere in policies and economic matters but enjoy life as long as you can and as much as you can (3: 12). For the poor he had only bad news. Nothing can change their situation (4: 1–3; 5: 12).[3]

Pause and reflect

READ THE BOOK OF ESTHER: Find out which empire provided the background to the book. What kind of hegemonic values does it reinforce—feudal? patriarchal? Go through chapter 1, and find out what sort of social, economic, and political situation is described there. List the people who are mentioned. Who are they? Which social and economic backgrounds do they come from? What kind of social life do they lead? Now go through the chapter again and see what kind of people are totally absent from the text? Which class of people are left out?

LOOK AT THE ROLE OF ESTHER AGAIN: How does she respond to the text's hegemonic agenda? Does she accept patriarchal and imperial values or use them as a means of survival. What was the underlying purpose of the narrative—gender struggle or national survival?

As a helpful guide to the background, read: Itumeleng Mosala, 'The Implications of the Text of Esther for African Women's Struggle for Liberation in South Africa', *Semeia: An Experimental Journal for Biblical Criticism*, 59 (1992), 129–37.

Professional code: This is produced by trained experts, scribes, rabbis, and doctors of law. The importance of scribes emerged during the exile when there was the necessity to translate and interpret Scriptures to maintain the rule of law and stability. The professional writers codify rules about diet, worship, handling of slaves, cultivation of lands, dealing with debts, and obligations to women and children. These rules serve to promote hegemonic interests. Examples of professional codes in the Bible are Leviticus and Deuteronomy and household codes in the New Testament letters. Though these were primarily collections of rules and regulations dealing

with ordering and maintaining society, they often provided radical programmes as well. Thus, when the prophets of Israel exposed the deepening
disruption of society, it was the priestly writers who thought through and
rendered their prophetic anger constructive by putting forward social
reorganization programmes. The Deuteronomic and Levitical codes were
prophetically inspired reinterpretations of the Torah by the priestly
writers. The radical social reordering represented by the Jubilee code and
the Sabbath law is an indication that, though professional writers were
associated with the dominant class by their status and function, and articu-
lated the concerns of this group, scribes often worked independently and
could take a position which worked against the interests of the group with
which they were aligned.

Pause and reflect

READ THE HOUSEHOLD CODES recorded in Ephesians 5: 21 to 6: 9; Colossians
3: 18 to 4: 1; 1 Peter 2: 18 to 3:7. At the outset, these codes promoted authority,
obedience, and family values. How do these square with values like human
rights, justice, and equality?

READ A FEW STANDARD COMMENTARIES and find out the historical circumstances out of which these codes emerged? Choose a couple of commentaries
written by male and feminist scholars and scrutinize how they exegete these
passages? What kind of value-system do they promote and advocate?

As a guide to the background, read: David L. Balch, 'Household Codes', in
David E. Aune (ed.), *Greco-Roman Literature and the New Testament:
Selected Forms and Genres* (Atlanta: Scholars Press, 1988), 25–50.

Negotiated code: While this acknowledges the legitimacy of hegemonic
elements, it operates within temporal and spatial limits. It carries with it
the potential for adaptation in varying contexts. Thus, an episode or event
or experience is retold and reconfigured to suit different contextual needs.
For instance, the first three gospels report a lawyer approaching Jesus with
a pertinent question (Mark 12: 28–34, Matt. 22: 34–40, Luke 10: 25–37). In
each case, he asks Jesus: which is the chief or the first commandment?
Though the question remains the same, the three gospel writers locate it in
three different settings to meet different ecclesiastical needs. In Mark, the
questioning is not part of the hostile atmosphere in which Jesus found
himself prior to this event. The scribes turn to Jesus with a view to solving

a problem. They come to Jesus because of his ability to answer well (Mark 12: 28). The enquiry is part of the rabbinical dialogue, and the scribes come to find out where he stands within it. Hence the question from one of the scribes: 'Which commandment is the first of all?' The issue here is what hermeneutical principle Jesus applies to produce his answers. Matthew's context is slightly different. After the fall of the Jerusalem temple, Rabbis were constantly asked to codify and summarize the 613 commandments for Jews who were trying to configure their faith and practice without the benefit of Temple teaching. At the same time, the nascent Christian community was trying to articulate its own faith and practice without the benefit of the Temple and the Torah. Faced with a different context from that of Mark, Matthew changes the question and words it differently: 'Teacher, which is the great commandment in the law?'(Matt. 22: 36). For Matthew and his community, it was important to know how one could do justice to the 613 commandments. For Luke and his readers/listeners, on the other hand, the paramount question is not about knowing the commandments but whether one can really practise and make them workable. That is why, in his narrative, Luke connects what appears as a controversy-dialogue with the story of the Good Samaritan, and shifts the emphasis from knowing the law to its actual implementation (Luke 10: 29–37).

Pause and reflect

READ THE PASSAGES THAT DEAL WITH THE POOR AND THE RICH IN LUKE'S TWO VOLUMES: How are the poor represented? How are the poor understood? Are they somewhat needy or real destitutes? Do they speak in Luke–Acts or they are spoken to? How is the role of the rich understood in Luke–Acts? In the Lucan account of the Young Ruler, how is wealth portrayed? Is wealth itself a problem, or the way one uses it?

SELECT A FEW COMMENTATORS AND EXAMINE HOW THEY VIEW THE QUESTION OF THE RICH AND THE POOR: How do they view economic inequality? Do they see it as God-given? Or changeable ? Are such questions relevant compared to the higher truths these narrative try to promote? What kind of solution do they advocate—charity? reconciliation? or redistribution of wealth?

As a guide to the background, read: George Soares-Prabhu, 'Class in the Bible: The Biblical Poor a Social Class?', in R. S. Sugirtharajah (ed.), *Voices from the Margin: Interpreting the Bible in the Third World* (London: SPCK, 1991), 147–171.

Protest/oppositional code. This is discerned in the voices of those who are on the periphery but whose concerns creep into the text despite the fact that it is recorded by the group whose interests are linked with the establishment. In spite of this elite focus, subversive elements are evident, if only partially. An example is the case of the five daughters of a man called Zelophehad, who, when their father died, stood up in front of Moses, Eleazar the priest, and other leaders, and demanded the right to the name and inheritance of their father (Num. 27: 1–11). Moses took their claim to the Lord and the narrative says that they were right in their demand: 'You shall give them possession of an inheritance among their father's brethren and cause the inheritance of their father to pass to them. And you shall say to the people of Israel, "if a man dies, and has no son, then you shall cause his inheritance to pass to his daughter"'(Num. 27: 7–8). But this victory is short lived. Nine chapters later, in Numbers 36, restrictions are placed upon the marriages of these women. They cannot marry outside their tribe, lest the property be transferred to another tribe.

A postcolonial reading will also be alert to the covert ways the marginalized protest. The encounter between the dominant and the subordinated is laden with duplicity—keeping secrets or lying, hiding goods, sabotage, and deception. These are subversive mechanisms employed by the subordinated to resist the system of oppression. It is a method of achieving personal and group goals by people in a socially disadvantaged position. The ingenious explanation given by the Israelite midwives, Shiphrah and Puan, of their inability to comply with Pharaoh's command to kill all the Hebrew boys at birth (Exod. 1: 15–19)—'Because the Hebrew women are not like the Egyptian women; for they are vigorous and are delivered before the midwife comes to them'—is a serious case of deception from the point of view of the Pharaoh, but an act of defiance by the midwives.

The act of subversion of the oppositional voice need not be open, aggressive, and vocal. It may be mediated through sheer silence. The silence of Jesus depicted in John before the Roman Procurator, Pontius Pilate, is an example of this. He does not defend himself or offer an answer. Jesus's silence, could be read as a sign of his powerlessness, and his non-intervention a sign of his marginalization, but his refusal to participate in a hostile milieu which was the creation of the colonial power is an indication that he is not willing to appeal to the expectations of the powerful. His silence is a challenge to colonial authority. In fact Pilate reminds Jesus of the power he has as a Roman Prefect: 'You will not speak to me? Do you not know that I have power to release you, and have power to crucify you?' (19: 10). Although Jesus makes no riposte to this claim, his silence itself gathers an element of power to itself and makes Pilate's power a relative thing. When eventually Jesus gives an answer—'You would have no power over me unless it had been given you from above'—what he is asserting is that the truly powerful one is God from whom the power of emperors, kings, and governors is derived.

Another oppositional case depicted in the New Testament is the Crucifixion, the pivotal event from which Christian faith emerged. Topographically and culturally, the event took place in a marginalized space—Golgotha, outside Jerusalem, the Holy City. The Crucifixion was an act of humiliation, torture, and execution designed to deal with those considered most threatening to the establishment and its interests. It was the Romans who initiated and enacted this form of punishment meted out during the Jewish festival of Passover. It included a public demeaning for the victims. How the cross, which thus symbolized powerlessness, in turn became a powerful symbol during the period of colonial expansion is another story. Nevertheless, the Crucifixion is for those who challenge and work towards dissolving hegemonic and imperial codes. Postcolonial criticism not only celebrates the presence of oppositional voices within the text but also marks out silenced voices and spaces in texts which fly in the face of hierarchical and hegemonic modes of thought.

It is apparent that these codes—hegemonic, professional, negotiated, and oppositional—are not rigid and closed systems. As we have seen, they may represent more than one concern, and occasionally register interests that contradict their declared ideology. Their usefulness is largely that they are able to provide indicators to scrutinize how texts embody and codify the vested interests of those who produce them.

Pause and reflect

It is a cliché but true that almost all written documents are produced by winners, and that protest voices are rarely registered. One has to search carefully to note their presence. There are at least two biblical characters who are often written out and under-exegeted but who in their own way make their presence and their protest. Go back to the Book of Esther again and look at the role of Queen Vashati. What do you make of her refusal to attend the royal court? Would you regard her act as a revolt against patriarchy?

READ THE STORY OF RUTH: While Ruth, the Moabite, is willing to assimilate with the dominant culture and espouse ethnic and cultural harmony, her sister-in-law, Orpah refuses to be part of the hegemonic agenda and goes back to her mother's house, and thus to her own gods and goddesses and to her ancestors. Would you see her act as a revolt? How do commentators represent these women—Vashti and Orpah—who are not part of the dominant ethnic group and outsiders?

As a helpful guide to the exercise read: Laura Donaldson, 'The Sign of Orpah: Reading Ruth through Native Eyes', in R. S.Sugirtharajah (ed.), *Vernacular Hermeneutics* (Sheffield: Sheffield Academic Press, 1999), 20–36.

Jesus and the colonial context

Whenever a new theory bursts onto the scene or a contemporary issue crops up, it is customary to look at Jesus and fit him into the theoretical framework or draw fresh insights from his teachings. What postcolonial criticism does is to depart from such attempts and bring out the limitations and ambiguity that surrounds the material that concerns Jesus. Those who are familiar with the New Testament record of his teachings would admit that the material we possess is unsystematic and sporadic in nature. His style was to face challenges with a riposte or a retort. In his response to questions, Jesus rarely gave a direct answer. He spoke in parables, pithy sayings, and paradoxes.

Jesus's life and work were undertaken at a time when Galilee was under imperial occupation. Though the Roman empire was noticeably different from modern empires, certain features are common to all empires—they subjugate people, deprive them of freedom, inculcate the values of the invaders, and seize the cultural heritage and property of the invaded. Roman rule in Palestine engaged in all these activities. Galilee was ruled for Rome by Herod Antipas (4 BCE–CE 39), one of the sons of Herod the Great, who carried on his father's policy of building on and fortifying the land he ruled. The gospel narratives do not record any explicit resistance by Jesus against the colonial occupiers. So far as we can infer from the gospel records, Jesus did not urge anyone to desert the imperial army. Such desertions took place only a hundred years later at the time of Marcus Aurelius (161–180 CE), when it was reported that soldiers joined the Jesus movement (Micklem 1920: 104). It was not Jesus, but John the Baptist whose activity paralleled that of Jesus, who raised a vocal protest against Herod. This protest, however, was not against him as an imperial ruler. John the Baptist's condemnation was aimed at Herod's marriage to Hero-dias. The basis for the censure was the immorality of such an act rather than political protest against the Roman oppression. John the Baptist's indignation was directed against Herod's marrying a woman who was already married to his brother, Philip. Incidentally this is the only narrative in Mark in which Jesus is not central to the narrative. Rather than promot-ing a head-on clash with the occupiers, what we read in the gospels is that Jesus's attention was turned towards local profiteers and those with vested interests, who, in collusion with the Romans, took advantage of the temple system. Some of Jesus's postures and actions might indicate that he was indirectly very much against the Roman presence, but not that he got involved in a direct way.

Jesus and earthly rulers

There are at least four reported sayings of Jesus in which kings and earthly rulers figure. What emerges from these sayings is that they provide an occasion for Jesus to contrast the standard of behaviour expected in the counter-cultural egalitarian society envisioned and advocated by him with the standard of behaviour promoted by those of 'the world'. The first reported saying was prompted by a dispute among the disciples, initiated by the ambitious request of the sons of Zebedee with regard to places of honour in the Kingdom. This provided the immediate context for Jesus to differentiate between the style of leadership envisaged by him and that of the earthly powers (Mark 10: 42–5; Matt. 20: 20–8; Luke 22: 24–7). Whereas Matthew and Luke spoke directly of the kings of the gentiles, Mark was decidedly ironic in speaking of 'those who supposedly rule over the gen-tiles and wield lordship over them'. Earthly rulers 'wield lordship' and 'exercise authority' over those whom they rule. This way they dominate and exploit the people they govern to their own advantage. But this is not how the followers of Jesus are expected to behave: 'It shall not be so among you.' The exercise of authority among his followers cannot be like that practised by earthly powers—exploitative and domineering—but directly opposite to this—serving and sacrificial. Jesus himself offered his life as a model. This reference to the gentile rulers might be seen as an implied criticism, and a generalized comment, but it is not a direct attack upon imperial occupiers. There is no allusion to Herod or any reference to his style of governance.

The second reported saying occurs in Jesus's statement about John the Baptist's identity. The disparaging rhetorical observations about people in royal houses wearing soft raiments (Matt. 11: 8; Luke 7: 25) was meant to compare the simple attire and frugal habits of John with the opulent living and lavish clothing of the rich (Matt. 3: 4). This saying was aimed at those who lived flamboyantly, exploiting people. Jesus's response was to provide an alternative redistributive system which would benefit the needy and the poor, namely the sharing of goods and the rejection of normal securities like money (Matt. 6: 19–21, Luke 12: 33–4, 16: 13).

The third saying is placed in the context of Jesus hitting back at the accusation that he was in alliance with Beelzebub (Mark 3: 23–5; Matt. 12: 25, Luke 11: 17). Here Jesus invoked the image of a kingdom, a city, or a house divided within itself, in order to show that it could not survive such division. The intention was to contrast two diametrically opposed kingdoms—that of Satan and that of God. Here again, the allusion to Herod or the Roman ruler is indirect, although the hearers/readers who have been raised up with the apocalyptic understanding of the Danielic vision of 'the saints of the most high' (11: 23) replacing earthly kingdoms, especially tyrannical ones, will have seen here either the Herodian dynasty or the Roman rulers, the most immediate sources of oppression, symbolizing the current evil age (Freyne 2000: 200).

There is a fourth reported saying of Jesus about a king going to war without counting the cost, which occurs only in Luke (14: 31). This could be a reference to the strained relationship between Herod Antipas and Aretas, the King of the Nabateans, which led to the war in CE 32. Whether this was a direct reference to an immediate problem or an event that was introduced to suit Luke's theological needs is not clear. What is common with the other sayings is that the reference to imperial power was only indirect, and that Jesus seems to have advocated a code of behaviour which was the opposite of the one espoused by worldly powers.

What is strikingly clear is that Jesus's alternative vision did not challenge or seek to radically alter the colonial apparatus. First, the reported sayings of Jesus do not contain any scathing attack on the expropriation of land by the colonizer. Jesus's sayings ignore the question of land belonging to the imperial power. Recent studies indicate that the peasants of Galilee, Southern Syria, and Transjordan lost significant parts of their land as large estates came under the control of the Herodians and other powerful families during the New Testament era. Since land was the basis of most of their living and yields were unstable, the debt burden of the peasants resulted in loss of their lands. The peasants had to support the temple, the priesthood, and the Herodian regime, and also pay tribute to the Romans (Luke 3: 13–14; 19: 8; 20: 22; 23: 2). It is difficult to calculate the percentage accurately, but between 15 and 30 per cent of their of total income was diverted for these purposes. Apart from this, they had to meet cultivation costs and find money for their personal needs. Both economically and politically, the peasants became captive in their own lands. Many became landless labourers, slaves producing crops for absentee landlords. Many were insolvent debtors and were threatened with imprisonment (Luke 12: 58–9), but there was a conspicuous silence on the part of Jesus with regard to the land which was the cause of such contention at the time. While there was a radical sharing of food, clothes, and wealth in his movement, the land was inexorably left out of his own sayings.

It is also clear that Jesus's alternative vision presupposes the continuance of the status quo rather than materially altering the unequal relationship between the oppressed and the oppressor. As indicated earlier, the payment of tax was a burning issue of the time. The only explicit occasion when Jesus had the opportunity to deny the legitimacy of the Roman imperial presence in Palestine was when a group consisting of Pharisees and Herodians quizzed him directly about paying tribute to the imperial authority (Mark 12: 13–17; Matt. 22: 15–22; Luke 20: 20–26). The inclusion of Herodians here suggests that they were supporters of Roman rule. Though Jesus's enigmatic reply—give unto Caesar what is Caesar's and to God what is God's—caused considerable difficulty not only to the original hearers/readers but also to later interpreters, there was nothing in the saying which questioned the unfairness of the tax system. Contrast Jesus's reply with John the Baptist's answer to those tax collectors who came to be baptized by him, and asked him what they should do, 'Collect no more than is appointed to you' (Luke 3: 13). Under the Roman empire the system of collecting the revenue put extreme pressure on the poor. There is no textual evidence to suggest that Jesus was concerned to see the repressive tax system changed, or that he urged the tax-collectors to revolt against it. Instead, he believed in the better nature of the people, who were propping up the system to reform it from within. His table-fellowship with the tax-collectors, and especially his dealing with Zacchaeus, a chief tax-collector and a rich person, who was part of the corrupt system of economic oppression, is indicative of Jesus's attitude (Luke 19: 1–9). Biblical interpreters tend to see Jesus's dealing with Zacchaeus from the perspective of a sinner being won over by Jesus. To an extent they are right, but what they fail to note is the apolitical nature of this encounter. Jesus did not call upon Zacchaeus to give up his profession nor did he request him to work against the system, the very system which had made him rich. Instead, Jesus believed in a person's, in this case Zacchaeus's ability to transform things from within, beginning with his own change of heart. Jesus's response to an oppressive structure had more to do with personalizing the issue and appealing directly to individuals to act fairly than with calling for a radical overhaul of the system. Jesus challenged the system by appealing to the moral conviction of individuals, and raising their consciousness. It was such a conviction which provided the courage to take the next step. Zacchaeus's response was to go beyond the law's requirement for restitution (Exod. 22: 1 and Num. 5: 5–7). It was the strength of that inner transformation which induced Jesus to go and dine with him. The people around Zacchaeus, too, noticed the difference. The result of such an approach is that we end up as good individuals with pure intentions who put up with oppressive institutions and allow power structures to remain unaltered. The struggle seems to be not against structures or invaders but within oneself.

The only incident where the gospels record a harsh remark by Jesus aimed at the ruler is when he called Herod 'that fox' as reported in Luke (Luke 13: 32). Those raised in urban Western understanding of the psychology of the animal kingdom tend to view the fox as a cunning, sly, deceitful animal. But in the rural West and the Mediterranean world, perception of the fox is slightly different. Its nature is seen as rapacious and gratuitously destructive. The fox is also seen as a threat to hens and chickens. The reference to the fox here is quite revealing, because, in the same passage, Jesus goes on to compare himself to a mother hen who offers protection: 'How often have I desired to gather your children together as a hen gathers her brood under her wings' (Luke 13: 34). Jesus is seen as a protector of the weak rather than as a protester against the system which produces and perpetuates predatory conditions. It is clear that Jesus was remembered for his telling comments on royal status, privilege, power, and lifestyle, and that the alternative vision he envisaged was incongruent with the courtly power. The very use of such contrastive standards, hinting at and exposing their vain, exploitative, and predatory nature, was, in its context, bold and challenging. The particular nuances of Jesus's position as we have identified it here make much sense when seen in the light of the prevailing apocalyptic understanding. For instance, it has been suggested that the inspiration for Jesus's sayings is essentially 'the apocalyptic understanding as this had received expression in various Jewish writings in the Second Temple period and which viewed the foreign rulers as belonging to the present evil age which was soon to be replaced by God's just rule on behalf of the oppressed' (Freyne 2000: 203).[4]

Colonial trauma and madness: The case of the Gerasene Demoniac

One of the tasks of postcolonial biblical interpretation is to expose the colonial presence concealed in the text. Richard Horsley, in his reclamation of Mark's gospel as a work of resistance written for a subjugated people, which spoke against the Roman empire and its henchmen, the Judaean and Galilean leaders, has unmasked the tendency of Western biblical scholarship to read the earliest gospel as a 'passion narrative with a long introduction', thus effectively erasing all traces of its opposition to foreign rule, and its atrocities, and the role of the local aristocratic collaborators whose support helped to prop up the system (Horsley 1998: 156). Unlike Luke–Acts, where most of the action takes place around urban centres, Mark locates most of his narrative of Jesus's activity in and around the Galilean villages. Although the empire appears directly in Mark only in the question of paying taxes to Caesar (Mark 12: 14) and in the persons of the governor and soldiers who executed Jesus as an insurrectionary (Mark 15: 1–32), his text is dense with colonial and military allusions and associations. One such instance is Mark's recording of the incident of the Gerasene

Demoniac (Mark 5: 1–20). The terminology in this narrative resonates with such connotations.

The incident, however, has been exegeted in at least three ways that take no account of the colonial context. The most prominent among them is a reading of the narrative from a mission perspective. The event taking place spatially outside the Jewish territory at Gadara, is taken to indicate the gospel reaching the gentile world and, by extension, the pagan world, meaning Asia, Africa, and Latin America. Another interpretation has the behaviour of the Demoniac explained in terms of social scientific categories and Western psychological theories. This is an attempt to mine new insights applying current critical categories to ancient data. In a third interpretation, African biblical interpreters have recently tried to vernacularize the incident by reading it in the light of African belief-systems regarding demon possession, witchcraft, and the spirit world (Avotri 2000: 311–25; Masoga 1995: 53–69). Here the emphasis is on Jesus's ability to domesticate and control supernatural powers. These three readings fail to take into account the colonial background against which the narrative is set.

On being asked his name, the Demoniac replies, 'My name is Legion.' This term has caused considerable difficulty to exegetes. It occurs in only one other place in the gospels. This is in Matthew, in connection with the report of the scene in the Garden of Gethsemane (Matt. 26: 53). Writing during the colonial period, Mary Baird was the first to uncover its colonial associations, and is unequivocal about its meaning: 'Now, there is no example in Hellenistic Greek of this word being used with other than a definite *military* connotation. Therefore it would appear in the N.T. contexts the word should be interpreted *literally*' (Baird 1920: 189; italics in original). The Tenth Roman legion was garrisoned in Palestine at the time when Jesus was engaged in his activities. The drowning of 2,000 pigs could be symbolic of the destruction of the colonial power.

'He begged him eagerly not to send them outside the country.' This request of the Demoniac that he should not be sent (*aposteile*) (5: 10) outside the country is interesting. The term *aposteile* means dispatch, as in the case of an officer sending a contingent of troops (Derrett 1979: 5). Like any other occupying colonial power, the Romans recruited people whom they had subjugated. It is evident from Josephus's writing that, from the time of Herod the Great onwards, Jews were drafted along with other

subjugated nationalities to serve in the imperial army and to be stationed throughout the Roman regions. At the funeral of Herod those in
attendance were Thracians, Gauls, Germans, and Jewish Guards. From
the time of Archelaus, Rome looked to Syria and Judea to supply ever-
increasing numbers of legionaries for service within the empire, and
filled gaps in the legions with the heftiest men from the province. The
Demoniac, according to the narrative, was a man of great physical
strength—'no one had the strength to subdue him' and must have been
a potential recruit. In the light of the Roman recruitment policy, the
man's request that he should not be sent outside his country seems to be
reasonable. The Greek word *agale* is translated as 'herd' but could also
mean 'a band of trainees' (Derrett 1979: 5). There may well have been a
training element in the Roman occupation forces which were stationed
in or around Gadara with a view to making a profit from the mercantile
routes which ran to Southern Arabia and India (Waetjen 1989: 116). Had
the terror of Roman military tyranny, and the thought of expatriation,
deranged his mind, leaving him obsessed night and day with the thought
of imperial service? Thus, when Jesus asked the man his name, the word
that sprung to his mind was the cause of his trouble—legion. It was the
fear of military service which made him plead with Jesus not to be sent
out of the country. The healing of the Demoniac was bringing back
sanity to a person who had been mentally unsettled by the colonial
presence and the prospect of severe military duty outside his own country. The command of Jesus (*epitrepien*) could mean a military command,
and *hormesen* is a natural term 'for troops rushing into battle' (Derrett
1979: 5). The reaction of those who benefited from colonial rule—the
townspeople and cattle-owners—is revealing. In order to maintain their
stranglehold on the people of the occupied territory, the colonizers allied
themselves with local merchants, business people, and landowners. Both
parties profited at the cost of the well-being of the people. These are the
'traitors and knaves' who seem to 'get on well with the occupying
powers and do their best to get on within the framework of the colonial
system' (Fanon 1990: 89). These cattle-owners and townspeople, in this
interpretation could well belong to the group of people who were mobilized by the colonial power, and who saw Jesus as a public threat. They
might well have feared that his action would upset their paymasters,
hence they beg Jesus to leave the territory. The symbolic allusions and

military overtones embedded in the text, then, are important aspects of this narrative.

There are two possible consequential ways of looking at this narrative: One is to treat Jesus's exorcism as an act of defiance against the ill-effects produced among a subject people as a result of the Roman occupation. Colonialism, in Fanon's view, is 'a favourite breeding-ground for mental disorders' (Fanon 1990: 201). In his study of the effects of French occupation on the Algerians, Fanon states: 'In the period of colonization when it is not contested by armed resistance, when the sum total of harmful nervous stimuli overstep a certain threshold, the defensive attitudes of the natives give way and they then find themselves crowding the mental hospitals. There is thus during this calm period of successful colonization a regular and an important mental pathology which is the direct product of oppression' (Fanon 1990: 201). Put at its simplest, demon possession is one of the defences the ordinary people resort to in order to face and withstand the stranglehold of colonialism, and Jesus's action is a disclosure of his hostility to colonial presence.

A second way of looking at this is to treat the action of Jesus as neutering the only option the oppressed had in declaring their opposition to the colonial occupation. Demonic possession was a type of social coping mechanism developed by the colonized to face the radical pressures imposed by colonialism. Jesus's dramatic removal of the condition not only disrupted the existing social way of dealing with demoniacs, but could also have been seen as a threat to an accepted mode of open hostility towards the Roman oppressors. Has Jesus simply treated the symptom without confronting the system which produces such behaviour? Has he in the light of his apocalyptic expectations, effectively removed one of the potential tools in the hands of the subjugated people?

Transcending the text, visualizing the reality

For too long, the focus of biblical criticism has been on verbalization. It has been seen as a literary activity dealing exclusively with texts and words. Ever since the emergence of Protestantism at the time of the development of printing, a high value has been placed on the written word, and the

Bible seen as a collection of texts which have to be read silently, analysed and interpreted. Scriptures are not simply texts, however, but narratives and scenarios for episodes of life, and along with reading, these invite and call for a more varied expression of interpretative avenues—theatrical performance, iconography, visualization. What postcolonial biblical criticism tries to do is to liberate the field from one-sided literary emphasis and identify and encourage other forms of expression. The imagining of biblical texts has spawned a number of examples which have not only enlarged visual conventions but also radically altered received interpretations. To illustrate this, let me cite two examples, one from the medieval period and the other a current one. Velazquez's 'Kitchen Scene with Christ in the House of Martha and Mary' (1618) overturns a well-known biblical story (Figure 1). The two sisters and Jesus are relegated to the background, and are hazily visible through a serving hatch. Looming large in the foreground is a young female cook, not mentioned in the Lucan story, with a pestle and mortar, preparing food. Her pose suggests that she is obviously paying attention to the conversation that was going on between Martha, Mary, and Jesus. Martha requests Mary's help, but Mary's silence

Figure 1 Velazquez, *Kitchen Scene with Christ in the House of Martha and Mary*, c.1618. Reproduced by kind permission of the National Gallery of Ireland, Dublin.

is indicative of her wish to listen to Jesus. Traditionally the Lucan passage (10: 38–42) has been used as a site to compare two opposite but interrelated themes—Christian action and contemplation. Mary is seen as the pious, prayerful one, and an exemplar of contemplative life, whereas Martha is less 'spiritual' but actively engaged in practical aspects of life. Quite contrary, though, to the conventional reading, Velazquez's portrayal marginalizes both the sisters through a servant girl who is actually involved in kitchen work, and, more importantly, did not have the choice that the two sisters had—to be either active or contemplative. Drury comments: 'Never before had a Christian painter taken the losing side of a hard-pressed cook as his way of interpreting St. Luke's story of Martha and Mary' (Drury 2000: 168).

Visualizing a well-known text can have much more radical consequences. Recently, the peasants of Solentiname, without the benefit of historical-critical tools, have used both verbal and visual hermeneutics to challenge the oppressive rule of General Anastasio Somoza, and as a way of subverting biblical narratives.[5] Just as with their verbal commentaries, the peasants' visual representation of biblical stories bridges and mediates

Figure 2 Matt. 2: 16. Reproduced by kind permission of Hermann Schulz.

between the biblical and Latin American contexts. In their painting to illustrate the massacre of the innocents (Matt. 2: 16) (Figure 2), the soldiers of Herod do not carry swords but automatic weapons. They are dressed in the uniform of the dreaded National Guards of General Somoza. These artistic changes are illustrative of the historical parallels between a Palestine dominated by the Romans and a Nicaragua controlled by Somoza. By reframing the biblical event, with its elements of both exploitation and emancipation, to suit the Nicaraguan context, the incident is no more seen as an event that happened in the past, but as an ongoing part of the lives of the peasants.

Propagandist literature or confessional writings

As indicated in the second chapter, since the arrival of the Bible with the modern missionary movement, its depiction, dissemination, and explication has been enmeshed in the context of propaganda and Church expansion. The Bible, especially the New Testament, has been projected as a document with a missional thrust facilitating missionary endeavours and promoting Christian values. In such a context the Bible provided the evaluative critical language to judge other peoples' cultures and texts.

Postcolonial biblical criticism aims at repositioning the New Testament writings as documents depicting inner doctrinal and creedal differences among the various parties and factions within the numerous groups of the rapidly and massively expanding early Jesus movements. Writing in the halcyon days of the British empire, T. Walker, a missionary in South India, was clear about the Bible's role in missionary expansion and its continued relevance to Britain as an occupier of other peoples' lands: 'In particular the Acts describe *the first evangelization of the Roman Empire* comprising at that period the main portion of the civilized world, as the first great instalment of that universal dissemination of the Gospel which the divine purpose had in view' (Walker 1911: 19; italics in original). He then went on to draw a parallel between the numerous provinces of the Roman empire and the outlying provinces of the British empire such as India, Ceylon, Sierra Leone, Uganda, and British North America. For him, the plan of the book 'shows us the Gospel spreading further and further, like circular waves propagated from a centre and growing larger and larger till they reach the distant shore' (Walker 1911: 18–19). Such missionary motifs are evident even in current readings which claim to be liberationist. Thus, in reclaiming the conversion of the African gentile Ethiopian eunuch for the African-American empowerment, Clarice Martin, almost echoing Walker, sees the narrative as the inauguration and advancement of the gospel to all lands:

The Lucan theme of universal salvation and world mission unfolds throughout Acts as the Gospel advances northward from Palestine through Antioch (Acts 9: 32–12: 24), westward through Asia Minor (12: 25–16: 5), Europe (Acts 16: 6–19: 20), and finally to Rome (Acts 19: 21–28: 31), the 'capital' of the Gentile world. Universalism in Luke–Acts underscores the certainty that the mission of Jesus and his church are 'united in the plan of God for the salvation of all nations'. The conversion of an Ethiopian eunuch provides a graphic illustration and symbol of the diverse persons who will constitute the Church of the Risen Christ.   (Martin 1989: 115–16)

What postcolonial biblical criticism tries to do is to treat the literature of the early Christian movements as confessional writings rather than a 'document' attempting to attract new converts. Textual claims on behalf of the Christian faith, such as 'I am the way, and the truth and the life' (John 14: 6), 'There is salvation in no one else, for there is no other name under heaven given among mortals by which we must be saved' (Acts 4: 12), and 'there is one mediator between God and humankind, Christ Jesus' (1 Tim. 2: 5), should be seen in the light of the constituency of intended readers, the narrative setting of these sayings, and, more importantly, as supportive of internal theological positions within the early Christian communities. In other words, they are not to be seen as statements made with Hindus, Buddhists, Sikhs, and countless indigenous people in mind. These assertions, if we read them with the above-mentioned perspectives, look much less triumphalistic. For instance, to take the case of the reported claim of Jesus in John's gospel. When the writer of the gospel stated that Jesus was the only way, truth, and life, he was addressing a community composed of Jewish Christians. Gentiles as such were conspicuous by their absence. The only gentile character one encounters in John is Pilate. Spatially, Jesus rarely leaves the Jewish territory and there is no reference to gentile mission as such. Instead of the Syrophoenician/Canaanite woman, the fourth gospel speaks about a Samaritan woman who identifies herself with her

Jewish forbears (4: 12). Similarly, and in contrast with the synoptic gospels, a royal official takes the place of the centurion, and there is no suggestion that he was a gentile, nor is there any comment on his faith (4: 46–54). Likewise, the community shows no urge for evangelism. The word *euaggelion*, a key term for the synoptic writers, does not figure in the fourth gospel, instead it employs *angelos* (message). Jesus does not gather the twelve nor does he send them out to preach. All the converts to the Johannine community are Jews—Nathaniel, the ideal Israelite (1: 47); Nicodemus, the ruler of the Jews and the teacher of Israel; Joseph of Arimathea, a member of the ruling class (19: 38), and the man born blind, an ordinary Jew (9: 1–39). Thus the statement at John 14: 6 was not aimed at gentiles, nor was it made in a missionary context. It was addressed to people who had already accepted Jesus. A variant reading of John 20: 30 puts this in its proper perspective: 'But these are written so that you may continue to believe that Jesus is the Messiah, the Son of God.'

To pursue this point a little further, this episode was part of the narrative setting (chapters 13 and 14) where the disciples, during the last days of Jesus, are shown to be apprehensive about their task and restless about their future. The questions they pose indicate this. Simon Peter wants to know where Jesus is going (13: 36), and Philip is anxious that Jesus should show them the father (14: 8). It was in this tense and troubled context that a worried Thomas posed his question. The reported answer was a consoling word for the distraught disciples, and it was not made to counter the claims of present-day Hindus, Buddhists, and Muslims. In other words, this and other exclusive claims were not missionary statements aimed at the adherents of other faiths. Neither do they tell us what Jesus the Galilean peasant thought about himself. What they convey is the confessional statement of a community that was struggling to redefine itself in the aftermath of its leader's demise. What we need to do is to read and judge Christian texts on their own terms, and find ways to respond creatively in situations where texts and stories are so often used to separate people and even whip up communal division and alienation.

To conclude: postcolonial biblical criticism does not possess its own tools. It largely depends on the existing methods but employs them as counter-tools and uses them as an act of disobedience directed against the text and its interpretation. Postcolonialism's critical undertaking is a fusion of a variety of methods ranging from the now unfashionable historical-criticism to contemporary literary methods. One of the significant aspects of postcolonialism is its theoretical and intellectual catholicism. It thrives on inclusiveness and is attracted to all kinds of tools and disciplinary fields, as long as they probe injustices, produce new knowledge which problematizes well-entrenched positions, and enhances the lives of the marginalized. Any theoretical work that straddles and finds a hermeneutical home in different disciplines is bound to suffer from certain eclectic theoretical deficiencies and contradictions. Its selective bias, though unsafe, is sometimes necessary in order to press on for the sake of the task at hand.

What postcolonialism attempts to do is to demonstrate that the Bible itself is part of the conundrum rather than a panacea for all the ills of the postmodern/postcolonial world. However much Dalits, feminists, and other crusaders against oppression may tantalizingly recuperate the emancipatory potential in the text, the Bible continues to be an unsafe and a problematic text. For every redeeming aspect of the narrative, there is an unredeeming feature linked to it. For instance, the South African artist Azariah Mbatha's wood-cuts of Joseph's story have been canonized by Gerald West as a supreme example of vernacular hermeneutics. Mbatha, in his reworking of the story, relocates it in Africa and tries to suggest African aspects relevant, especially to Zulu culture, enmeshed in the narrative. Mbatha's portrayal rescues the story from its customarily individualistic readings tainted by Western influence, and places it within the African understanding of clan and community. West, attempting to act as midwife in elucidating Mbatha's intentions, comments: 'It is a story of *ubuntu:* a person is a person because of other people' (West 1999: 45). Although the biblical story is about a father and his sons, and the role of women is peripheral to the plot, African notions of 'first wife', 'favourite wife', and 'helper to the wife' are brought in as an interpretative key to explain the matrilineal presence and power and to determine the roles of Leah, Rachel, Bilhah, and Zilpah. The story is mined for symbolic aspects which signify power and powerlessness. This hermeneutical proposal, however, framed within the dominant African cultural values, overlooks and fails to examine the other aspect of Joseph's life at Pharaoh's court where his food policy eventually led to the enslavement of his own people.[6] Joseph used famine to gain control of the land and created a labour force to acquire power. He used food as a commodity to control people. When there was extreme famine, the people used their money to buy food. When their money ran out, he demanded they pay with their cattle, flocks, and asses—their means of income. When money and the source of income were gone, he asked for their land, and made them work in exchange for food. Finally without money, without cattle, and without land, the people were left with nothing but themselves and their labouring skills. Out of desperation they were willing to trade these too. As the text puts it: 'The land became Pharaoh's and as for the people; he made slaves of them from one end of Egypt to the other' (Gen. 47: 21, 22). The person who was himself bought and sold twice now becomes the perpetrator of the same crime.

A similar under-interpretation happens in the Exodus narrative. Even a cursory reading of Exodus will reveal that it endorses both freedom and enslavement. For instance, one of the earliest acts undertaken after the deliverance was to do with the purchasing and trading of slaves (Exod. 21: 1–11). All along we have assumed liberation and human rights—high points of the Enlightenment—to be part of the biblical ethos. Before the advent of the Enlightenment's radical critique of religion, however, the medieval natural law advocated by Thomas Aquinas upheld the view that people had no rights, only duties. It may be possible for the advocates of liberation, applying Enlightenment values, to mine the Bible for its libera-tive strands. However, it is important to be mindful that this same Bible contains elements of bondage and disenfranchisement. What postcolonial biblical criticism does is to make this ambivalence and paradox clear and visible.

Subjecting the Christian Bible to a postcolonial scrutiny does not reinforce its authority, but emphasizes its contradictory content. At a time when, outside of fundamentalist circles, Christian doctrines carry little weight, and moral questions are less likely to be settled by biblical teach-ings, the Bible's place has to be rethought. Under such a scrutiny, it will be approached not for its sacred status but for its content, and especially as an archive which contains stories of victims and victors, exploitation and benevolence, enslavement and emancipation. The Bible will not be seen as a rampaging and intruding text but as a chastened and ambivalent text. The temptation is that, in our enthusiasm to expose colonial intentions in texts, we may end up restoring the text and making it safe. The purpose is not to recover in the biblical texts an alternative, or to search in its pages for a fresher way of coming to terms with the aftermath of colonial atrocity and trauma, and the current effects of globalization. The purpose is to interrupt the illusion of the Bible being the provider of all answers, and to propose new angles, alternative directions, and interjections which will always have victims and their plight as the foremost concern.

NOTES

1. For examples of postcolonial biblical criticism, see R. S. Sugirtharajah (ed.), *The Postcolonial Bible* (Sheffield: Sheffield Academic Press, 1998); R. S. Sugirtharajah, *Asian Biblical Hermeneutics and Postcolonialism: Contesting the Interpretations* (Sheffield: Sheffield Academic Press, 1999); R. S. Sugirtharajah, *The Bible and the Third World: Precolonial, Colonial and Postcolonial Encounters* (Cambridge: Cambridge University Press, 2001); Fernando F. Segovia (ed.), *Interpreting Beyond Borders: The Bible and Postcolonialism 3* (Sheffield: Sheffield Academic Press, 2000); Musa W. Dube, *Postcolonial Feminist Interpretation of the Bible* (St Louis: Chalice Press, 2000).

2. For the social and historical circumstances of Qoheleth's world, and the reasons for his scepticism and pessimism seen from the comparative sociology point of view, see Robert C. Harrison, Jr, 'Qoheleth among the Sociologists', *Biblical Interpretation: A Journal of Contemporary Approaches*, 1997, 160–80.

3. For a contrary view which sees the Preacher as a renegade aristocrat who offered a word of resistance, see Elsa Tamez, *When the Horizons Close: Rereading Ecclesiastes*, trans. M. Wilde (Maryknoll, NY: Orbis Books, 2000).

4. I have drawn on the work of Sean Freyne here, esp. *Galilee and Gospel: Collected Essays* (Tübingen: Mohr Siebeck, 2000), 199–203, although my perspective is slightly different from his.

5. For the textual commentaries of the peasants of Solentiname, see Erneto Cardenal (ed.), *The Gospel in Solentiname*, trans. D. D. Walsh, vols. i–iv (Maryknoll, NY: Orbis Books, 1982); for visual commentaries, see Philip Scharper and Sally Scharper, *The Gospel in Art by the Peasants of Solentiname* (Maryknoll, NY: Orbis Books, 1980). For Asian examples, see Masao Takenaka and Ron O' Grady, *The Bible through Asian Eyes* (Auckland: ACCA and Pace Publishing, 1991), also *Image*, a quarterly which specializes in Asian art, published by Christian Art Association, Jogkarata, Indonesia.

6. West acknowledges the difficulty of the selective reading of the Joseph story, but does not explore the hermeneutical implications raised by it.

4

CONVERGENT TRAJECTORIES? LIBERATION HERMENEUTICS AND POSTCOLONIAL BIBLICAL CRITICISM

An oppressed Bible oppresses and a liberated Bible liberates.

(Itumeleng Mosala 1992: 137)

Up until now liberation hermeneutics has been seen as the distinctive contribution of Third World biblical interpreters. Recently another critical category, postcolonialism, has emerged as its rival, and has staked claim to represent minority voices. On the face of it, both liberation hermeneutics and postcolonial criticism share a common interpretative vocation—for instance, de-ideologizing dominant interpretation, a commitment to the other, and distrust of totalizing tendencies. More significantly both are committed to social and political empowerment of the oppressed, and critical reclamation of the cultural resources of people who were histori- cally denigrated. However, a closer look will reveal that liberation hermeneutics is still stuck with some of the vices of the modernistic project—excessive textualism, disparagement of both major and popular religions, and homogenization of the poor. Also, it seems shy about breaking with them.

This chapter has three aims. First, it will draw on the recent use of the Bible by liberation hermeneutics to illustrate how liberation hermeneutics ends up reproducing a microcosmic version of the very hegemonic interpretation which it tried to dislodge. Second, it will highlight the modernist/postmodernist leanings of liberation hermeneutics, and third, it will map out the affinities between these two endeavours and argue that liberation hermeneutics can align with postcolonial criticism without compromising its commitment to liberation.

Marks of classic liberation hermeneutics

Liberation hermeneutics is principally associated with Latin American liberation theologies. There is no need to rehearse here the origins and development of these theologies. Based on the available literature, one can see three phases within liberation hermeneutics.[1] One, Latin American liberation theology, undertaken at a grand macro-level, engages in a universal discourse of liberation. It provides overarching categories which make sense only from a cosmopolitan perspective. In the interpretation of the texts, its aim is to read the text 'in the light of our Latin American reality', or through 'Latin American eyes' and, by extension, including all those in distant continents who are oppressed. It is stripped of all Latin American particularities, and aims to speak for all the oppressed. For instance, in Gutiérrez's seminal work, *Theology of Liberation*, his own country, Peru, is hardly mentioned. In his introduction to *Job*, he writes: 'In this reading of the Book of Job I shall keep my attention on what it means to talk of God in the context of Latin America, and more concretely in the context of the suffering of the poor—which is to say, the vast majority of the population' (Gutiérrez 1987: p. xviii).

In the process of working out its hermeneutic, liberation theology bypassed all specificities and assumed some kind of universal proportion and intention. In her preface to the North American edition of *The Amnesty of Grace*, Elsa Tamez reminds her readers of the universal implication of her work: 'Even though this study has arisen in a context of exclusion, oppression, and poverty, its message is for everyone' (Tamez 1993a: 8). I would like to call this mode of interpretation classic liberation hermeneutics.

The second phase is the reading of the Bible undertaken at the grassroots in the base Christian communities, by non-trained readers. They see the Bible as the product of a community and see their task as recovering it from an individualistic, 'spiritual' apolitical reading, for the empowerment of the community. This reading practice was initiated in Latin American based ecclesiastical communities and indigenous communities. The appropriation of the Bible during the Samoza regime by the peasants from Solentiname became an important hermeneutical occasion. This mode of interpretation later flowed into other parts of the world, particularly to South Africa and the Philippines. I would like to call this approach the People's Reading.[2]

The third phase is the emergence of specific-reference liberation reading engaged in by a wide variety of minority voices—Dalits, women, *burakumin*, indigenous people, and people who were victimized by both internal and external forces. Liberation theology is no longer seen as a single genre but as a series of genres, many of them interconnecting and speaking on behalf of many voices. In the 1980s the victim culture began to emerge, and historical suffering became a kind of certificate of legitimacy. It was the 'product of damage'. People stopped hiding their ethnicities and gender differences and saw their goal as awaking and nourishing their wounded identities. Victimhood became not only a rallying point but a central focus of identity. I would like to call this identity-specific reading.

It is with classic liberation hermeneutics that I am concerned in this chapter. At the risk of oversimplifying it, let me recount the basic tenets of liberation hermeneutics. There is no need to rehearse the origins and development of Latin American liberation theologies. There is enough literature dealing with it. However, let me highlight some of the interpretative features which have become the hallmarks of liberation hermeneutics:

- commitment to eradicate poverty comes first, and the reading of the text follows as a critical reflection upon it, tangibly accomplishing the intentions behind the sacred writings;

- affirmation that reality is one and liberation is seen as an all-encompassing phenomenon. Traditional dualism such as sacred/secular, individual/communitarian is coalesced into one unified history. History is seen as the medium of God's self-disclosure, and the site of the historical activity of God;

- privileging the poor as a significant hermeneutical category. Every new situation rescues a new interpretative concern which earlier interpreters had either neglected or overlooked. Liberation hermeneutics made the poor a favoured exegetical concern;

- it also made a compelling case for biblical scholarship to come to grips with the problems of people and serve them rather than taking refuge in theories and philological debates;

- abhorrence of the idea of a neutral reading of the text. An interpreter has to take an option, and liberation theologians unapologetically, openly, and consciously side with the poor, and it is from this perspective that a reading is undertaken;

- the credibility of the Bible rests on a proper pre-understanding. The Bible has meaning only when it is read with a particular viewpoint. Reading the Bible from a specific perspective does not threaten the catholicity of the Gospel, rather it liberates the Gospel message from its neutrality and brings out its multifaceted dimension.

Liberation hermeneutics was responsible for introducing two hermeneutical categories—'hermeneutical circle' and 'hermeneutics of suspicion' which have since then entered the lexicon of biblical scholarship (Segundo 1976: 7–38). It was Segundo who first mooted the idea of a hermeneutical circle. According to him, one first analyses the everyday reality of the context with all its problems and conflicts, then one goes to biblical texts to listen to their message, and then one returns to the context bringing in that newness the Gospel introduces to the situation. The hermeneutic of suspicion, on the other hand, seeks to expose the ideological bias in biblical interpretation. José Miguez-Bonino identified in the early days of liberation theology that what is often mistaken for an objective reading is ideologically biased. This was before it became fashionable to see a link between social location and interpretation. For instance, looking at the way the sayings of Jesus regarding the rich and poor have been exegeted by the dominant hermeneutics of the time, Bonino was able to expose how these readings reflected class values: 'Even a cursory look to [sic] biblical commentaries in the Protestant tradition shows the almost uniform ideological train of thought: riches (in themselves) are good—therefore Jesus could not have condemned them as such, nor rich people as such—consequently the text must mean something else' (Miguez-Bonino 1995: 60).

Such ideological blindness, Bonino went on to declare, was found even in honest and responsible exegetes. Bonino cites the example of Joachim Jeremias:

He—perhaps correctly—argues in the parable of the rich man and Lazarus, 'Jesus does not want to comment on a social problem'. But when verse 25 (Luke 16: 19–31) poses the reversal of the condition of the poor, Jeremias argues for the 'ideological supposition' and asks: 'Where had Jesus ever suggested that wealth in itself merits hell and the poverty in itself is rewarded by paradise?' (Miguez-Bonino 1995: 60)

To which Bonino himself came up with answers which an interpretation free from bourgeois presupposition could not have failed to see:

One: that Jesus never speaks of wealth *in itself* or poverty *in itself* but of rich and poor as they are, historically. The 'in itself' abstraction is clearly a piece of liberal ideology. Second: a whole number of texts, or rather practically all texts dealing with the subject (with the exception of Matthew 13.12 and parallels if interpreted in this connection), point in the clear direction of this reversal, whatever explanation we may want to give them. Moreover, its relation to one trend of the prophetic tradition—to which Jesus is evidently related in several other aspects of his teaching—makes it all the more clear. We reach the real ground of Jeremias' interpretation in the strange affirmation that 'Jesus does not intend to take a position on the question of rich and poor'. (Miguez-Bonino 1995: 60–1)

Next, as a way of highlighting liberation hermeneutics' use of the Bible, I would like to look at Gutiérrez's *On Job* (Gutiérrez 1987) and Elsa Tamez's *The Amnesty of Grace* (Tamez 1993a).

Gutiérrez's Job

The starting point for reading Job, for Gutiérrez, is God-talk—how do we talk about God particularly from within the situation of innocent suffering? The theological focus for him is not the one which Western theology has been trying to wrestle with since the holocaust—how do we speak about God after Auschwitz? Rather, how does one engage in theological discourse while Ayacucho lasts?[3] It is talking about God while ordinary people daily experience violation, deprivation, and death in Latin America. It is not about a theological reflection based on a past event like Auschwitz, important though it is; the Latin American question is about the present innocent suffering of the poor when everything in their daily life seems to be a denial of the presence of the love of God. With these questions, Gutiérrez turns to the Book of Job because he finds in it that the 'innocence that Job vigorously claims for himself helps us to understand the innocence of an oppressed and believing people amid the situation of suffering and death that has been forced upon it' (Gutiérrez 1987: p. xviii). While conceding that the Book of Job addresses other pertinent theological issues such as the transcendence of God, the problem of evil, personal suffering, and grief, Gutiérrez's conviction is that central to the narrative is the question of innocent suffering.

Gutiérrez acknowledges that the Book of Job does not provide a neat answer for the question of innocent suffering, Job's faith has prompted him to inquire into finding an appropriate language about God that makes sense to the suffering people. Job conveys that there are two ways of speaking about God—prophetic and mystical—both are interlaced and reinforce and inspire each other. Prophetic language allows one to draw nearer to God because of God's predilection for the poor. An aspect of this language is justice. In the early stages, Job was too concerned about his own suffering, and this becomes the site for his protest. Gradually Job realizes that he is not alone, and that suffering is not something peculiar to him, and that there are many like him. From then on his protests become stronger because he is open to other sufferings, and they include the plight of others as well. Now he protests in the name of all innocent victims. It is this kind of prophetic language, Gutiérrez urges, that Christians should recapture in their discourse and praxis.

Mystical language, on the other hand, speaks about the gratuitous love of God—the unmerited love God has for the poor. The poor are privileged not because they are morally superior or materially deprived, but because of the gratuitousness and universality of God's utter freedom to love. God is committed to the poor not because they are inherently good, but because God is good and God prefers the least in the world. Gutiérrez writes: 'The ultimate basis for the privileged position of the poor is not in the poor themselves but in God, in the gratuitousness and universality of God's *agapeic* love' (Gutiérrez 1987: 94; italics in original).

For Gutiérrez, both languages—prophetic and mystical—are necessary and therefore inseparable. The language of contemplation acknowledges that everything comes from God's unmerited love and it opens up 'new horizons of hope'; and the language of prophecy attacks the structural causes which deprive the poor and keep them in the unjust situations in which they find themselves. It is the language which looks for ' "the suffering features of the Christ the Lord" in the pain-ravaged faces of an oppressed people' (Gutiérrez 1987: 97). This twofold language, in Gutiérrez's view, is the language of Jesus presaged by Job. While Job stutters, Jesus speaks out clearly and explicitly. It is on the cross that Jesus talks with great expressiveness about God. Gutiérrez's contention is that we 'must humbly allow the cry of Jesus on the cross to echo through history and nourish our theological efforts' (Gutiérrez 1987: 103).

In reading *On Job*, we see a shift in methodological orientation in Gutiérrez's thinking. The celebrated phrases which he wrote in *Theology of Liberation* and which became a kind of a manifesto for liberation theology—commitment as a first act, and theology as a critical reflection upon praxis as a second act—(Gutiérrez 1973: 9) have now given way to contemplation and praxis as the first act, and reflection on it as the second act.[4] In his changed understanding of speaking about God, Gutiérrez writes:

The point I want to make can be stated thus: God is first contemplated when we do God's will and allow God to reign; only after that do we think about God. To use familiar categories: contemplation and practice together make up a *first act*; theologizing is a *second act*. We must first establish ourselves on the terrain of spirituality and practice; only subsequently is it possible to formulate discourse on God in an authentic and respectful way. Theologizing done without the mediation of contemplation and practice does not meet the requirements of the God of the Bible.   (Gutiérrez 1987: xiii; italics in original)

The accent here seems to be placed more on contemplation and emancipatory spirituality, than on action and social transformation for which liberation theology came to be known in its heady days. In a statement which suggests the repudiation of one of the basic tenets of liberation theology, Gutiérrez goes on to say: 'The ultimate basis of God's preference for the poor is to be found in God's own goodness and *not in any analysis of society or in human compassion*, however pertinent these reasons may be' (Gutiérrez 1987: p.xiii; emphasis added). These changes in thinking could be attributed, among other things, to pressures from the Roman Catholic hierarchy, and the apparent failure of the socialist experiment in Eastern Europe. In face of these, liberation theology seems to be distancing itself from an earlier liberative critical theory and practice and moving to a more conservative type of theological discourse.

Tamez's Paul

Tamez engages in a similar theological pursuit, but this time her hermeneutical aim is how to talk about justification in Latin America when there is cultural, social, and psychological dehumanization. The doctrine of justification, as it is perceived in Latin America, offers good news to the oppressor rather than to the poor. It is viewed in an abstract, individualistic, and generic sense. Going beyond confessional and denominational debates which focus on faith and works, law and grace, Tamez tries to make justification meaningful to the excluded and she redefines sin as being structural and as the cause of the deaths of innocent millions in Latin America (Tamez 1993a: 14). Unlike the denominational theologies which see sin in private and pietistic terms, Tamez places it in a social context, and hence her contention is that justification has to be seen in social terms. In her rereading of Paul's Romans, Tamez detects correspondences between the Pauline and the Latin American contexts. Her claim is that Paul himself addressed questions about the power of the structural sin which has enslaved all humanity, and which Paul recognized as an indestructible power. Tamez reckons that sin is a reality woven into Paul's historical context. To triumph over this, Paul engages in two types of interrelated languages. Echoing Gutiérrez's view of prophetic and mystical languages, Tamez sees in Paul a similar twofold theological vocabulary: one talks about the faithfulness of God, and the other about the redemption of the poor and about human solidarity among them as a consequence of such an act of God. Tamez explains Paul's position thus:

One type of language speaks about faith in God: the absolute certainty of the solidarity of God with the condemned, which is manifested in the love of God in Christ. No one and nothing will be able to separate us from that love (Rom. 8: 38–39). The other type of language speaks of the faith response in the human being: 'In all these things we are more than conquerors through him who loved us' (Rom. 8: 37). (Tamez 1993a: 112)

To overcome the perceived subjectivism and individualism of justification, Tamez sees justification as God's loving care on the Cross. The resurrection constitutes an integral component of justification. On the Cross, God not only heard the cry of his son but the cries of all those who were abandoned. In raising Jesus, God offered to the excluded the possibility of resurrection. Without resurrection one would remain in the former life— the life of hopelessness. For Tamez, justification has more to do with the affirmation of life than with forgiveness of sin. Reconciliation with sinners is only an aspect of justification, but the very essence of justification is God's solidarity with those who are on the periphery and are threatened with death. She writes

The revelation of the justice of God and its realization in justification proclaim and bring about the good news of the right to life for all people. The life granted in justification is recognized as an inalienable gift, because it proceeds from the solidarity of God, in Jesus Christ, with those who are excluded. Such a life of dignity makes human beings subjects of their history. God 'justifies' (makes and declares just) the human being in order to transform the unjust world that excludes, kills, and dehumanizes that same human being. (Tamez 1993a: 14)

Such an act of solidarity, according to Tamez, has vitalized the excluded into regaining their dignity as free people of God. The logic of grace declares an amnesty for all those who are excluded. No more are they the objects of law or manipulated by the structures. Now, as the result of the work of Jesus on the Cross, they emerge as fully humanized subjects, to do 'justice and rescue the truth which has been imprisoned in injustice'. To put it differently, justification is God in solidarity with humanity in Jesus Christ—the prototype of the excluded, and as result of which, human beings discover their dignity and self-affirmation.

To sum up. There are certain similarities between the hermeneutical enterprises of Gutiérrez and Tamez. Both speak from within the context of Latin America, and try to recontextualize the biblical message within that context. In this, their interpretive practices resonate with Clodovis Boff's notion of 'the correspondence of relationships'. Unlike 'the correspondence of terms' which sees facile parallels between the present context and past texts, 'the correspondence of relationships' is a much more finessed mode where the current political, social, and economic struggles of people are seen as the prism through which to look at a similar political, social, and economical engagement depicted in biblical narratives (C. Boff 1991:

9–35). Both exegete at the redacted level of the texts, and their commentarial style reflects the current narrativel way of commenting rather than the technical line-by-line approach. They both use the Bible as a check and a corrective to the prevalent teachings of the Church. For both, the credibility of the Bible is defined by and based on its essential content—Jesus Christ 'The life of Jesus Christ, his death and resurrection of which we read in the Scriptures,' in Tamez's view, must be 'reinterpreted with the purpose of giving life to every human being' (Tamez 1993a: 122). It is Jesus who replaces the Bible as the authority. Finally, Gutiérrez and Tamez concur in their theological proposal, too. Both emphasize the generosity and compassion of God, and social responsibility, and the benevolence that prevails among the disadvantaged, prompted and inspired by God's graciousness.

While rejecting the universalizing tendencies of Western theologies, these two interpreters end up reproducing a microcosmic version of the very theology they tried to reject. The Book of Job and the Pauline writings are reread, not using any specific Latin American theological nuances, or indigenous cultural resources, but from the perspective of liberal and modernist values of solidarity, identification, and liberation.

Their hermeneutics retain some features of liberal theology. The understanding of justification based on the reconstruction of Paul, and the message that God shows unmerited love towards the poor, are actually closer to liberal thinking. The justification for Tamez, and the gratuitousness of God's love, for Gutiérrez are ultimately effected through the death of Jesus, and the difference is that it is the poor who replace sinners as recipients. In their use of the Bible too, Gutiérrez and Tamez replicate the classical liberal view which advocates that the Bible must be related to the context wherein God's presence is already evident. Their hermeneutical proposal sounds as though it is replicating the liberal message, couched in liberation language: Jesus loves me. This I know for the Bible tells me so.

Liberation hermeneutics and its entanglements

In its desire to espouse liberation at a time when there is cynicism and weariness about the emancipatory causes, liberation hermeneutics has valiantly and almost single-handedly helped to maintain liberation at the centre of theological discussion. To keep the momentum of liberation alive, liberation hermeneutics has drawn on both modern and postmodern tendencies. It embraces features of both, and at the same time distances itself from them. Liberation hermeneutics' chief focus is liberation which itself comes out of a modernistic agenda. Liberation is one of the grand stories of modernity which is still to play out its potential in many Third World countries, and liberation hermeneutics has rightly aligned itself with this modernistic cause. Where liberation hermeneutics becomes redundant is when it implicates other grand stories of modernity in its interpretative pursuits. Two such narratives which dominate liberation hermeneutics are 'salvation in history', and 'Jesus Christ saga'. Liberation hermeneutics operates within the existing biblical approaches, and it accords God's self-disclosure through historical events in the life of Israel a primary status in its hermeneutical endeavours. It was this very model which was appropriated by missionaries and colonialists in order to subjugate and subdue other peoples' culture and history. The salvation in history model raises the question of the experience of God. It emphasizes a fuller account of history and historical consciousness. This approach tends to project an interventionist image of God—a God who lives outside history and who, from time-to-time, intervenes in the affairs of the world. This means having to wait patiently from event to event to see how God operates in the ongoingness of life.

The other grand story that liberation hermeneutics reifies is the Jesus Christ saga. In its approach, liberation hermeneutics is overtly Christocentric. The authoritative Jesus reconstructed by liberation theology is not the Jesus behind the text, but within the text. His actions are seen as acts of God mediated in solidarity with humanity as depicted in the canonical texts of the New Testament. In fulfilling this task, the interpreter assumes an apostolic and canonical status in interpreting the significance of Jesus for the marginalized community of faith. The notion that Jesus is at the heart of the Bible gives rise to an unconscious conviction that the Bible cannot err. In relation to the Bible, liberation hermeneutic is postmodern and postcritical, especially when it looks for 'images' and 'types' in the Bible. Clodovis Boff writes:

We need not, then, look for formulas to 'copy', or techniques to 'apply' from scripture. What scripture will offer us are rather something like orientations, models, types, directives, principles, inspirations—elements permitting us to acquire on our own initiative, a 'hermeneutic competency', and thus the capacity to judge—on our own initiative, in our own right—'according to the mind of Christ,' or 'according to the Spirit,' the new, unpredictable situations with which we are continually confronted. The Christian writings offer us not a *what*, but a *how*—a manner, style, a spirit.   (Boff 1991: 30; italics original)

Such an approach helped to veer liberation hermeneutics away from being literalistic. But at the same time what is so striking about liberation hermeneutics is its textualism. It emphasizes the written word. For liberation hermeneutics, ultimately it is in the Bible that the message of liberation is to be found, and it is recoverable through a variety of critical means. Raul Vidales asserts that liberation theology's 'starting point is the original, pristine witness of Scripture' (Vidales 1980: 38). The text remains the centre of debate. The hermeneutical suspicion with which ideological interpretation of the text is viewed, is not accorded to the Bible. Pablo Richard maintains that 'the problem is not the Bible itself, but the way it has been interpreted. The Bible gives us the testimony of the word of God, it is also the canon or criterion of discernment of the Word of God today' (Richard 1990: 66). There is an inherent biblicism in its approach. The texts which speak of dehumanizing aspects are conveniently passed over.

In its attempts to recover the biblical message, liberation hermeneutics employs the now suspicious historical-critical tools, the very tools worked out at the foundry of modernity. But where it deviates from modern shortcomings of historical criticism is in its usage. These tools are marshalled to serve the modernist project of making the gospel relevant to the educated, secularized middle-class Christians who are unsure of their faith. Liberation hermeneutics makes use of the very same tools to liberate the gospel, and make it serve the non-persons whose faith remains unshakeable in spite of the emergence of rational thinking. Liberation hermeneutics has made historical tools more ethically responsible. Though historical criticism retains its archeological and philological pursuits, it is now employed by liberation theologians to discern the interconnection between the social-political world of the text in its past context as well as in the contemporary context.

Liberation hermeneutics is postmodern in its desire to take the other— the poor, women, indigenous, and all the marginalized peoples seriously. In doing so, it rightly overrides the Enlightenment concern with the nonbeliever, and focuses on the non-person. But this does not preclude reifying the poor, and it functions within the Enlightenment paradigm of dichotomous thinking—rich/poor, oppressed/oppressor, and have/have-nots. Moreover, it is prone to romanticize the poor. What Pablo Richard says about the indigenous people of Latin America is true of other marginalized peoples as well:

The indigenous peoples, with their millennial history, with their cultural and religious tradition, and recently, with their own native method of evangelization and their native theology, are much better prepared to read and interpret the Bible than the Western European Christian who has a millennial history of violence and conquest, impregnated with the erudite, liberal and modern spirit. (Richard 1995: 271)

Eleazar López goes still further and accords a privileged access to the poor because of their deprived status. In his view, indigenous people are the conservers of the gospel content, and it is much more 'preserved among our peoples, because of the purity of heart possessed by the poor, than in the contaminated vessels of the Church' (Richard 1995: 271).

Liberation hermeneutics is modernistic in its attempt to speak for all, and in setting hermeneutical goals. It sees its role as a testimony, a testimony to what it has witnessed of human suffering and degradation. Not all liberation hermeneuts are economically disadvantaged. They believe that interpretation has a witnessing function, as did the sages of old who urged: 'Open your mouth for the dumb, for the rights of all those who are left desolate, open your mouth, judge righteously, maintain the rights of the poor and needy' (Prov. 31: 8–9). In its overzealousness to represent the poor, liberation hermeneutics has ended up as a liberation theology of the poor rather than a theology of liberation by the poor. The goal now is not social change but pastoral concern. Political activism is replaced with the Church's traditional concern for good work and charitable projects.

Religion and liberation

Liberation hermeneutics has to reconcile its position with the theology of religions, with religious pluralism, and the religiosity of popular religions. It still operates within the Judaeo-Christian notion of what religion is. One of the reasons for its failure to get to grips with religions, according to Aloysius Pieris, is that liberation theology reels under the captivity of two 'Karls' of dialectical disposition—Karl Barth and Karl Marx. In his view, Marx's dialectical materialism failed to perceive the potentiality for revolution in religion, and Barth's dialectical theology failed to acknowledge that there was revelation in religion (Pieris 1988: 91). Though liberation theology has taken the poor seriously, as we noted in the previous chapter, it has hitherto dismissed the religious agency of the poor, expressed through mystical visions and dreams, healings and exorcisms, veneration of saints and relics, and through feasts, fasts, and religious processions. In their study of liberation theology's attitude to African religions and cultures, Sathler and Nascimento conclude that liberation theology tends to maintain the purity of the Christian gospel and frown upon the liberative potentiality of the indigenous religions. They have demonstrated that even a person like Leonardo Boff, who pleaded for syncretism, maintained an offensive position towards Afro-Brazilian religious practices: 'He reduces their social elements to psychopathologies and acknowledges their members as underdeveloped subjects that need a true, universal, psychic, social, and religious salvation which can be given only in the Catholic Church. So he comes close to the orthodoxy' (Sathler and Nascimento 1997: 114). Pablo Richard himself, an advocate of indigenous reading of the Bible, eventually sees the Bible as adjudicator in matters related to Indian religions and cultures. 'The indigenous peoples must construct a new hermeneutic to decolonize the interpretation,' writes Richard, but in the final analysis, the Bible is 'an instrument, a criterion, a canon, for discerning the presence and reevaluation of God in indigenous culture and religion' (Richard 1990: 66). There is no concession to the religious claims of other faith traditions, only an apology for Christian truth. Postcolonialism, on the other hand, represents the contemporary restlessness concerning religious pluralism, the validity of different confessional traditions, and the empowerment of repressed voices through visual, oral and aural means. It is distinctly postmodernistic, since it has argued from the start for a pluralistic outlook and has encouraged the possibility of alternative ways of thinking, valuing, and acting. It is sceptical about the monopolistic and prescriptive nature of Christianity.

Postcolonialism and liberation hermeneutics as companions in struggle

As I pointed out earlier, liberation hermeneutics and postcolonial criticism should be companions in arms, fighting the good fight. For both, commitment to liberation, however modernist the project may be, still has a valid purchase, for liberation as a grand narrative provides hope for countless millions of people who daily face institutional and personal violence and oppression. Both liberation hermeneutics and postcolonial criticism take the 'other', namely the poor, seriously; both want to dismantle hegemonic interpretations, and do not hesitate to offer prescriptions and make moral judgements, while acknowledging the perils of such decisions. However, to reiterate a point made in the last chapter, the entrenchment of liberation hermeneutics within the modernistic framework acts as an inhibition, and prevents it from embracing some of the virtues of postmodernism for its liberative cause. Postcolonial critical theory, on the other hand, as an offshoot of postmodernism, while it collaborates with it, distances itself from its errors and unsavoury aspects.

While liberation hermeneutics has successfully undermined the certitude of dominant biblical scholarship, it is triumphalistic about its own achievement. Postcolonalism, on the other hand, understands the Bible and biblical interpretation as a site of struggle over its efficacy and meanings. There is a danger in liberation hermeneutics making the Bible the ultimate adjudicator in matters related to morals and theological disputes. Postcolonialism is much more guarded in its approach to the Bible's serviceability. It sees the Bible as both safe and unsafe, and as a familiar and a distant text. Liberation hermeneutics wants to redeem the Church and its past colonial atrocities through the very book which perpetuated them. In legitimizing the Bible's role in this redemptive act, Pablo Richard states that the Bible as 'an instrument of prophetic discernment of Christianity and a radical critique of Christendom, . . . [the Bible] can regain the credibility which colonial Christianity destroyed' (Richard 1990: 66). For him, and other liberation hermeneuts, the 'problem is not the Bible itself, but the way it has been interpreted' (Richard 1990: 66). Postcolonialism, on the other hand, sees the Bible as both problem and solution, and its message of liberation is seen as far more indeterminate and complicated. It is seen as a text of both emancipation and enervation. Postcolonial reading advocates the emancipation of the Bible from its implication in dominant ideologies both at the level of the text and at the level of interpretation. For postcolonialism, the critical principle is not derived only from the Bible but is determined by contextual needs and other warrants. It sees the Bible as one among many liberating texts. Liberation hermeneutics could usefully avail itself of some of the insights advocated by postcolonialism without abandoning or toning down its loyalty to the poor.

In its choice of biblical paradigms, and in its preoccupation with certain favoured texts and with reading them at their face value, liberation hermeneutics fails to appreciate the historical or political ramifications such an interpretation will have for those who face displacement and uprooting in their own lands and countries. For instance, in espousing and endorsing the Exodus as the foundational text for liberation in its early days, liberation hermeneutics failed to note that its suitability as a project had limited value and force. While liberation hermeneutics claimed that the Exodus was read from the point of view of the oppressed, it did not pause to think of the plight of the victims who were at the receiving end of its liberative action, and who were forced to embark upon what Robert Allen Warrior calls a 'reverse Exodus' from their own promised land. How inappropriate the narrative is for Native American, Palestinian, and Aboriginal contexts is well documented. It also raises awkward theological questions as to what kind of a God is posited both by the Bible and liberation theology. God is the one who emancipates Israel, but also in the process destroys Egyptians and Canaanites. What postcolonialism does is to read the narrative from the Canaanite point of view, and discern the parallels between the humiliated people of biblical and contemporary times.[5] Similarly in reading Ruth, liberation hermeneutics sees her as the paradigmatic convert and assimilator. Her inclusion into the mainstream, assimilating its key values, was seen as an important strategy. Laura Donaldson, as a Cherokee woman, tries to reposition Ruth in the light of the specific cultural and historical predicament of an American Indian woman (Donaldson 1999: 20–36). In the face of the constant demand for ethnic minorities to assimilate into the mainstream culture, Laura Donaldson recovers another often written-out and under-exegeted indigene character—Orpah, the sister-in-law of Ruth, who, unlike Ruth, returns to her mother's house. Donaldson's contention is that it is Orpah who signifies hope and provides emancipatory vision for

Cherokee women, because it is she who embraces her own clan and culture. When read from Orpah's point of view, we see a different Ruth. Both liberation hermeneutics and postcolonialism share reading as resistance, but postcolonial critical practice sees reading and resistance as a far more complex activity.

Liberation hermeneutics creates an impression that liberation is intrinsic to the Bible. All along we have been made to believe that liberation, human rights—high points of the Enlightenment—were part of the biblical ethos. Before the advent of the Enlightenment's radical critique of religion, the medieval natural law advocated by Thomas Aquinas upheld the view that the people had no rights but only duties and responsibilities. It may be possible for the advocates of liberation to mine the Bible for its liberation streak. To whatever extent the Dalits, feminists, and other crusaders of oppression may tantalizingly recuperate the emancipatory potential, the Bible continues to be an ambivalent and unsafe text. Even a cursory reading of Exodus will reveal that it endorses both freedom and enslavement. For instance, one of the earliest acts undertaken by Israelites after the deliverance from Egypt was to do with the purchasing and trading of slaves (Exod. 21: 1–11). What is important is to be mindful that the Bible contains elements of bondage and disenfranchisement. What postcolonial biblical criticism tries to do is to make this ambivalence visible and clear and to demonstrate that the Bible is part of the conundrum rather than a panacea for all the ills of a postmodern world.

For liberation hermeneutics, the project of liberation remains within the bounds of Christianity and its construction is informed by Christian sources. Liberation hermeneutics sees liberation as something lodged and located in biblical texts, or in ecumenical and Christian Church documents, and as something which can be extracted from these textualized records. As Marcella Althaus Reid has pointed out, however, liberation as a concept 'obeys certain masters, a certain framework of thought which in the end regulates the available strategies for freedom, even pre-empting the notion of freedom in itself' (Althaus-Reid 1998: 268). It still works with the binary notions of Christian and non-Christian and sees religious pluralism as an exception rather than a norm. Postcolonialism, on the other hand, is able to draw on a larger theological pool, and is not confined to a particular religious source. Liberation for postcolonialism is not imposing a pre-existing notion, but working out its contours in response to voices within and outside the biblical tradition.

Postcolonial space refuses to press for a particular religious stance as final and ultimate. As a point of entry, individual interpreters may have their own theological, confessional, and denominational stance, but this in itself does not preclude them from enquiring into and entertaining a variety of religious truth-claims. It is the multidisciplinary nature of the enterprise which gives postcolonialism its energy. It sees revelation as an ongoing process which embraces not only the Bible, tradition, and the Church, but other sacred texts and contemporary secular events as well. What postcolonialism will argue for is that the idea of liberation and its praxis must come from the collective unconscious of the people. It sees liberation not as something hidden or latent in the text, but rather as born of public consensus created in a democratic dialogue between text and context.

Both liberation hermeneutics and postcolonialism endorse the other—the poor, the marginalized—as the prime site for doing theology. The former's view of the poor, however, is largely a restrictive one, confined to the economically disadvantaged. Aloysius Pieris, the Sri Lankan theologian whose commitment to the poor is impeccable, does not explicitly include the Tamils who are impoverished on the basis of their ethnicity and language. His writings fail to integrate the concerns of the minorities. Where postcolonialism differs is that it recognizes a plurality of oppressions. Unlike liberation hermeneutics, postcolonialism does not perceive the other as a homogeneous category, but acknowledges multiple identities based upon class, sex, ethnicity and gender. In their preferential option, there is a tendency in liberation hermeneutics to romanticize the poor. For instance, when exegeting the gospel account of the widow's mite (Mark 12: 41–4), José Cárdenas Pallares, the Mexican who wrote a commentary on Mark from the liberation perspective, falls a victim to liberal interpretation when he sees in the widow an exemplar of ideal piety. Her piety and sacrifice are differentiated from the barrenness of the scribal faith or the facile and pretentious offering of the rich:

In contrast with the sterility of official religion, which gets along on miracles and money alone (Mark 11.12–22), the poor widow demonstrates true faith in God (11.22–24). Her strength and her security are God. (12.44). The interpretation Jesus and the first Christians make of this poor person's behaviour is an absolute and utter reversal of values, a contradiction of everything that motivates a class society, a commercial society. For this poor person, as for the poor Jesus and the poor primitive communities, what counts is God. (Pallares 1986: 57–8)

A similar liberal view is advocated by John Vincent, a leading proponent of liberation hermeneutics in England, who sees the widow as the ideal giver whose action is worthy to be emulated (Vincent 1991: 126–7).

Ultimately, in the name of liberation, what is offered to the poor is an old-fashioned evangelical exhortation to faith in God and trust in God's faithfulness. What postcolonialism does is to read the gospel incident from the point of view of the widow, and see it not as an approval of her action but as an exposure of abuse by the temple treasury authorities. If one sees it from the widow's angle, Jesus was not applauding her action but making an assault upon an institution which generated poverty in Israel. This is evidenced by the judgement prefigured in Jesus's condemnation of an institution which destroys the poor and costs very little to the rich. Post-colonial reading will not see the widow as being singled out by Jesus as a model for piety but as a poor widow who was manipulated and conned by the system into parting with what little she had. Linked with the poor is the idea in liberation hermeneutics of the poor as the new people of God. That a recent volume on Dalits, *burakumin*, and aborigines has the title, *God, Christ and God's People in Asia*, is an indication of such a claim. The identification and correspondence between the biblical people of God and the current oppressed is a concept needing much more careful articulation.

In conclusion, this is not the time to assess the impact of liberation theology, but I would like to end with a couple of comments which come from a sense of solidarity and shared concern. One is tedious, and the other is serious. Liberation hermeneutics when it emerged on the hermeneutical scene, provided a high profile and respectable status for Third World theological discourse. The unhappy by-product of this pre-eminent status was a collective amnesia which consigned the earlier works of the Third World interpreters to near oblivion. The often exciting and creative output of previous generations was forgotten, and the works of liberation theologians were seen to be more interesting as they were recent as well as appealing and because of their interweaving of modernistic tendencies. Let me provide anecdotal evidence. At a recent international meeting to discuss the state of Third World biblical interpretation, it came as a surprise to both the experts and audience gathered there, to know that even before the emergence of liberation hermeneutics there had been in existence a vigorous biblical interpretation in the Third World, which was worthy of serious study. The second concern as I said causes genuine worry. When liberation theology emerged, it gave the impression that it was going to be a great force in altering the way we do theology itself, and would usher in an era of radical changes. Sadly this failed to materialize. In its interpretative proposals, liberation hermeneutics continued to be conservative. In its appropriation of the Bible, in its expositions, in its obsession with Christ-centred hermeneutics, it adhered to conventional patterns. A theology which started out as socially progressive, remained largely conservative and theologically cautious. It did not engage in an overall reappraisal nor did it desire a reconfiguration of the basic theological concepts. This reluctance could be attributed to several factors: a lack of critical self-reflectivity which is crucial to any emancipatory theory and practice; pressure from conservative forces within the Church hierarchy; overeagerness to get the methods correct; and the seductive effects of dialoguing with Western theologians. Whatever the reasons, over the years, without much self-criticism and a willingness to re-perceive ancient doctrines, liberation hermeneutics has faded into a pale imitation of itself. Instead of being a new agent in the ongoing work of God, liberation hermeneutics has ended up reflecting upon the theme of biblical liberation rather than being a liberative hermeneutic.

Liberation hermeneutics and postcolonialism share mutual agendas and goals, and hope for and work towards an alternative to the present arrangement. If liberation hermeneutics could eschew its homogenization of the poor, incessant biblicism, and hostility to religious pluralism that plague its interpretative focus, it should be able to join forces with postcolonial thinking to fathom and fashion a different world from the one we live in.

NOTES

1. Literature on liberation theology is enormous. For a helpful introduction to the methodologies, see Peter C. Phan, 'A Common Journey, Different Paths, the Same Destination: Method in Liberation Theologies', in E. S. Fernandez and F. F. Segovia (eds.), *A Dream Unfinished: Theological Reflections on America from the Margins* (Maryknoll, NY: Orbis Books, 2001), 129–51 and also Curt Cadorette et al., *Liberation Theology* (Maryknoll, NY: Orbis Books, 1992).

2. For examples of the reading of Solentiname peasants, see Erneto Cardenal (ed.), *The Gospel in Solentiname*, trans. D. D. Walsh, vols. i–iv (Maryknoll, NY: Orbis Books, 1982). For their visual representation of biblical narratives, see Philip Scharper and Sally Scharper, *The Gospel in Art by the Peasants of Solentiname* (Maryknoll, NY: Orbis Books, 1980).

3. Ayacucho is a rampantly poor and violent city in the Peruvian mountains.

4. For a moving personal account of shift in his methodology, see his introduction to the revised edition of *A Theology of Liberation*, trans. C. Inda and J. Eagleson (Maryknoll, NY: Orbis Books, 1988), esp. pp. xxviii–xxxvi.

5. For a different take on Exodus from a Filipino-American perspective which sees the Exodus as not Exodus from Egypt but Exodus to Egypt, see Eleazar S. Fernandez, 'Exodus-toward-Egypt: Filipino-Americans' Struggle to Realize the Promised Land in America', in E. S. Fernandez and F. F. Segovia (eds.), *A Dream Unfinished: Theological Reflections on America from the Margins* (Maryknoll, NY: Orbis Books, 2001), 167–81. For further discussion on this, see this volume, pp. 186–7.

PART II

POSTCOLONIAL PREOCCUPATIONS

5

THE VERSION ON WHICH THE SUN NEVER SETS: THE ENGLISH BIBLE AND ITS AUTHORIZING TENDENCIES

> The Bible [The Authorized Version], at this moment, is the *only* version in existence on which *the sun never sets*.
>
> (Anderson 1845: p.xi)

> [I]f as sometimes asserted, 'a camel is a horse designed by a committee', then the Authorized Version is the ultimate camel.
>
> (Prickett 1996: 84)

Writing at the turn of the twentieth century on the history of the English people, J. R. Green observed that no 'history, no romance, hardly any poetry save the little known verse of Chaucer existed in the English tongue' until the emergence of one book:

No greater moral change ever passed over a nation than passed over England during the years which parted the middle of the reign of Elizabeth from the meeting of the Long Parliament. England became a people of a book, and the book was the Bible. It was yet one English book which was familiar to every Englishman; it was read at churches, and read at home, and everywhere its words, as they fell on ears which custom had not deadened, kindled a startling enthusiasm.   (Green 1903: 935)

One of the most extraordinary events in the history of the English people was the translation of the Bible into English. Through this act of translation, Protestant England was trying simultaneously to recover the original spirit of Christianity, and to redefine itself in the face of pressure from papal Rome. The version which came to symbolize these aspirations was the King James Version, popularly known as the Authorized Version. James I, by all accounts was not a particularly attractive personality or a progressive monarch, yet it was during his rule that the two most significant books in the English language emerged—the Authorized Version of the Bible in 1611 and the first folio of the collected works of William Shakespeare in 1623. The former was initiated by the King's authority and the latter had royal backing. In the history of the translated Bible, no other translation has achieved what the Authorized Version did by domesticating itself permanently into English life and the English psyche by extending and deepening its hold on English language, character, and culture. A. Clutton-Brock wrote that, although the Bible came from the East, it had now been 'naturalized in the West, and that the Englishman had fathered what the Jew so long ago begot' (Clutton-Brock 1938: 78). English writers, both secular and theological, often refer it to as 'our English Bible', 'the supreme monument of the English language' (Henson 1938: 12).

The Authorized Version is the nearest the English have had to a national epic. It was Thomas Huxley who first mooted the idea of the Authorized Version as a national epic: 'Consider the great historical fact that, for three centuries, this book has been woven into the life of all that is best and noblest in English history; and it has become the national epic of Britain, and is as familiar to noble and simple from John-o'Groat's House to Land's End, as Dante and Tasso once were to the Italians' (Cook 1909: 42–3). Recently the notion of national epic has been reiterated by Peter Levi: 'In its range and in the use we have made of it, one would say it was an epic; and there is no other English national epic' (Levi 1974: 10). A. Clutton-Brock went on to claim that what Italian painters had done for their country in pictures, the Authorized Version had done in words, thus turning it into an 'English book, so that we can without any incongruity make pictures out of it in our minds full of English things' (Clutton-Brock 1938: 74). He wrote: 'We think of its stories as happening in England, of Ruth as standing in tears amid the alien corn, because the translators have made these stories their own and ours, expressing their feelings in them as fully and directly as if there had been no original text to control them' (Clutton-Brock 1938: 74). The British and Foreign Bible Society, in one of its popular reports, made it clear that of all contributions the English had made to civilization,—literature, cricket, cathedrals, the English countryside, manor houses and mansions, the British constitution—the most precious of them was—'our English Bible' (*Our Heritage* 1934: 16). Mahatma Gandhi, once wondered, 'what would have happened to the English if they had not had an authorized version of the Bible' (M. K. Gandhi 1944: 173). It is some indication of the hold the Authorized Version continues to have in the imagination of the English today, that the Edinburgh-based publishing firm, Canongate, has recently brought out the Bible in the form of single books in the King James Version. This was a publishing sensation of the late 1990s, running into more than a million copies. The King James Version whose translators opposed comments or marginal notes now comes in these single books with a series of introductions by eminent people to attract attention. Each volume is introduced by a writer not necessarily associated with the Christian tradition, and encouraging readers to approach them as literary works in their own right.[1] We will return to 'Canongate Bibles' later.

A collection of writings which was redacted and codified even before the English could read and write has now penetrated deeply into the bone and spirit of the English. Although the vernacular English Bible was a late-comer to English life, H. W. Hoare, in his *The Evolution of the English Bible*, wrote that 'the Bible story has been among us from our national infancy' (Hoare 1901: 4). It is amazing to note how a record of beliefs, laws, and customs of one particular people has now became a national epic of another. As George Steiner has pointed out, 'in the history of art very probably the most successful domestication is the King James Bible' (Steiner 1976: 347).

The context of the English Bible

The translation of the whole Bible into English for the common people began only with John Wycliffe. The medieval institutional Church was opposed to a vernacular Bible. It permitted a restricted availability to monks and nuns who were not conversant with the Latin of their offices, and to learned people of the time, but free access to all was considered risky. An anonymous pre-Wycliffe translator claimed that his translating venture might lead to his death (Mozley 1955: 127). But by the seventeenth century, safeguards and qualifications were no longer necessary before laypeople could be allowed to read the Bible. The King James translators, in their Preface note: 'But we desire that the Scripture may speak like itself, as in the language of *Canaan*, that it may be understood even of the very vulgar' (Carroll and Prickett 1998*b*: p. lxviii).

The appearance of the vernacular Bible in England was due to the simultaneous emergence of a variety of factors. First, the arrival of a middle class which enjoyed increasing prosperity and mobility. It was this upwardly mobile class which agitated for their voices to be heard in political issues and clamoured for a quality literature in English which would address both their secular and spiritual needs. The answer was the English Bible, a literature in their own vernacular. David Lawton sees the pressure for the English Bible as a natural reaction of Protestantism 'against an international establishment, the Church, which lays down the law in Latin, and which claims, in Latin, to be the ultimate authority—spiritual, moral, political and intellectual' (Lawton 1990: 54). Thus, the vernacular Bible was not an outcome of an ideological conflict between the proletariat and the elite, but between the rising middle class and the ecclesiastical establishment. A further factor was that this same class was turning to worldwide commercial ventures and colonial enterprises. Though other European nations such as the Portugese, the Spanish, and the Dutch were already flexing their muscles, British colonialism was in its infancy. Four hundred years later, however, both colonialism and the English Bible had made their global presence felt and left their imprint across the world. The English Bible eventually became the Bible of the British empire so that quoting the Psalms, it was said that 'its sound has gone forth into all lands, and its words unto the ends of the world' (Hoare 1901: 228). In the course of the development, it was made to perform ideological acts way beyond its textual propensities, such as endorsing the civilizing mission of European empires, and it was projected next to Shakespeare as the book of the empire.

The rise of the English Bible

The King James Bible was not of course a new translation. Though initiated by the Puritan demand for a new translation, the translators' note to the readers made it clear that theirs was not a new translation but simply an improvement of the existing ones: 'Truly, good Christian Reader, we never thought from the beginning that we should need to make a new translation, nor yet to make of a bad one a good one; . . . but to make a good one better, or out of many good ones one principal good one' (Carroll and Prickett 1998b: p. lxv). The end result was that the 1611 version was not a fresh translation. Neither was it the effort, as in the case of the previous versions, of a single translator such as Tyndale or Coverdale. It represented the last stage of a process of development and was the product of a corporate venture, a conflation and 'crowning refinement' of the then existing versions. It was 'in effect a palimpsest of the best of previous translations, corrected and winnowed through almost a hundred years of development' (Prickett 1996: 82). The idea of a palimpsest is a helpful way of understanding the King James Version. It is a version where previous translations have been erased and overwritten yet remain as traces within the present text. No single version can be singled out as the original, since all are related and intertwined with one another in an endless and multiple process of selection and deselection. More importantly, the concept of palimpsest prevents the emergence of one single version as the 'pure', 'final' 'ultimate' translation. Since the King James Version was deemed to be only a revised edition, it was not entered in the Stationer's Register, thus we do not have any information as to the month in which it was issued (Pollard 1911: 61).

Contrary to popular perception, the King James Bible was never formally authorized. Despite its being known as the Authorized Version, it was never publically authorized by parliament, convocation, privy council, or king. Although there was an injunction by Thomas Cromwell in 1538 which obliged every parish to provide with 'one book of the whole Bible of the largest volume'[2] before the feast of Easter (6 April 1539) (Bray 1994a: 179), this was followed by a fresh proclamation on 6 May 1541, which set the feast of the All Saints (1 November) as the deadline, and thereafter a fine of 40s for every month of delay (Pollard 1911: 21). According to Pollard there is no order in council 'having enjoined parishes to buy copies with inconvenient haste' (Pollard 1911: 65). The wording on the title page read 'Appointed to be read in Churches', not 'Authorized'. As to the question by what authority it came to be used in Church services, Lord Chancellor Selborne, in the correspondence column of the *Times*, 3 June 1881, came up with this surmise: 'Nothing is more probable than that this may have been done by Order in Council. If so, the authentic record of that order may be lost, because all Council books and registers from the year 1600 to 1613 inclusive were destroyed by a fire at Whitehall on the 12 January 1618 (O.S)' (Bruce 1970: 100). In Pollard's view, 'Appointed' presumably meant 'assigned' or 'provided' and the words ' "Appointed to be read in the Churches" literally expressed the fact that this Bible was printed by the King's printer with the approval of the King and the Bishops for use in the churches, and that no competing edition "of the largest volume" was allowed to be published' (Pollard 1911: 60). What the wording 'Appointed to be read in Churches' implied was that, from now on the new version should take the place of the Bishops' Bible which was then in use in the English parishes, just as the Bishops' Bible of 1568 had been a revision of the Great Bible of 1539, the translation of Miles Coverdale based on Tyndale's work and the Latin Vulgate.

The literary style and the language of the King James Version did not entirely reflect the linguistic style of the seventeenth-century. Unlike the Tyndale version, which had deftly turned phrases of the common Greek of the New Testament writings into a compelling vernacular of its time, the language of the King James Version was often antiquated and Latinized. The Hampton Court translators abandoned the English syntax which had its origins in the Middle Ages, and since then had exercised a tremendous influence on English Bibles, from the Tyndale version to the Bishop's Bible. Rather than making the Bible available in the recognizably contemporary idiom, they studiously adopted a style which was archaic to give the translation 'textual authority', a venerable status. Words and phrases like 'verily', 'it came to pass', and sentences with transposed syntax such as 'And there was taken up of fragments' (Luke 9: 17), point to an earlier or alien generation. A. C. Partridge surmises that this antique style could be attributed to Miles Smith, of the final editors (Partridge 1973: 112). The preponderance of Latin terms seemed to serve two purposes. It provided an ecclesiastical tone and flavour to the translation, and it significantly placed interpretation once again in the hands of ecclesiastical experts and Church authorities. Such a move reversed the initial aim of Tyndale, who, true to the Reformation ethos, wished to make the Bible a daily companion and guide to ordinary people without the mediation and intervention of priests and bishops: 'If God spare my life, ere many years I will cause a boy that driveth the plow to know more of the Scriptures than thou [a theologian] dost' (Daniell 2001: 1).

The eventual triumph of the KJV over all rival versions was not due to its 'own intrinsic superiority over its rivals' as Westcott triumphantly proclaimed (Westcott 1868: 158), or to its '*unassisted* merit' as Herbert Hensley Henson, the Bishop of Durham asserted (Henson 1938: 5). The English heritage industry and elements in the literary establishment, and in publishing, together with traditionalists would want us to believe that it was through sheer literary Darwinism that the Kings James Version survived and eventually prevailed over competing versions. The pre-eminent place of the Authorized Version as the supreme literary production needs demythicizing. These successive English translations were undertaken at a time when English as a language had no literary status. It was only much later that the Authorized Version came to be praised for its literary qualities. In seventeenth-century England it was the Geneva Bible which was seen as the people's Bible. This had the advantage of being printed attractively and produced in a convenient size for private use. David Norton, in charting the eventual triumph of the King James Version, pointed out that it was commercial considerations and political influences rather than its literary or its scholarly merits which played a crucial role in its elevation. The King's printer and the Cambridge University Press which had the monopoly of the Authorized Version secured the suppression of the Geneva Bible in spite of its superior printing and its easy accessibility. More importantly, the anti-monarchical notes in the Geneva Bible did not find favour in the court of James I. The Authorized Version prospered not because of its popularity with the general reading public but because of a deliberate political and commercial decision made by the Church establishment and printing companies. David Norton puts it bluntly: 'economics and politics were the key factors. It was in the very substantial commercial interest of the King's Printer, who had a monopoly on the text, and the Cambridge University Press, which also claimed the right to print the text, that the KJB should succeed' (Norton 1993: 212). Along with the commercial reason, one could add the change of political landscape in

Britain for the ensuing success of the Authorized Version. After the restoration of Charles II in 1660, the Authorized Version became the book of the eventual winners. With the end of the Civil War, the Geneva Bible gradually lost the spell it had over people. In the new political context, the Authorized Bible came to be identified with the winning side, and with peace and prosperity. Progressively the King James Bible attained the status of being God's own preferred version, and in certain conservative circles it gained a reputation as being written by God himself.

In their introduction to the Oxford World's Classic, *The Bible*, Carroll and Prickett note that the 'Authorised Version was not, as is sometimes argued, simply the product of the English language at a peculiarly rich stage of its evolution, but of a deliberate piece of social and linguistic engineering' (Carroll and Prickett 1998*a*: p. xxviii). Furthermore, they point out that 'it was designed to control the language of salvation, and to occupy the linguistic high ground in such a way as to allow its rivals, whether the Puritan Geneva or the Catholic Rheims and Douai Bibles, less verbal space, less legitimacy, less power' (Carroll and Prickett 1998*a*: p. xxix). It was a political as well as a religious undertaking. As Peter Levi aptly put it, 'If ever successful establishment prose existed, this is it' (Levi 1974: 35).

The Englishness of the Bible

The production and provision of vernacular Bibles in English occurred at a crucial cultural boundary-crossing of the English people. The medieval Catholic culture with its preoccupation with and emphasis on oral and visual expression of faith was now being gradually replaced by a literate culture which legitimized its faith and authority in the written word in the form of a printed Bible. When Wycliffe began his translation work, the Middle Ages were in decadence, and when he completed his task, the Renaissance was transforming Europe into a modern world. The Catholic faith, which was expressed in the Middle Ages through cathedrals, shrines, sculptures, pilgrimages, and other popular visual and emotional expressions, had now given way to a Protestant form of faith which emphasized the Word of God in the form of the written word. The English vernacular Bible emerged at a time when the written word was seen as the harbinger of modernity. Clutton-Brock stated: 'In no other nation was the same feat accomplished. Germany and France have their national epics; but they were made before the modern world began, and they are not religious. . . . Sayings from them are not constantly in the mouths of the people; nor are they read aloud weekly in any kind of assembly. We alone have the good fortune to possess the Scriptures which are thus familiar to us all, and at the same time full of a beauty which our own tongue has given to them and of a poetry which expresses our faith' (Clutton-Brock 1938: 72). Clutton-Brock's reference to reading aloud is interesting because punctuation marks in the King James Version were elaborate and designed to aid the reader 'in effectual delivery' (Partridge 1973: 112). It is ironic that the same Henrician injunction of 1538 concurrently abolished 'pilgrimages, offering of money, candles or tapers to images or relics, or kissing or licking the same, or saying over a number of beads, not understood or minded on, such like superstition' (Bray 1994a: 180), and ordered the Church to provide a new icon in the form of a Bible in English so that the parishioners 'may most commodiously resort to the same and read it' (Bray 1994a: 179).

The English Bible came to be seen as the quintessence of Englishness and as the measure of human character. No other text evinced such a national or racial superiority among the English. Like the role of football today, the English Bible was used to invoke nationalistic tendencies among an earlier generation of English commentators. In comparison with other European languages, the English language was seen as the proper vehicle to convey the biblical literature. Commenting on Psalm 23, David Daiches saw it as a natural English phenomenon, nay an Anglican poem. The mark of English acclimatization was the introduction of phrases which invoked genteel English rural and pastoral life, such as 'green pastures' and 'still waters'; those who are familiar with the original would know that these were not a literal rendition of the Hebrew text. Whereas the German version of Psalm 23, Daiches pointed out, had greenness, but in its rendition, the water was fresh rather than still. In Daiches's view, Luther's version lacked the flow of the Authorized Version and he declared it a 'clumsy mouthful' due to its accumulation of consonants. Similarly, he found the translation of Joshua 24: 26 in the King James Version demonstrating 'overtones of familiarity', 'simple customariness', and 'dignity', whereas the German rendition was 'stark in its own way, but with the starkness of a report written by an efficient civil servant' (Daiches 1967: 194). Daiches's contention was that, only the English version had the simplicity of the Hebrew (Daiches 1967: 192). His comment on the French Bible was equally xenophobic. He found that the French version of Isaiah 40: 1, 'Comfort ye, comfort ye my people, saith your Lord' sounded to 'English ears rather like a ticket agent announcing politely to a crowd of customers that all his tickets are sold out and they must comfort themselves as best they can' (Daiches 1967: 197). In his estimation, the Authorized Version, more than any other European Bible, had a 'flowing limpidity combined with ritual overtones'. The French Bible was 'discreet', and the German had a 'solid middle-class ring about it' (Daiches 1967: 197), but the English version was a monument of 'divine eloquence' (Daiches 1967: 203).

James Baikie, too, in his history of the English Bible, pointed out the inferior position of the Bible among Southern Europeans, especially among the Latin races, because of the privileged place accorded to 'ceremonial and sacramental acts' at the expense of the written word. In contrast, echoing the words of the historian J. R. Green, Baikie claimed that 'the English race is emphatically "The People of the Book", though he was candid enough to add that—'that book was an alien one' (Baikie 1928: 8). Just as a coin added value to the metal from which it was minted, the spirit of the ancient book entered a new body and 'reincarnated' (Dixon 1938: 51) into an esteemed English book.

The English Bible is seen as the mirror of English character and genius. Unlike vernacular versions on the continent, which were exclusively the work of individuals, as in the case of the German Bible by Luther, the English Bible was seen as the result of a corporate effort of generations of translators which demonstrated the spirit of the English. Dixon stated: 'Only if we remember that unlike the other translations, unlike, for example, the German Bible, Luther's version, it is not the work either of one man, of one generation, or one period. Its language as Hallam noted, "is not the language of James I". This was its good fortune, the happy circumstance that it represented the mind not of one man or time, but of many, that it had upon it the stamp not of Henry, or Elizabeth, or James, but of England herself. 'The genius of the country led the way, and into it has been distilled the peculiar character of the people and the spirit of their speech' (Dixon 1938: 55). It is this, according to Dixon, which made the English Bible 'so national, so representative, so English, a mirror of the country's character and genius' (Dixon 1938: 49). Moreover, its evolution was likened to that of the Hebrew Bible—slow and gradual in its growth, exerting its influence and perfecting its contents, as the English people as a nation stirred and were inducted into its great heritage of spirituality. Baikie asserted:

In short, our Bible became the English Bible in the way that we have come to regard as most characteristically English—the way in which our constitution and our laws have grown up; not by violent changes in which each new stage is unrelated to what went before it, but by a slow process in which all that was good in earlier attempts was conserved, and handed down to future generations with whatever of improvement the time then present could make upon the fabric. (Baikie 1928: 294)

Hoare asserted that English Christianity owed its religious enthusiasm to Celts and its ecclesiastical organization and discipline to Rome, but the Bible was essentially an English national product: 'Its record is interwoven with our native instincts of independence, of freedom, of personal religion. It is the true child of our ancestral Teutonism, a genuine home growth, stamped on every page of its history with our indelible Saxon Character' (Hoare 1901: 239).

What differentiated the English Bible from the translations undertaken by other people was that it came through the furnace and martyrdom of pioneers like William Tyndale and John Rogers. It was the ordeal of the first translating giants which lent the English Bible a special strength and distinction. Westcott claimed that the English Bible was greater than the Vulgate because nobody had died for the latter:

But the English Bible has what the Latin Bible, as far as we know, had not. It has not only the prerogative of vitality while the other has been definitely fixed in one shape, but it has also the seal of martyrdom upon it. In this too it differs from the other great modern versions. Luther defied his enemies to the last. Lefèvre in extreme old age mourned that when the opportunity was given him he had not been found worthy to give up his life for Christ. Calvin died sovereign at Geneva. But Tyndale, who gave us our first New Testament from the Greek, was strangled for his work at Vilvorde: Coverdale, who gave us our first printed Bible, narrowly escaped the stake by exile: Rogers, to whom we owe the multiform basis of our present Version, was the first victim of the Marian persecution: Cranmer, who has left us our Psalter, was at last blessed with a death of triumphant agony. The work was crowned by martyrdom and the workmen laboured at it in the faith and with the love of martyrs. (Westcott 1868: 371)

The other mark of the Englishness of the Bible was that it was intimately associated with the English monarchy. It was not only produced under the patronage of ruling monarchs but was also often dedicated to them. It was Miles Coverdale's Bible which set the obsequious tone. This was the first of the English Bibles that was dedicated to the king: 'Unto the most victorious Prince, and our most gracious sovereign Lord, King Henry the Eighth, King of England and of France, Lord of Ireland etc. Defender of the faith, and under God the chief and supreme head of the Church of England' and signed by his humble subject and daily orator, Miles Coverdale. His edition of 1537 had these words: 'Set forth with the king's most gracious licence' (Baikie 1928: 206–7). The frontispiece in the Great Bible was further illustrative of the indebtedness to the monarchy. This was designed by Hans Holbein. In it we see a God-figure looking down on Henry VIII. Two Latin scrolls, Isaiah 55: 11 and Acts 13: 22, run down from the lips of this figure. The passage from Acts is addressed to Henry who kneels down with his crown on the ground uttering the words, 'Thy word is a lamp unto my feet.' Below, on one side is the primate Cranmer and on the other Lord Secretary Thomas Cromwell engaged in distributing scriptures. In one corner, at the foot of the engraving is a portrait of a preacher who addresses the crowd on the duty of praying for kings and all in authority, using 1 Timothy 2: 1, and to which the crowd respond, 'God save the King.' In the other corner, is a prison where prisoners look on, observing the loyalty of the crowd. Even such a radical version as the Geneva Bible, when its New Testament version came out first in 1557 was dedicated to the Scottish monarch. The monarchical connection was further reinforced in 1689 when the ceremonial gift of the Bible became part of the coronation of English monarchs (Wickham Legg 1932: 696). At the coronation ceremony, the Archbishop, along with presentation of other emblems such as the sword, mantle, orb, ring, and sceptre, which make up the traditional apparatus, also offers the Bible with the words: 'Our gracious majesty, we present you with this Book, the most valuable thing this world affords. Here is wisdom; This is the Royal Law; These are the lively oracles of God.'

The vernacular versions thus acquired totemic status in England. They validated monarchical authority, facilitated an autonomous status for English Protestants, and acted as a manual of morality and social subordination.

Simple people and the simplicity of the Scripture: The Geneva Bible

Among the English versions of the Bible, another very important one was the Geneva Bible published in 1560. Unlike the King James Version, the Geneva Bible was unauthorized and emerged as a project in exile. It was initiated by a group of Protestants escaping from the reign of Catholic Mary and domiciled in Geneva, a significant centre of Protestant scholarship at the time. If the Authorized Verison is a Bible of the establishment, then the Geneva Bible was the Bible of the people. William Whittingham, who later became Dean of Durham, probably acted as the chief editor and he may have had a larger hand in translating the New Testament (Pollard 1911: 25), but the whole enterprise was clearly an effort of several Protestant refugees like Anthony Gilby, Thomas Sampson, William Cole, and Christopher Goodman, and was paid for by the English Church in Geneva. The adoption of the Geneva Bible by the Puritans and its portable size made it a popular version, and it went through many editions:

It was the Bible of Shakespeare from about 1596, and the Bible of Milton, it survived well into the mid-century as the popular Bible of Scotland and took root in America with the Pilgrim Fathers in 1620. It was the source of the Soldier's Pocket Bible, which was sixteen pages of fighting texts that Oliver Cromwell printed for the Army in 1643. It was naturally Bunyan's Bible. The reason why it ceased to be printed after about 1644 and almost ceased to be remembered after about 1700 is political and social: it was identified with forces in English society which were stifled in those years. (Levi 1974: 28)

The more 'modern' attitude of the editors of the Geneva Bible was shown by their naming or not naming some of the books in the New Testament. For instance, in titling the Epistle to the Hebrews, unlike the Authorized Version, they left out the misleading 'Epistle of Paul the Apostle to the

Hebrews' and had simply 'The Epistle to the Hebrews'. In their preface to the Epistle they made clear the doubts about its Pauline authenticity: 'For as much as diuers bothe of the Greek writers and Latin witness, that the writer of this epistle of just causes would not have his name known, it were curiosity of our part to labour much therein. For seeing the spirit of God is the author thereof, it diminishes nothing the authority, although we know not with what pen he wrote it. Whether it were Paul (as it is not like) or Luke, or Barnabas, or Clement, or some other, his chief purpose is etc' (Baikie 1928: 244). Interestingly, it was the Geneva Version which called the epistles of James, Peter, 1 John, and Jude, the General Epistles rather than the 'Catholic Epistles', a practice based on the Vulgate and followed by other English versions (Bruce 1970: 86).

In a number of ways the Geneva Bible set the tone for future English Bibles. It was the first portable Bible in English. Though the state policy was to place a copy of the Bible in every church, the authorized versions did not find their way into the ordinary homes of the people. The Bibles that were found on the lectern in parishes during the time of Henry VII, Edward VI, and under Elizabeth were huge, heavy folios, too costly for the ordinary people to purchase them. It was the Geneva Bible which was set out to provide a new type of small Bible for a new generation. The Geneva Version was the first family Bible issued in relatively handy size. In its day it was the reader-friendly version. It was aimed at those who were 'not well practised' and those readers who might be 'discouraged' by unfamiliar Hebrew phrases. It used italics for explanatory and additional words. It provided maps and a concordance. In effect, what the Geneva Bible did was to provide the necessary tools for an ordinary reader to become a biblical critic of some sort. It was the first English version to divide the chapters into verses, a device first employed by the Dominican Santes Pagnini for the Latin Vulgate printed at Lyons in 1527 (Pollard 1911: 27). The breaking up of biblical narratives into verses reflected the Puritan penchant for quoting texts. What was then seen as a convenient way to handle biblical passages would be seen by future literary critics as destroying and dismantling the narrative's potential as a good story.[3] It was the Genevan use of roman type which gradually taught the English to prefer that style. It was the black gothic letters which became the national form for the vernacular. 'The significance of Whittingham's choice of roman may be measured if the first editions of the Geneva books, in roman are compared

with the first edition of the Authorized Version, which is in black-letter'
(Special Correspondent of the Times 1955: 134). These features were simply
reproduced in the King James Version.

Apart from ideological reasons, many turned to the Geneva Bible as a
matter of convenience. It facilitated private reading. It was much easier to
read and was available in octavo form and could be effortlessly held in the
hand easily. Since it was printed in Roman rather than the older Gothic
type, it was easy to read as well.

In reality, the Geneva Bible became the Bible of ordinary English Protestants despite the fact the Great Bible was the Bible of the Church and
sanctioned by ecclesiastical authority. Between its appearance in 1560 and
the production of the King James Version in 1611, Tyndale's New Testament
went through five reprints, the Great Bible, seven, the Bishops' Bible
which succeeded it, twenty-two, and the Geneva Bible over 140. F. F. Bruce
notes:

The Geneva Bible immediately won, and retained, widespread popularity. It
became the household Bible of English-speaking Protestants. While its notes
represented a more radical Reformed viewpoint than that favoured in the
Elizabethan religious settlement, and it was never appointed to be used in the
churches of England, its excellence as a translation was acknowledged even by
those who disagreed with the theology of the translators.   (Bruce 1970: 91)

The Geneva Bible could justifiably stake a claim as the first Bible of the
ordinary people. The preface to the reader made it abundantly clear that it
was aimed not at erudite ecclesiastical theologians but at ordinary people.
Its translatory decisions, choice of vernacular English phrases, textual
explanations, and marginal notes had one singular constituency in mind—
'simple readers'—who found the words and phrases obscure and 'seemed
so dark' in certain places (Bray 1994b: 362). In another respect, the Geneva
Bible was a genuinely popular document. It ignored the textual and theological issues which preoccupied English and continental theologians. It
paid less attention to technical disputes over biblical narratives, and took
only a limited interest in the reigning theology of the time—covenant
theology and the allied exegetical contention, 'national election', espoused
and propounded by theologians at Oxford and Cambridge at that time.
Rather, it focused on the principal message of the Scripture as propounded
by Martin Luther—justification by faith in Christ:

At every point in the commentary the reader's attention is focused unblinkingly on the person and work of Christ. . . . There was not one preface to an Old Testament book that did not explicitly focus on the life and person of Christ. Indeed, so conscious were the translators of the actual presence of Christ in the Old Testament that the references to the 'Angel of the Lord' were routinely identified as the pre-existent Christ who lay at the core of both Old and New Testament. (Stout 1982: 22–3)

What kept the Geneva Bible alive and made it a dominant cultural and religious force until the Civil War, were its explanatory and exegetical notes. This was in spite of the effort by the authorities to replace it with the King James Version. The innovative aspect of the Geneva Bible, its marginal comments, run to nearly 300,000 words. These were seen by authorities as 'very partial, untrue, seditious, and savouring too much of dangerous and traitorous conceits' (Pollard 1911: 46). It was no surprise that the notes annoyed James I.

The King James Version was the Church's third attempt at producing its own authoritative version, following the Great Bible and the Bishop's Bible. It was an attempt to drive out the popular Bible, that is the Geneva Bible, largely for theological but also for social reasons. In this it failed, initially but, as we saw earlier, political and printing history succeeded where the intrinsic merits of the Authorized Version failed. Ironically, in their preface to the Authorized Version, the court translators used the Geneva Bible for their biblical citations, the very Bible they loathed and wanted to banish (Bruce 1970: 92), and in dedicating it to James I, they simply copied Whittingham's dedication of the New Testament to James as Scottish monarch: 'To the Richt Excellent Heich and Mightie Prince James the Sext, the King of Scottis' (Special Correspondent of the Times 1955: 138).

The Geneva Bible's role as a charter of people's liberty and as a provider of vocabulary for an egalitarian framework in the face of tyranny is under serious re-evaluation. A closer reading will reveal that it reflected a mixture of popular rebellious feeling and conservative Calvinism. Whether its notes espoused radical social reforms fuelled by biblical teachings as Christopher Hill (Hill 1993: 47–78) and Richard Greaves (Greaves 1976: 94–109) claimed, or endorsed social conformity and spiritual solace as Stout suggests, their import remains tentative and contentious (Stout 1982: 25).

An example of the support of rebellion in the notes is found in that on Exodus 1: 19, where the Geneva annotators endorse the disobedience of the Egyptian midwives regarding the killings of Hebrew male children. On the other hand, the marginalia supported the ownership of private property. It tried to explain away the radical social vision of Acts about holding all things in common (Acts 2: 44, 4: 32, 5: 4) by saying that the early Church did not share property but voluntarily supported the needy. What was communal was not social possession but spiritual commonality. Not all annotations and marginal notes were politically motivated or denominationally influenced. Some bring out the English sense of humour by understatement. In Mark's account of the murder of John the Baptist, the editors betray their puritan attitude to recreation and amusement by slipping in the heading, 'The inconvenience of dancing' (Baikie 1928: 245).

What the battle of different versions, with their annotations and comments, in the sixteenth and seventeenth centuries indicates is the interpreters' strong belief that God's word spoke immediately to their context, and that biblical texts could be utilized profitably in the ongoingness of daily life. Within their pages they imagined the reflection of their national destiny, and conceived themselves as replicating and re-living the trials and tribulations of ancient Israel and the Church of New Testament times. More significantly, the production of the Geneva Bible, the translatory content, and its technical layout were an attempt to free the Bible from ecclesiastical control. In Hammond's view, 'of all English versions the Geneva Bible had probably the greatest political significance, in its preparing a generation of radical puritans to challenge, with the word of God, their tyrant rulers' (Hammond 1982: 136). The title page is illustrative of this. There was a woodcut of the Israelites about to cross the Red Sea. Encircled in this were the words: 'Great are the troubles of the righteous, but the Lord delivereth them out of all' (Ps. 34: 19). On the top were the words: 'Fear not, stand still and behold the salvation of the Lord, which he will shew to you this day' (Exod. 14: 13), and at the bottom: 'The Lord shall fight for you: therefore hold you your peace' (Exod. 14: 14).

A text for the empire: A post-imperial footnote

The textual choice of the King James Version by the Edinburgh publisher, Canongate, is an interesting and intriguing one. The aim of Canongate was to present the Authorized Version not as a religious text but as a work of literature with a profound and long-lasting impact on English literature and life. P. D. James, herself a contributor and reviewer of the first series wrote: 'No single book has had more influence on our national identity, our literature and the development of the English language than has the Authorised King James Version of the Bible' (James 1998: 21).

Two uneasy questions keep emerging. At a time when there were what R. J. Watson calls a 'seemingly endless series of piddling translations' (Watson 1993: 15), one wonders whether the Authorized Version offered the definitive version, as a work of literature as much as a holy writ which has stood magisterially holding its own in the face of numerous upstart and various renditions such as the New English, Jerusalem, Revised Standard, Good News, New International, Revised English. Is the use of the King James Version for the Canongate series some kind of nostalgia, putting the clock back to a time when the English had one main version? The concluding paragraph of P. D. James's review of the first series of the pocket Canon Bibles is indicative of such a wish: 'Is it too much to hope that the day may actually come when, even if the Church of England continues to neglect the Authorized Version in its worship, the King James Bible will at least be part of the reading syllabus of students of English Language and Literature? Or, in this timid, media-obsessed age of all faiths and none, would that be regarded as politically incorrect?' (James 1998: 21). The reclamation of the Authorized Version could be seen as a ploy to placate traditionalists or could be seen as a ruse to woo impressionable youth who would not dream of buying a copy of the Psalms written in an unfamiliar prose, had it not been introduced by Bono who professes an affinity with David as a fellow pop-star, whom he calls the 'Elvis of the Bible'.

The other uncomfortable question is whether, at a time when Britain and most of the Western world are becoming more multicultural, and a new configuration of belonging to a nation is emerging due to immigration and unprecedented social and geographical mobility, the reintroduction of the King James Version may encourage nostalgia for an imaginary single culture and for an old homogeneous glory. The Authorized Version was seen as a common bond which held together divergent peoples who were part of the British empire. The popular report of the British and Foreign Bible Society recorded that a large number of copies of the Authorised Version were being sent to the colonies to keep up the concord of the British Commonwealth, and it claimed that 'devotion to the ideals of the Holy Scriptures is at once the sign and instrument of that unity' (*In the Mother Tongue* 1930: 42). Now that the empire has gone, is this Canongate's way of recovering a singular and straight sense of English identity?

Colonial parallels

In the Canongate's marketing of the Bible in the West at the end of the twentieth-century, and the Bible's journey into non-Western cultures with the missionaries two hundred years previously, one notices certain parallels. Unlike the missionaries of the colonial period who wanted to bring culture and morality to the uncivilized, Canongate and its authors appear to humanize the Western population which is seen as decadent, secular, individualistic, materialistic, and theologically illiterate. As a way of introducing the Bible, most missionaries painted the colonies as morally and spiritually degenerate and in need of salvation. Thus the Bible was made to participate in the colonial project of 'improving' the natives and in the process destabilized people and their cultures. The Authorized Version became the quintessence of Englishness and an index of human character. But now with an ironic twist, the West is seen as needing salvation. The context out of which these introductions emerge are naturally Western and it is variously described as a 'secular age' (Morrison 1998: p. xvi) , a 'post-Christian' age (Wilson 1998: p. vii), 'a time of religious transition' (Armstrong 1999: p. vii), and the world of investigative journalism and science (Wilson 1998: p. vii). Karen Armstrong, in her introduction to Hebrews, writes: 'In many of the countries of Western Europe, atheism is on the increase, and the churches are emptying, being converted into art galleries, restaurants, and warehouses' (Armstrong 1999: p. vii). She could have also said that they have been turned into Hindu temples and Sikh Gurudwaras. In such a context, the Bible, the sacred text is advocated primarily as a literary text, and to be read like any other book.

But the opposite was at work in colonial India. For many in countries with a history of colonialism, the King James Version was not 'the noblest monument of English prose' as claimed by John Livingstone Lowes, but an intruding text that was deeply implicated in the colonizing enterprise. Christopher Anderson, who in 1845 published a two-volume history of the English Bible, surveying the territorial spread of the British empire from Hobart to Ottawa, claimed that the authorized Bible was at that time 'in the act of being perused from *the rising to the setting sun*' and he went on to claim that it was 'the *only* version in existence on which *the sun never sets*' (Anderson 1845: p. xi; italics in original):

> [T]he English Bible is at present in the act of being perused from *the rising to the setting sun*. . . . The fact, the singular and unprecedented fact, demands deliberate reflection from every British Christian, whether at home or abroad. His Bible, at the moment, is the *only* version in existence on which *the sun never sets*. We know full well that it is actually in use on the banks of the Ottawa and St. Lawrence, as well as at Sydney, Port Philip, and Hobart Town; but before his evening rays have left the spires of Quebec or Montreal, his morning beams have already shone for hours upon the shores of Australia and New Zealand. And if it be reading by so many of our language in Canada, while the sun is sinking on Lake Ontario; in the eastern world, where he has risen in his glory on the banks of the Ganges, to the self-same Sacred Volume, many, who are no less our countrymen, have already turned.   (Anderson 1845: pp.x–xi; italics in original)

In the colonies, the Bible as literature, became a disguise for the moral improvement of the natives and a source for a means of introducing biblical religion. The Authorized Version was first encountered in the colonies, particularly in India, as part of colonial education. It was part of the civilizing process that involved the moral improvement of the natives. Touring India soon after the Indian Revolt of 1857, H. Hipsley, a Quaker, questioned the apparent neutrality of the British government in matters related to religion, and advocated the introduction of the Bible in Indian schools as a remedy for the lawlessness of the heathen. He dismissed the self-governance of Indians as a 'theoretical fiction'. In India, he wrote, the English were the imperial power, and if they intended to continue in India their 'duty is to educate the people'. His prescription was the introduction of the Bible: 'We cannot call that education complete, even in a literary point of view, which ignores the English version of the Bible' (Hipsley n.d.: 14). To reinforce his case that Bible-reading produced law-abiding subjects, he pointed out that no single native Indian Christian was implicated in the Revolt (Hipsley n.d.: 17).

Colonial educators envisaged a dual project for the Bible—to use it simultaneously as a literary and a religious text. Having pronounced that the literary, scientific, and historical information contained in the vernacular literature was no patch on Western learning and literature, and that indigenous writings lacked the moral and mental power to equip the Indians (the famous/notorious 1835 Minute of Lord Macaulay: 'a single shelf of a good European library was worth the whole of native literature') colonial administrators and educators decided that carefully selected English texts infused with biblical references could shape the minds of Indians to appreciate and recognize the authority of British rule, but more specifically lead them to read the Bible without any compulsion from missionaries. With this view in mind, English writings which were suffused with biblical and Christian references were introduced into the Indian university curriculum. Shakespeare, Locke and Bacon were seen as texts which could supply and uphold Christian faith and inculcate morality and civility. Lengthy extracts from the Bible were also incorporated in textbooks, for example those which were part of the Bachelor's degree course for Calcutta University. The literary techniques employed in the Bible—narrative, plots, events, and characters were seen as a more effective way of attracting the attention of students than preaching or doctrinal teaching. The Bible might be the word of God, but the religious truth was conveyed through literary imagery and analogy. Or, to put it another way, the Bible came to be read as literature. It came to be seen as a human as well as a divine document. The new understanding meant that at the very least the Bible reflected human fallibilities, and was not free from error. It also became evident that cherished notions about the role and the authority of the Bible also had to be rethought, and, in many cases, its themes, doctrines, and concepts had to be configured and reconfigured to the extent that they bore little resemblance to the meanings traditionally ascribed to them.

The power of the Bible was seen as lying in its potent imagery. The objective was personal awakening and conversion through an appeal to this. Gauri Viswanathan, who has written on the inextricable link between English literature and the politics of the empire, observes: 'The horrors of sin and damnation were not to be understood through reason but through images that give the reader a "shocking spectre of his own deformity and haunt him, even in his sleep". . . . To read the Bible well, to be moved by its imagery, to be instructed by its "dark and ambiguous style, figurative and hyperbolical manner", the imagination first had to be fully trained and equipped' (Viswanathan 1989: 55).[4] The concern was not immediate conversion but to enable people to realize their degenerate spiritual state. However, colonial educators were very particular that the Bible should be put to use exclusively for imparting religious knowledge, and that it should not be subjected to secular pursuits such as 'parsing or syntactical and other grammatical exercises of linguistic acquisition—practices that necessarily reduced the Bible from its deserved status as "the Book of Books" to merely one among many books' (Viswanathan 1989: 53). Whereas currently the Bible as literature is viewed sceptically with regard to its religious potency, in the colonies the secular use of the Bible in the university syllabus was seen as a source of religious belief and moral improvement.

In Victorian England under the influence of the Arnoldian curriculum, the Bible as literature became a disguise for the moral power of Christian values, while in colonial India, English literary texts which were infused with Christian morality became a mask for spreading biblical civilization. The curriculum planners were looking in English texts for what they called the 'diffusive benevolence of Christianity'. Viswanathan writes: 'The process of curricular selection was marked by weighty pronouncements on the 'sound Protestant Bible principles' in Shakespeare, the 'strain of serious piety' in Addison's *Spectator* papers, the 'scriptural morality' of Bacon and Locke, the 'devout sentiment' of Abercrombie and the 'noble Christian sentiments' in Adam Smith's *Moral Sentiments*, which was hailed as 'the best authority for the science of morals which English literature could supply' (Viswanathan 1989: 86). The King James Version soon ceased to be treated as scripture alone, but came to be also seen as a literary phenomenon.

The English vernacular Bible had functioned as more than the Word of God. It had been turned into an icon to make the people obedient to their rulers. The English vernacular Bible played a vital role in Henry VIII's efforts to establish royal supremacy over the Church of England. This new supremacy was asserted in the name of the divine law as revealed in the word of God, and became crucial after the English Church's disjuncture with Rome. Henry's iconoclasm, too, was legitimated by a direct appeal to the Scriptures. This reliance on the Bible, according to Richard Rex, led to the 'official publication of an English Bible to reveal to people the scriptural authority claimed for his policies' (Rex 1993: 103). The Henrician enthusiasm for the word of God might at first glance look like an evangelical zeal for a plain and pure text of Scripture, over against the traditions, teachings, and non-biblical paraphernalia espoused by the Roman Church, but, according to Richard Sampson, it was a code to make the people obedient to the King rather than the Pope (Rex 1993: 25–6). Now the Bible had been turned into a paper Pope. The state's prime purpose in making the vernacular English Bible accessible to ordinary people was to promote obedience. Henry was neither moved by the Protestant principle of the efficacy of the plain text nor interested in the laity's need to have the Bible in their own vernacular. What, in fact, he was doing when he opened up the Bible for the ordinary people was to assert his own royal authority and presence rather than to make known the potency of the gospel. His intention was to raise an awareness of obedience to God's law among his subjects, especially that which pertained to the obedience to princes. Unlike the Reformers who saw faith and salvation as the core of the biblical tradition, Henry made obedience and conformity the key biblical virtues. Richard Morrison, one of the propagandists at the time, claimed that 'obedience is the badge of a true Christian man' and went on to say that of all commandments the most important one was 'obey ye your king' (Rex 1993: 26).

Similarly, in the colonies when the Bible was introduced, missionaries and the British and Foreign Bible Society which played a prominent part in disseminating the Bible were not necessarily enthused exclusively by the gospel truths of 'faith' and 'salvation'. As part of 'improving' the natives they were keen to introduce values such as law and order, obedience etc. In Papua, the missionaries saw the laid-back, no-rule, non-authoritarian lifestyle of Papuans as a sign of their primitiveness. They found that these communities lacked any central authority and well-defined purpose and control. They did not have a chief with the power to awaken aspiration and encourage commitment. There were no courts, no judges, no penalties, no officers of law and order, and no active sense of obligation, duty or rights. In such an atmosphere people were not only passive but also lacked the vocabulary to express their understanding of a purposeful life. For instance, in a no-rule, care free atmosphere, the early biblical translators had difficulty in translating the sentence in Jesus's parable 'Compel them to come in', and had to rephrase it as: 'Urge them to enter in'. The writer of the 1914–15 Report of the British and Foreign Bible Society, could now proudly inform readers that law and order had been introduced to an unruly country as a result of the joint effort of British rule and the New Testament:

> However, moral ideas are now being introduced. Compulsion has come into the lives of the Papuans by the introduction of English law and justice. It is becoming easier to explain the New Testament by means of reference to the British Government. To-day a centralized authority exists, which can impose laws, and punish the breach of laws; there are magistrates and judges and policemen, and prisons. But all these things are foreign; the ideas they convey are foreign; and they have still to be translated into terms of native life and thought. A fresh world is being opened up to the Papuans, and a new life with a new sense of responsibility. They are being constrained into practical recognition of that Categorical Imperative which the New Testament translates in terms of love. (*The Book and the Sword* 1915: 17)

The perception of the Bible as a document which urges people to obey and be subservient is demonstrated in 1912 by the following request to a missionary by a chief who found his people unmanageable and disobedient and felt they were in need of the Word of God to rein them in:

> Missionary, this country is growing worse. I would like you to teach my people, for my servants refuse to do as I tell them; even the slaves have no ears. Yes, the country is changed since the white man came. I had power to rule once; if a slave disobeyed, I could put him to death; but now, if you thrash one he goes to the magistrate and complains, and I am helpless. We need somebody here to be constantly teaching us. The land is before you; build where you choose; we are all in the dark, and need these words of God.   (D. F. Walker 1912: 260–1)

Concluding remarks

All translated Bibles exist in the shadow of the Authorized Version which has taken its place as *the* Bible. It has not only defined, designed, and forged the lexicon of other versions and the vocabulary they must adopt, but also acts as the yardstick by which other renditions will be judged. When a new Tamil translation was mooted in the nineteenth century, a resolution of the Madras Auxiliary of the British and Foreign Bible Society, made in 1841, tied the hands of the revision committee in Jaffna (Sri Lanka) at the outset by instructing them that the new translation should strictly adhere to the English Authorized Version of 1611:

That the translators and revisers of the Holy Scriptures in connection with this Society, be required, in all translations published by the Society, uniformly to retain that sense of the Textus Receptus of the original Scriptures which is found to have been adopted in the English Authorized Version, together with its position of words, arrangements of sentences and punctuation, in so far as the sense is, or can be affected thereby: that the marginal readings of the English version shall not be admitted into the text of the translation, but if inserted shall be placed in the margin as in the English. That when the sense of the English version appears to have been designedly left doubtful, such doubts shall, as far as possible, be retained in the translation, and that every insertion of supplemental words or other alterations supposed to be necessary on the ground of idiom shall be brought to the notice of the Committee of variations, in order that in regard to sense there be no variation whatever from the English version. (*A Brief Narrative of the Operations of the Jaffna Auxiliary Bible Society* 1868: 17).

The Authorized Version's tendency of setting the pattern did not stop with vernacular versions of the Bible. It extended its tentacles to sacred texts of other faith traditions. At a time when Orientalists were 'discovering' the texts of other people and were involved in their translations, William Jones (1746–1794), the eminent Indologist, was certain as to what publishing format these translations should follow. Commenting on Charles Wilkin's translation of the *Bhagavadgita* (1785), he commented: 'But, as a learner, I could have wished that it had been still more literal, and that the verses had been numbered, and every thing put in the Sanscrit printed in Italicks, like our excellent translation of the Bible' (Cannon 1990: 259).

In the postcolonial discourse, the reordering of other people's textual heritage by the British in the form of the English Bible, falls within the mode of negation. In the rhetoric of negation, the Western writing conceives 'the other as absence, emptiness, nothingness and or death' (Spurr 1993: 92). What negation does as a way of establishing and maintaining colonial control is to inferiorize other people's texts, erase them or divest them of their meanings. The purpose is to clear the space for Western imagination, and to replace the vacated space with the appropriate images, stories, and texts of the West. The Authorized Version which is seen as the custodian of the truth and 'a trustee of civilization', is now used as the *ur*-text to deny any claims or validity of other versions or texts. Now any version has to be measured against the 'monumental' standard of the King James Version.

I end with two images of the appropriation of the Authorized Version by the 'natives'. One, drawn from the days of colonialism and the other, from its aftermath. In both cases, the Englishman's book, as Bhabha has demonstrated in his oft-cited essay, 'Signs Taken for Wonders', has now become freely available, so that the natives can make use of it in their own way, free from any subordination (Bhabha 1994: 120). The recipients interact with it as they reconfigure it in their own terms. In the first case, the printed word of God, which was seen as the vehicle for God's revelation, has now only a non-theological use. It serves as packaging paper for the natives. William Canton recalls an incident in the Indian Revolt where pages of the Authorized Version were used as wrapping paper. When two English ladies and children were hiding in Sitapur and expected to die at any time at the hands of the Indian rebels, one of the children fell ill and a native doctor was allowed to send some medicine. It was wrapped in a sheet of printed paper and when the ladies opened it they found the verses from Isaiah 51: 12–15:

I, even I, am he that comforteth you: who art thou, that thou shouldest be afraid of a man that shall die, and of the son of man which shall be made as grass; And forgettest the Lord thy maker, that hath stretched forth the heavens, and laid the foundations of the earth; and hast feared continually every day because of the fury of the oppressor, as if he were ready to destroy? And where is fury of the oppressor? The captive exile hasteneth that he may be loosed, and that he should not die in the pit, nor that his bread should fail. But I am the Lord thy God, that divided the sea, whose waves roared: The Lord of hosts is his name.   (Canton 1914: 271–2)

In the other case, the book retains its narrative hold to move and stir but this time its power and authority are somewhat dented. In selecting his 'books of the millennium', K. Satchidanandan, a noted Indian literary critic and poet, named the King James Version as his first choice, the other two being *The Complete Works of Shakespeare* and *Kabir Ranchanavalli*. Strangely enough, all three were almost contemporaneous writings. Of the three, he went on to say that the Bible had been of special interest to him as a poet:

I hear in it the echoes of *Tao-te-Ching*, the *Upanishads*, and *Dhammapada*; I identify myself with Abraham in his anguish that even shakes his faith; the Book of Job fascinates me with its intense sense of tragedy; the Book of Genesis fills me with remorse, anger, hope; David's Psalms make me weep; I am elated by the Song of Solomon; Exodus to me is the journey of life; the sacrifice of Jesus, rather the murder, shocks me as I find Cain reborn again and again in history; the Book of Revelation with its surreal vision takes me to Dante, Moses, Aaron, Noah, David, Solomon, Job: material for a Vyasa or a Shakespeare. I read the Bible, particularly the Old Testament first in my undergraduate days when I came across the Communist Manifesto whose power is drawn to a great extent from the vision and the idiom of the Bible. Today I read a different Bible, its miracle and metaphysics, its magic and mystery, however, are still intact even when I carry into it my post-structuralist or feminist understanding of mind, discourse and history and the whole burden of the modern experience with its terror and hope, its heresies and awakenings.[5]

The opening sentence of Satchidanandan sets the new scene. The 'Book of Books' is now placed alongside other texts and has now become a book among books. The Englishman's book gains a new lease of life when it is read contrapuntally with other texts. What these two incidents indicate is the double nature of the book. In one case, it is merely a sheaf of paper to be used for wrapping things, and as the medium of religious authority has become virtually unrecognizable. In the other, the Book retains some of its power when read in conjunction with other texts. The recipients engage with the Book, but recast it to suit their needs. The Authorized Version which was projected as a religious text without parallel, is now seen as having many purposes.

NOTES

1. The essayists include prominent novelists: Fay Weldon (I and II Corinthians), Doris Lessing (Ecclesiastes), Louis de Bernières (Job), Ruth Rendell (Romans), P. D. James (Acts), Joanna Trollope (Ruth and Esther), Will Self (Revelation); a pop artist, U2's Bono (The Psalms); an atheist, Steven Rose (Genesis); Jewish writers David Grossman (The Exodus) and Meir Shalev (Books of Samuel); and the Buddhist, Dalai Lama (The Epistle

of James). For a detailed critique of these introductions, see R. S. Sugirtharajah, 'Marketing the Testaments: Canongate and their Pocket-sized Bibles', *Biblical Interpretation: A Journal of Contemporary Approaches* (forthcoming).

2. The identity of 'one book of the whole Bible of the largest volume' is difficult to ascertain. Although Cromwell had the Great Bible in mind, it did not make its appearance until April 1539. The Great Bible was Miles Coverdale's (1488–1569) revision of Matthew's Bible. Matthew's Bible was the work of John Rogers, a former associate of Tyndale, who used the pen name Thomas Matthew. See David Daiches, *The King James Version of the English Bible: An Account of the Development and Sources of the English Bible of 1611 with Special Reference to the Hebrew Tradition* (Chicago: University of Chicago Press, 1941), 35 n. and F. F. Bruce, *The English Bible: A History of Translations from the Earliest English Versions to the New English Bible*, new and revised edn. (London: Lutterworth Press, 1970), 689.

3. It took nearly three hundred years to rectify this. It was people like Matthew Arnold, H. G. Moulton and Ernest Sutherland Bates, James George Frazer among others who advocated the notion of the Bible as literature. Some of them even went on to produce Bibles without verse divisions. For example, see James George Frazer, *Passages of the Bible: Chosen for their Literary Beauty and Interest* (London: A. C. Black, 1927) and Ernest Sutherland Bates, *The Bible Designed to be Read as Literature* (London: William Heinemann Ltd, 1937).

4. The citations Viswanathan employs come from *Madras Missionary Register*, 2/1 (1836), 36 and *Calcutta Christian Observer*, 2 (1833), 87.

5. See the boxed item in *The Book Review*, 24/3 (2000), 19.

6

BLOTTING THE MASTER'S COPY: LOCATING BIBLE TRANSLATIONS

So the question was *which* translation and *why*.

(*White Teeth*, Zadie Smith 2000: 428)

Translator invades, extracts, and brings home.

(George Steiner 1976: 298)

I start with a disturbance, caused by the Bible translation, which occurred not in a colony in the British empire but in a city in Romanized North Africa in the fifth century CE. It took place in Tripoli (Oea) where the bishop of the diocese arranged for Jerome's new version of Jonah to be read. When some Greeks heard a word which differed from the translation they were familiar with, they criticized the new wording and condemned it as false. Apparently the offending translation was in Jonah 4: 6 where Jerome used 'ivy' instead of 'gourd'.[1] Augustine, the Bishop of Hippo, who was perturbed by the incident, wrote to Jerome that his Latin version was different from the one which had been read for 'so many generations', and which had been 'enshrined in the memory and hearing of all' (White 1990: 92). He added that if Jerome's translation were to be more generally read in many churches, it would not only cause difficulty, but much worse it could prove the earlier Latin and Greek translators wrong and be condemned (White 1990: 92). Augustine rather wished that Jerome would provide him with a translation of the Greek version of the canonical Scriptures, the Septuagint, known to be the work of the Seventy translators. This version, in Augustine's view, was a 'text of great importance' which had wielded power for nearly three centuries. Moreover, it had been published abroad and had a wide circulation, and even more significantly, it was the version which the apostles used (White 1990: 93). At present I will leave Augustine and his uneasiness about Jerome's translation and come back to it later.

Confusing and confused tongues

Bible translation has long been implicated in diverse imperialist projects in Africa, Asia, the Caribbean, and South America. In the colonial context, translation acted as a mediating agency between conquest and conversion. Vicente L. Rafael, who has seen a pervasive connection between translation and conquest in the Philippines, writes thus:

> The Spanish words *conquista* (conquest), *conversión* (conversion), and *traducción* are semantically related. The Real Academia's *Diccionario de la lengua española* defines *conquista* not only as the forcible occupation of a territory but also as the act of winning someone's voluntary submission and consequently attaining his or her love and affection. *Conversión* literally means the act of changing a thing into something else; in its more common usage, it denotes the act of bringing someone over to a religion or a practice. Conversion, like conquest, can thus be a process of crossing over into the domain—territorial, emotional, religious, or cultural—of someone else and claiming it as one's own. (Rafael 1993: p. xvii)

Since the invader and invaded spoke different languages and practised different religions, translation played a crucial role in conquering and converting the other. A virtual hagiography has emerged around missionary translations, describing the trying conditions under which these early translators toiled. Missionary literature is littered with instances of both a heroic and comical nature as these missionary translators tried to make sense of and introduce the written form for languages which were untouched by Christianity and Western civilization. Revd A. A. Lind's experience with the Mardia tribe of the Upper Godavari River in India may be an extreme case but illustrates the extent to which missionary translators were willing to go. He wrote to his supporters back home: 'I grunted like a pig, quacked like a duck, neighed like a horse, howled like a jackal, and so forth. I also had to exercise all my artistic abilities in drawing various kinds of animals, birds, and sects' (*The Book and the Sword* 1915: 14).

The role of colonialists in translation invoked both indebtedness and indifference. It was the translated Gikuyu New Testament which provided ammunition for the Gikuyu women to fight against female circumcision in the colonial days. When faced with the argument that female circumcision was a central ritual in Gikuyu culture, the women, reading from the translated Gikuyu version, discovered for themselves the absence of any reference to female circumcision in the Bible. They found out that God commanded not Sarah but Abraham to be circumcised, and came to the conclusion that there was no biblical warrant for female circumcision (Njoroge 2000: 35). The efforts of missionaries to reach the natives in their own language might conjure up a compassionate and benevolent face of the colonial project. The flip side was the domestication of languages. Rather than harmlessly retrieving vanishing languages, missionaries aided by the colonial apparatus reconfigured the vernacular lexicon, moulding the thinking of indigenous people to fit with Christian thought patterns, and thus prescribing alien ways of conceptualizing language and displacing native religious and linguistic conventions.

Faced with mutually incomprehensible languages in the mission field, missionary translators showed both a grudging fascination and a downright detestation. One of the popular reports of the British and Foreign Bible Society comments that it is 'a mistake to imagine that savage folk always use crude and elementary forms of speech. Many African languages, for example, are in structure far more complex than English' (*For the Healing of the Nations* 1916: 12). Although these languages were seen as ungrammatical, there was an admiration for them. Bantu languages were praised for their terminations at the beginning, so that the words are inflected, conjugated, or defined by means of a system of prefixes. The same report goes on to mention that 'the Bantu languages are generally "agglutinative"—which means that they build up whole sentences round a simple stem, until the original word is buried and hardly discoverable' (*For the Healing of the Nations* 1916: 12). Similarly, the Ila language of the tribe in Northern Rhodesia (now Zimbabwe) was highly thought of for its sophistication. A verb in Ila possesses eight voices, sixty tenses and has at least two hundred different forms of the pronouns each with its own peculiar use (*For the Healing of the Nations* 1916: 12). While some of the languages were singled out for their intricacy and sophistry, others were deemed as vacuous, gibberish, and as grunts. An anonymous missionary, on his arrival in China, wrote to the British and Foreign Bible Society: 'When I arrived in Cochin-China, and heard the natives speak, particularly the women, I thought I heard the twittering of birds, and I gave up all hope of ever learning it' (*Have Ye Never Read?* 1913: 6).

Missionaries found the proliferation of languages in the colonies as a 'Babel' and a 'terrible obstacle to missionary enterprise' (*In the Mother Tongue* 1930: 24). Their answer was to standardize and unify the languages. The profusion of dialects and languages was seen as detrimental to progress. A common form of language was projected as the pathway to progress and civilization. Embracing the notion that language exists in a process of transition, missionary translators routinely repeated the historical example of England and France which benefited from the standardized form of English and of French, respectively. During the period of the seven kingdoms of Anglo-Saxon England, people from Northumbria hardly understood what the people from Kent had to say. But when England became one kingdom, and gradually as the centuries progressed, a standard form of English evolved which everyone could understand. A similar evolutionary pattern was envisaged for 'barbarous and half-civilized' races (*For the Healing of the Nations* 1916: 20), which was reflected in the editorial work of the Bible Society. One of the Bible Society's annual popular reports described the process thus: missionary enters a 'savage' country and discovers 'a strange confusion of tongues, each tribe speaking a language of its own' (*For the Healing of the Nations* 1916: 20). The Gospels are rendered into several of these languages and printed by the Society. Over the years as the country becomes more open, communications become better and civilization advances, and the tribes which have been hostile for generations draw together, 'all their differences of dialect are slowly fused into a common tongue which they all use and understand.' Then the Bible Society steps in, and in the words of the report: 'When this comes to pass, the time grows ripe for our Society to organize and prepare one common standard version of the Scriptures, which gradually supercedes the early tentative dialect versions that have prepared the way for it and made it possible' (*For the Healing of the Nations* 1916: 20). Thus, the Bible Society, in conjunction with the Universities' Mission to Central Africa, the Church Missionary Society, the German Mission, and with government experts, encouraged the use of a standardized Swahili which they hoped would ultimately bind the whole of British East Africa (*The Common Bond* 1935: 49). Similarly, the Bible Society with the help of missionaries unified *Lingala*, the language of the Congo basin (*The Common Bond* 1935: 50).

In India missionaries resorted to different sorts of action. The existence of numerous Indian vernaculars acted as a barrier between the ruler and the ruled. They also provided protection for Indians against any manipulation by missionaries and the colonial administration. One of the ways to get access to these languages was to reduce them to a bland uniformity which was controllable and negotiable. The proposed method of achieving this was to use 'cheap, distinct, popular Roman letters' for Indian languages. Missionary translators thought that such a substitution of alphabets could fill India with Bibles and Testaments and religious books. The idea was mooted by C. E. Trevelyan. His argument was that by romanizing the indigenous languages, the essence of their vernacular grammar could be retained, and by changing the outward form of the 'clumsy' and 'complicated' characters of the vernaculars, they could be purged of their corrupting influence so that Europeans could learn and read Indian vernaculars easily. Using Roman characters for Indian languages, in Trevelyan's view, was advantageous in two ways. First, it would make it easy for foreigners. Trevelyan wrote: 'I think you will agree with me that a German student could read Bengali *fluently* in half an hour, in the Roman character' (*The Thirty-fifth Report of the British and Foreign Bible Society* 1939: 59; italics in original). The second was much more significant. It was the simplest way to introduce English to native youth:

But the greatest advantage of all the use of these letters is, that it will cut up the existing native literature by the roots, and give rise to a new and purified literature, unconnected with the abominations of idolatry, and impregnated with the Spirit of Christ, from whose blessed religion it will derive its origin and support ... You will now understand what I mean by cutting up the existing corrupt native literature by the roots. In three years we might, without any extraordinary exertion, publish more native books in the Roman character than now exist altogether in the old characters. We might fill India with Bibles and Testaments, and religious books of all kinds, and school-books, at one third of the existing price. All the middle and upper classes, who already know the English letters, would prefer them. All those who know no letters at all, including the vast majority of the grown-up population, and all the raising generation, would prefer them. Their superior cheapness and superior simplicity—(you know the number of intricate compound letters in the native alphabet, the length of time which is consumed in merely learning to read, and the hesitating imperfect style of reading which, after all, is usually attained)—and the example of the upper and middle class would insure this (*The Thirty-fifth Report of the British and Foreign Bible Society* 1939: 58).[2]

Trevelyan's aim was that such alphabetical changes would result in 'one character and one system of notation for them all' (*The Thirty-fifth Report of the British and Foreign Bible Society* 1939: 59). Unruly languages were now turned into manageable propositions so that they could serve the interests of the colonial project.

One of the lessons missionaries learnt in the process of translation was that the Christian message was not necessarily universal nor easily applicable to those of different cultural backgrounds. They found that the languages were either sullied with pagan notions or lacked a Christian equivalent. In India, for example, missionary translators discovered that the Hindi word for salvation—*mukti*—was tinged with the Hindu notion of release from the cycle of birth, death, and rebirth. So the translator had to discard *mukti* and use a neutral term which was used for deliverance of any kind (*The Book and the Sword* 1915: 16). Similarly when translating the word 'sin' in Korean, translators found out that the corresponding Korean word really meant 'crime'. The Korean word 'love', too, created a problem. It meant the feeling of a superior for an inferior, so that God might love humankind but they in turn could not reciprocate that love (*For the Healing of the Nations* 1916: 15–16). In Burma, while translating St. Mark's gospel, translators realized that the authority in a village or in a family was exercised differently. It rested on common consent rather than on any power of compulsion. The Burmese vocabulary lacked words such as 'must', 'necessity', 'to command, to compel', 'to order' . Therefore, the Markan phrase, 'to exercise authority' had to be rendered, 'to hold in the grip of one's hand' (*For the Healing of the Nations* 1916: 15). To rectify pagan associations, or to remedy any lack of a proper Christian correspondent, the translators remedy was to convert and baptize these languages into 'a Christian sense' (*For the Healing of the Nations* 1916: 15).

Dismissing and embracing

When missionary translators faced languages such as Chinese, Tamil, and Arabic, which had a long written and literary tradition, their response was ambivalent. On the one hand, their tendency was to dismiss them as elitist, irrelevant, and as used only by a minority and on the other, it was to use those same languages to appease and attract the very people who spoke such high flown languages. The missionaries found the Bible in the Wenli, the elaborate literary form of the Chinese language, to be intelligible and appealing only to the educated minority. In the case of Tamil, L. P. Larsen when revising the Tamil Bible remarked that Tamil had 'a literature which has grown up in the course of more than a millennium and a half. On many points literary standards have been fixed, and those engaged in translating the Bible cannot afford to act as if they were laying the foundations of a literature and a literary language' (*In the Mother Tongue* 1930: 30). Languages which were systematized by grammarians and ennobled by great literary traditions were dismissed as treasured possessions 'of a comparatively few scholars, and was unknown to the great majority of the people' (*In the Mother Tongue* 1930: 31). They were seen as not reflecting the everyday speech of the ordinary people, and thus hardly appreciated by them. Although Arabic had the 'perfect form', it had over the years become archaic and artificial. Literary Arabic which was 'highly esteemed by scholars is imperfectly understood by multitudes of half-taught Muslims' (*In the Vulgar Tongue* 1914: 27). To the credit of missionary translators, they did produce versions to appeal to ordinary people. Their Chinese Mandarin version and various translations of the colloquial Arabic of Tunisia, Algeria, Morocco, and the Sudan did make the 'Book' accessible to the masses, or as the Bible Society report put it, it circulated the Bible 'to the masses in the only tongue they knew—the home-speech' (*In the Mother Tongue* 1930: 32).

The egalitarian notion of presenting the Bible in the language of the ordinary people was not always followed scrupulously. Biblical translators in colonial India, with a view to attracting converts from high caste communities, were often willing to tailor translation to suit high culture. They achieved this in two ways. One was to Sankritize the biblical renditions. Most British colonialists worked on the premiss that India was fundamentally a Hindu nation and its religious and literary treasures were locked away in brahminical texts written in Sanskrit. They made considerable efforts to endow it with a classical status akin to that of Greek and Latin. Thus, Sanskrit loomed loftily as the classical language, and other Indian languages such as Tamil (which itself has a classical status), and Bangla were reduced to mere vernacular status. The missionary translators, in order to give textual authority to biblical narratives, used Sanskrit as a base for vernacular theological vocabulary. For instance, Tamil versions were highly derivative from Sanskrit and relied heavily on it. Even when there were Tamil equivalents available for words like 'grace', 'God', 'salvation', biblical translators, according to Dayanandan Francis, continued to avoid these terms for the last two hundred years or so and substituted them with Sanskrit terms (D. Francis 1989: 17). In the process they helped to evolve what came to be known as Christian Tamil which was a hybridized form of Sanskrit and Tamil vocabulary.

The other way was to purge the Bible of any images that would cause offence to high caste converts. Abbé Dubois (1770–1848), a Roman Catholic missionary who worked in India (1792–1823), found that the Bible contained accounts which would deeply hurt the feelings of the high caste Hindus and prejudice them against the Christian faith. It is well worth quoting what Dubois thought of how high caste Hindus might react to biblical passages which contained accounts such as the killing of cows and the offering of blood sacrifices which were sacrilegious to them:

But, above all, what will a Brahmin or any other well-bred Hindoo think, when he peruses in our holy books the account of the immolating of creatures held most sacred by him? What will be his feelings, when he sees that the immolating of oxen and bulls constituted a leading feature in the religious ordinances of the Israelites, and that the blood of those most sacred animals was almost daily shed at the shrine of the god they adored? What will be his feeling when he sees, that after Solomon had at immense expense and labour built a magnificent temple in honour of the true God, he made *pratista* or consecration of it, by causing 22,000 oxen to be slaughtered, and overflowing his new temple with the blood of these sacred victims? He will certainly in perusing accounts (in his opinion so horribly sacrilegious) shudder, and be seized with the liveliest horror, look on the book containing such shocking details as an abominable work, (far be from me, once more, the blasphemy, I am expressing the feeling of a prejudiced Pagan) throw it away with indignation; consider himself as polluted for having touched it, go immediately to the river for the purpose of purifying himself by ablutions from the defilement he thinks he has contracted, and before he again enters his house, he will send for a Poorohita Brahmin to perform the requisite ceremonies for purifying it from the defilement it has contracted, by ignorantly keeping within its walls so polluted a thing as the Bible. (Dubois 1823: 16)

Abbé Dubois's solution to this awkward problem of appeasing the high caste Hindus was that if translation of the Bible were to be undertaken, it should be selective, heavily abridged and indeed summarized liberally. He also advocated avoiding all mention of Jesus having been a son of a carpenter, or for instance, having surrounded himself with 'twelve low-born' ignorant and illiterate fishermen (Dubois 1823: 17), lest it upset the high caste Indian readers. Furthermore, in Dubois's view, translations or summaries of the Bible as literary productions 'ought to be on a level with the Indian performances of the same kind among them, and be composed in fine poetry, a flowery style and a high stream of eloquence, this being universally the mode in which all Indian performances of any worth are written. As long as the versions are executed in the low style in which we find these, you may rest assured that they will only excite contempt and tend to increase the aversion already entertained by the natives against the Christian religion' (Dubois 1823: 22).

Abbé Dubois also narrated an experience which happened to him in 1815. Soon after he had preached on the parable of the Prodigal Son about how the father had killed the fatted calf to entertain his friends to welcome his son home, some Christians told him that his mentioning of a fatted calf was very improper. Their worry was that Hindus who were often present at such services, on hearing of the fattened calf would get their worst fears confirmed, 'that the Christian religion being a low or pariah religion'. The caste Christians' practical advice to Dubois was that, should he ever give an 'explanation of the same parable, to substitute a lamb instead of the *fatted calf*' (Dubois 1823: 18; italics in original). In a recent article in a Tamil literary journal, A. Sivasubramaniyan has shown how the Roman Catholic literature produced in the 1920s often changed fatted calf to lamb to appease caste Christians and to make Christianity appear untainted with low caste associations.[3]

Translations and their preoccupations

Biblical translation is obsessed with right meaning and the question of truth. But the history of the battle for Bible translation has demonstrated that truth questions are eventually settled not by the intrinsic authority of the text but by extra biblical factors. Notwithstanding their expressed preference for the Scripture principle (the Bible alone as the sole arbiter in matters related to Christian faith and practice), Protestants, in solving translation conundrums, continue to invoke an authority other than the text. The history of translation is full of such incidents. In the initial stages of the vernacular Bible production, it was the anti-Roman bias which prompted Tyndale to cleanse biblical texts which supported the primacy of papacy or advocated rituals. He denied papacy its favourite proof-text—Matt. 16: 18 by translating *ekklēsia* as congregation. Similarly, it was his opposition to medieval piety which led him to render *eidōllatrēs* (1 Cor. 15: 11) as 'worshippers of images', and not as 'idolater'. The political bias in the linguistic selection of the court translators of the King James Version is well documented.[4] Recently, the New English Bible (NEB) rendered Mark 9: 1 'There are some standing here who will not taste death before they see the kingdom of God come with power' into 'There are some of those standing here who will not taste the death before they have seen the kingdom of God already come with power.' The addition of phrases such as 'already' and 'have seen' were the result of catering to the theological position which came to be known as the realized eschatology advocated by the chair of NEB, C. H. Dodd.[5] More than linguistic fidelity, what was crucial was ensuring the faith of believing communities and the maintenance of the stability of the Church as an institution. This was precisely what worried Augustine about Jerome's translation. Augustine feared that the new version could make the Latin Churches 'out of step with the Greek ones, especially as anyone who puts forward objections will be easily proved wrong when the Greek text is produced' (White 1990: 92). For him, if the translation varied from version to version, it would be 'intolerable' and no one would have the confidence in either using 'quotations or proofs from it' (White 1990: 94) lest it be different from the Greek translation made by the Seventy. In Augustine's view, Christians recognized themselves as Christians on the basis of an ecclesiastically validated translation which was familiar and ingrained in the memory of the worshippers. More importantly, it was read by so many generations, thus ensuring stability. But Jerome's intervention, according to Augustine, forced the Bishop to correct Jerome's version because he 'did not want this crisis to leave him without a congregation' (White 1990: 93). The linguistic choice ultimately boiled down to the very root of the Reformation—the Word of God or the institutionalized Church. The Protestant scriptural principle inevitably had to negotiate an array of competing interests such as the linguistic and contextual ambiguity of the text, the spiritual thirst of congregations, the doctrinal interests of institutionalized churches, and literary sentiments associated with repeatedly quoted or misquoted words. When translators decided to use 'virgin' instead of 'young woman' in Isaiah 7: 1, the question, as rightly raised by Thuesen, was whether their decision had to do with institutional politics, or because the Church hierarchy wanted it, or because of its implications for messianic expectations, or had to do with the complex philology of Hebrew or Greek (Thuesen 1999: 121–43).

One of the by-products of translation is to revitalize the language in which translation is undertaken. The one conspicuous case in point is the King James Version and its impact on the English language. It was this translation which naturalized the Bible permanently into the English language and English consciousness. According to George Steiner, the 'translators of the Authorized Version made of a foreign, many-layered original a life-form so utterly appropriated, so vividly out of an English rather than out of a Hebraic, Hellenistic, or Ciceronian past, that the Bible became a new pivot of English self-consciousness' (Steiner 1976: 348). Macneile Dixon claimed: 'The English people instinctively, and with one accord, took it to their hearts. It rooted itself in England as a native tree, like one of her own oaks' (Dixon 1938: 44). The poetry and piety of biblical Jews have been naturalized into English speech and coalesced and knitted into the texture of English language. He went on to claim that the King James Version was even better than the original:

Translation is translation, and cannot claim to be anything else. None the less we have here something unparalleled. Somehow we have made it ours. To say that it is good English, the best English, ours in language, is not enough. The metal was there, but as a coin may add a new and splendid quality, a new beauty to the metal of which it is composed, so the English language took possession of the material and minted it afresh. The spirit of the book entered into another body. It was reincarnated. The English Bible is only a translation. . . . But the wonder of this translation is that, if anything, it excels the original. (Dixon 1938: 51–2)

As we saw earlier, Huxley hailed the Authorized Version as a 'national epic of Britain'. How 'Europe, with its cool temperate climate and abundant rainfall, was able to assimilate and successfully make use of the everyday imagery of a semi-nomadic Near Eastern desert people as part of its cultural and poetic heritage', as Stephen Prickett queried, remains an amazingly under-studied subject, and accorded little scholarly attention (Prickett 1996: 68–9). The King James Version was an example of how the original was so much transformed that the translated literary form became ineluctably part of the target language, and was much more popular in that language than in the original. Some of the Hebraic and Greek phrases had migrated to and were entrenched in the everyday language of the English. One often forgets the biblical origin of such phrases as: 'the land of the living' (Job 28: 13; Ps. 27: 13; 52: 5), 'like the lamb to the slaughter' (Isa. 53: 7); 'salt of the earth' (Matt. 5: 13), 'a thorn in the flesh' (2 Cor. 2: 17). The translated Bible in English became the literary expression of English Christianity. Indian translations of the Bible into vernaculars never reached such dizzy literary heights as the King James Version, nor achieved such easy naturalization as the Authorized Version did. No Indian Bible translation contributed noticeably to the enrichment of Indian languages, except in reassuring new converts that they could access their new-found faith in their own vernacular. The significant contribution of Bible translation to India's literary tradition had more to do by far with the introduction of the printing press to India than with the vernacular Bibles reviving indigenous languages. This made the printed word possible, and turned India's literature, written on palm leaves, into modern format—the bound books (Mukherjee 1994: 80).

Translation practices have paid undue attention to what people think rather than what they do and feel. In translation activities 'culture' is defined as a cognitive category and is related to what people think, not what they do. These practices are heavily biased towards a visual mode of thinking and equate seeing, especially seeing the text, with knowing. This has resulted in explaining away some of the biblical passages related to olfaction. In the Hebrew Bible there are numerous references to olfactory images. The aroma of sacrifice is frequently referred to. In Exodus and Leviticus we read of how the attention of Yahweh is drawn towards those who sacrifice. But in the passages dealing with sacrifices, it is apparent that while many operations surround cultic sacrifices—prayers, offerings, liturgical formula, ablutions—the attraction of God is not captured by any of these. It is not until the odour of the sacrifice reaches heaven that the deity turns towards humanity and comes down to answer their prayers. Only when the deity smells the odour of sacrifice rightly made does he respond. For instance, we read in Genesis 8: 2 when Noah makes the sacrifice to the Lord after the flood: 'And when the Lord smelled the pleasing odour, Lord said in his heart, I will never again curse the ground.' Humanity is reconciled to God through the smell. But on the other hand, bad behaviour has the opposite effect. Leviticus 26: 31 is a warning against disobedience: 'I will lay your cities waste, will make your sanctuaries desolate, and I will not smell your pleasing odours' (also see Amos 5: 12, Isa. 65: 3, Jubilees 21: 13–14).

The importance of olfaction as a rite of passage and transition, in some African cultures, could also open up some of the difficult biblical passages which exegetes, raised in the Enlightenment mode of thinking, try to expurgate or explain away. One such verse is Isaiah 11: 3. Modern translations read: 'And his delight shall be in the fear of the Lord.' If translated literally, it would read: 'He shall smell in the Lord.' Such a translation causes uneasiness among cultures which fail to see a potent link between odour and discriminatory powers. God discerns through the senses of smell and taste just as much as through the oral and visual. In African traditional religions this is a common practice. In these religions there is a Chief Sniffer whose role is to sniff every entrant at the worship with a view to checking whether the intentions of the worshipper are good or evil. Some African independent churches have instituted the role of a Chief Sniffer. Ian Ritchie who has studied this phenomenon and has been arguing for the democratization of the means of knowing, points out that olfaction in many African religions is considered as 'a means of discernment equal to, and in some key respects superior to, any other sense. It can reveal important things not perceptible through any other sense—the inner state of the person' (Ritchie 2000: 65).[6] Because of the disuse of olfactory language among contemporary commentators, there is a reluctance to accept the idea of a God or Messiah who would discern by a sense of smell. The Hebrew Bible is full of olfactory images, olfactory language and olfactory metaphors of knowledge. The current Western hermeneutical paradigm is heavily biased towards a visual mode of knowledge and equates seeing, especially seeing of the text, with knowing. African culture, like the Hebrew, is free of this exclusive textualist and visualist paradigm and is in an advantageous position to appreciate the Isaian and similar passages in the Bible.

A postcolonial gaze at the New Revised Standard Version (NRSV)

Next, as a way of evaluating how modern translations fare when it comes to addressing colonial tendencies embedded in biblical texts, I would like to look at the New Revised Standard Version (NRSV), one of the most scholarly versions to come out in our time. Although it is a great improvement on the earlier versions, it, too, exhibits marks of previous translations. It is determinedly literal. Its mandate has been: 'As literal as possible, as free as necessary' (Metzger 1989: 3). And there is a declared wish to alter sexist language. But the latter wish is followed by almost a contradictory qualification: 'without altering passages that reflect the historical situation of ancient patriarchal culture' (Metzger 1989: 3). My interest in looking at the NRSV is largely confined to highlighting some of the marks of colonialism found in its renditions.

Christological title—kurios/Lord/Sir

The title 'Lord' is not a significant problem in Acts 11: 20 when Jesus is given the title *kurios* instead of Messiah as Christianity moved into Greek-speaking culture. As far as its usage in the Gospels is concerned, the matter is not that complex. The proper rendition of the title has some relevance for the postcolonial world. For those who have experienced endless lordship from the Raj, the image is not the best for speaking about Christ in a way that connotes power, authority, and domination. Faced with this uneasiness, Indian theologian Russell Chandran, advocated a softer, gentler image of Christ: 'Please do not use the word "Lord" when you speak of Jesus in Asia. This idea of the lordship of Christ carries echoes of Western aggressiveness, of colonialism, and imperialism. It is the humble Christ, the Christ who quietly serves and sacrifices, it is this Christ who reaches towards our heart' (cited in Hargreaves 1972: 101). On two notable occasions, the NRSV continued with the old and imperialistic renditions: 'Have mercy on me Lord' (Canaanite woman) (Matt. 15: 22), and 'Lord, have mercy on my son' (from the father of the epileptic boy) (Matt. 17: 15). Why does NRSV perpetuate this translation when we know that the primary meaning of *kurios* is 'owner' or 'master', and the meaning 'sir' is readily available and appropriate for the situation at this stage of the Gospel narrative? Most modern versions put 'sir' or 'master' in these two verses and elsewhere. In the case of the Canaanite woman, the Revised English Bible daringly just ignores *kurie* and puts nothing in though there is no textual reason for such an omission. To present the image of Jesus in terms of how he was ordinarily known and how he ordinarily lived especially at this juncture of his life in Palestine, would make him more humane than would investing him with the lordly titles which were later conferred on him by the early Church after his death and resurrection.

The Beatitudes

'Blessed are the poor in spirit' (Matt. 5: 3). Traditional English translations of these words in the Beatitudes are regarded by some as sacrosanct, and too devotionally built into the patterns of prayer, too risky, to be tinkered with. But as with *dikaiosune*, I think, the Hebrew prophetic background to these words has to be borne in mind. William Barclay, when he was engaged in biblical translation work, wrote with passages like Isaiah 61: 1 in mind—*ptochos* meant 'not simply poverty but destitution; it describes not the man who has too little, but the man who has nothing. In Hebrew the word is *'ani. 'Ani* began by meaning "poor", and then went on to mean "down trodden" and "despised by men." It then proceeded on to describe the man who has no earthly resources and who has therefore put all his trust in God' (Barclay 1968: 333). Perhaps the reality of oppression now in various parts of the world can push translators into coming up with wordings such as 'Blessed are the poor and vulnerable'. No modern, main versions have so far risked alerting the 'the poor'.

'Blessed are the meek, for they will inherit the earth' (Matt. 5: 5). Here some modern translations have made a change from the traditional translations used by the NRSV. The Revised English Bible has 'Blessed are the gentle . . .' In a world of much oppression, we need to look for a word which would bring out the relationship between gentleness and righteous indignation. Here again Barclay, who translates it as 'those whose strength is in their gentleness', goes to the point: 'In the modern language "meek" has tended to come down in the world, until it describes a rather colourless and spineless kind of a person. Into the translation two things have to be introduced—the idea of humility and the idea of strength of self-control' (Barclay 1968: 330). The word 'gentle' in modern English still connotes a number of strong, positive nuances, but in a worldwide usage of English these subtleties may not be fully appreciated. Moreover, poor as meek perpetuates the notion that they lack inner resources, thus needing to be rescued from their misery. To bring out the intricacies in the Beatitudes, the translation should reflect 'gentleness-strength' which the word 'meek' originally contained.

Promise of the land

'For all the land you see I will give it to you and your offspring for ever' (Gen. 13: 15). This, according to the narrative, was God's promise of land to Abraham and his offspring. The phrase 'for ever' is obviously of enormous importance in relation to the Zionist interpretation and reading of the biblical promise to Abraham of the land he was entering. As a Palestinian, Naim Ateek Naim reminds how the Hebrew phrase, 'ad 'olam, reflects a Semitic Eastern expression meaning the length of a person's life, as in Deut. 15: 17, but not indefinite time. It means 'for all your life', rather than 'for ever'. Naim Ateek claims that this is obviously the meaning in 1 Samuel 1: 22, where Hannah says Samuel will remain in the temple 'all his life' ('ad 'olam). Or it could mean 'always', as translated in most modern English Bibles (Ateek 1995: 276). In Israel where land and its possession is both a theological and political issue, and where biblical texts are cited to make claims, a translation which holds on to 'for ever', as the NRSV does, and translates it as 'remain there for ever' will alienate Palestinians who also have a right to the land.

Justice and righteousness

The translation of these two words, justice and righteousness, continue to cause considerable difficulty. The debate has centred around whether to render them as 'seeing right done', or 'being upright.' The NRSV sticks to what might be called the traditionalist interpretation of the phrase, 'In it [the gospel] the righteousness of God is revealed . . .' (Rom. 1: 17), unlike the notable rendition of the 1970 New English Bible 'Here is revealed God's way of righting wrong', which was later disowned by the 1989 revision of it in the Revised English Bible (New Jerusalem Bible: 'God's saving justice'). Admittedly there is no final agreement among biblical scholars regarding this verse and its translation. Was Paul using *dikaiosune* in the sense of it standing for the sort of *sedaqa* of God which the Second Isaiah and the Psalms were often talking about, namely the active righting of wrong by God? Or was he using *dikaiosune* to represent the old juridical background of *sedaqa*, in the sense of a quality of uprightness and blamelessness in God to be shared with humanity? Let me give two examples of how the NRSV fares in comparison with other modern translations.

'Blessed are those who hunger and thirst for righteousness' (Matt. 5: 6). But surely, the Revised English Bible brings in some 'justice' idea better, with its 'Blessed are those who hunger and thirst to see right prevail' (Luke 18: 7–8). 'Will not God grant justice to his chosen ones who cry to him day and night. . . . I tell you he will quickly grant justice to them.' Here the NRSV almost gets it right. But the Jerusalem Bible gets it even better 'will not God see justice done. . .? I promise you, he will see justice done.' At a time when there is so much injustice and oppression of varying kinds, from economic to sexual, postcolonial translation would advocate 'God's way of righting wrong' as a preferable alternative.

Some notes on postcolonial biblical translation

The Bible as such has a relatively minority status today. It is facing a much more crowded market with other religious texts. Theorizing about biblical translation was often undertaken and emerged within the framework of missionary practice. All new translations are seen as effective instruments of evangelization. The tradition of biblical translation being coloured by evangelical interests goes back to the time of the Septuagint. Initially, it was translated for Hellenistic Jews, but it has become an important tool in their hands for proselytization. As minorities living among nations, Jews in diaspora found echoes of their existence in the books of Isaiah, Ruth, and Psalms, and became alert to the meaning of God's plan for nations, and the place of proselytes and the need to bring them to the worship of the one true God. Richey Hogg reckons that the Septuagint was more than a translation. Its translation perspectives were not only shaped by Hellenistic thought patterns but also its texts made diasporic Jews become aware of God's plan for other nations. Hence Jews in diaspora saw the translated Septuagint as serving 'God's outreach among the Gentiles' (Hogg 1984: 394). Any new revision and newly updated, or aesthetically fine, version was regarded as an essential weapon in spreading the gospel among people. The hope was that an improved Bible would arouse the attention of people thereby instigating an extensive study of the Word of God. When the Revised Version was published, *New York Tribune* expected that it might signal the revival of religion in general: 'Possibly we are on the eve of a great revival of Christianity' (cited in Thuesen 1999: 49). The recently published NRSV, too, stands within a tradition of evangelical revival. The closing paragraph in 'To the Reader' declares that the aim of the new translation is to enable 'all persons and communities who read it' to understand clearly what there is in the biblical message and respond (Metzger 1989: 4). Biblical translation has to move beyond the narrow understanding of mission as a simple revival of a textualized biblical faith that is intolerant, smug, and superior. At a time when there is so much animosity and suspicion among peoples of faith, the task of interpretation is to promote tolerance and understanding. Though these values may sound worn-out modernistic clichés, for people who live and come from communities which are torn apart by religious conflicts, they are worth promoting and aiming for. What postcolonial biblical translation attempts to do is to relocate the task of translation within a postmissionary context, and to promote a less predatory nature of the Christian faith.

Biblical translations, even the best ones, proceed from a received presupposition. They want to turn Hebrew, Greek, and Latin into Tamil, Chinese, and Acan and so forth. Biblical translators have a far greater reverence for ancient languages than for the spirit of the languages into which they are being translated. The fundamental fault of translators is that they preserve the state of established biblical languages instead of allowing these languages to be powerfully affected by languages other than the biblical ones. Translation must expand and deepen biblical languages by means of Asian, African, Latin American, and the Pacific languages. In the process of translating, non-biblical languages should be allowed to interrogate and even radically disrupt biblical languages. Biblical languages must be willing to be affected by the 'other' rather than merely affecting the 'other'. In other words, biblical languages have to be transformed and rendered more open to the claims of other languages and cultures.

Biblical translators have often worried about fidelity to the original and the authenticity of translation. Indian literary tradition hardly considered faithfulness to the original as a virtue. Westcott's claim that the Authorized Version was better because it was 'more faithful to the original, than any which had been given in English before' (Westcott 1868: 364–5) is unthinkable in the Indian context. In a continent which brims with cultures, religions, and languages, where translation is seen as natural as breathing, translation is considered as an independent creative act. It is seen as an expression of freedom rather than dependence on the *ur*-text. In precolonial India, translation of texts within the same culture was considered not as paraphrasing but as an act of intertextuality allowing plenty of fluidity and diversity. Only with the advent of colonialism and the intervention of colonial translators did faithfulness to the original text become a hallowed tenet, creating inhibitions and a feeling of treacherousness about deviating from the so-called original text. Accountability to the original text began in earnest with the production of the King James Version. It was a Puritan, John Reylands, president of Corpus Christi College, who, at the Hampton Court conference convened by King James in January 1603, requested the monarch: 'May your majesty be pleased that the Bible be new translated, such as are extant not answering the original' (Sykes 1955: 140), because he found 'those which were allowed in the reign of Henry VIII and Edward VI were corrupt and not answerable to the truth of the original' (Lovett 1909: 157). One of the first rules for translators, among the fourteen set down by the monarch, was that 'as little altered as the original will permit' (Sykes 1955: 141). This was to have repercussions and set the tone for the future. The *ur*-text or the original has never been accorded an exceptional status, and Indian translators and poets worked on the premiss that it can never be perfectly restated. On the contrary, Indian literary tradition has admired the imaginative freedom of different translators of the *Ramayana*, whose different tellings are even more admired than the features common to them. For Indians, translations have been a revitalization of the original through the imagination of the writer.

Biblical translators could take a cue from Indian attitudes to the original. Faced with numerous oral, visual, and written reproductions of the Hindu epic the *Ramayana*, the cultural critic A. K Ramanujan came up with a theory. He postulated the notion of many *Ramayanas* and advocated jettisoning the hitherto held binary notion of the 'Ramayana' and 'its versions or variants'. For him, the binary mode of thinking implied that there was an invariant, an original, or *ur*-text, usually Valmiki's Sanskrit *Ramayana*, the earliest and most prestigious of them all (Ramanujan 1991: 25). Instead he saw the various *Ramayana* traditions being related to each other through a common code or common pool. Each author, narrator, teller, artist, or performer 'dips into it and brings out a unique crystallization, a new text with a unique texture and a fresh context'. Ramanujan concluded: 'In this sense, no text is original, yet no telling is a mere telling—the story has no closure, although it may be enclosed in a text' (Ramanujan 1991: 46). His postulation persuades us to treat each text as a telling rather than as a variant, since 'variant' implies deviation from the original. Ramanujan's theorization emphasizes many different tellings of Rama's story—oral, written, read, and performed, recited and depicted in various forms—without representing each one primarily in terms of its relationship to Valmiki's original telling. His model does away with the idea that some versions are intrinsically better than others and that there is a pecking order of relationship between various tellings within the *Ramayana* tradition. It also encourages us to consider how each telling is informed and decidedly shaped by social location, religious affiliation, literary practices, and the linguistic conventions of the narrator/teller/writer/performer.

Conventional translation practices work on the assumption that target languages are enclosed entities. As a result of the history of the empire, languages are completely layered, stratified, socially and culturally differentiated for both individuals and groups. In postcolonial contexts where languages alarmingly intermix, borrow, and cross traditional boundaries with ease, it is difficult to uphold the notion of a single source language or single target language. What has resulted is that the question of native/ mother/first language has become problematic. Samia Mehrez, the Egyptian academic, has shown how in francophone North Africa a hybridized and hierarchized form of Arabic and French exists:

These postcolonial texts, frequently referred to as 'hybrid' or 'métissés' because of the culturo-linguistic layering which exists within them, have succeeded in forging a new language that defies the very notion of a 'foreign' text that can be readily translatable into another language. With this literature we can no longer merely concern ourselves with conventional notions of linguistic equivalence, or ideas of loss and gain which have long been a consideration in translation theory. For these texts written by postcolonial bilingual subjects create a language 'in between' and therefore come to occupy a space 'in between'. In most cases, the challenge of such space 'in between' has been double: these texts seek to decolonize themselves from two oppressors at once, namely the western ex-colonizer who naively boasts of their existence and ultimately recuperates them and the 'traditional,' 'national' cultures which shortsightedly deny their importance and consequently marginalize them.   (Mehrez 1992: 121)

What Mehrez says of francophone North Africa is equally true of India. Indian novelists who write in English, as G. J. V. Prasad points out, write in 'an English suitable for the task at hand, to convey the particularities of the situation and region portrayed. Each writer is aware of the task and makes a conscious attempt at it through various linguistic experiments as well as the use of imagery' (Prasad 1999: 44–5). R. K. Narayan, the doyen of Indian writers in English, spoke for many when he said that often writing in English seemed 'imitative, halting, inept or an awkward translation of a vernacular rhetoric, mode, or idiom; but occasionally brilliant', and went on to say that Indian writers 'are still experientialists' (Narayan 1990: 22–3).

English has become a more influential and widely used language. The expansion of English has been taken to be legitimate, neutral, and advantageous. It is the medium which helps to circulate knowledge, images, and information disproportionately within and between countries. Its prestigious and important position in academic, business, and professional fields has been well recognized. The downside of the global triumph of English has been that English is no longer seen as the sole property of any particular people. Native speakers of English are now being heavily outnumbered by people who speak English as a second language or in some cases third or fourth language. According to a study, by the end of the year 2000 as many as 750 million people will speak English well enough to use it for business, and as many as a billion people are thought to be learning English at any given time.[7] Recently, Terry Eagleton observed that 'for the first time in history, English language was no longer one with English culture. The exiles and emigrés have driven a wedge between the two.'[8] In the face of these changes, it is becoming increasingly clear that there is no such thing as single, monolithic English, but rather there are many varieties of English, each coming out of a different locality with its own indigenous flavour. Recently sociolinguistics have been paying much attention to the appropriation of English across the globe. Kachru and Nelson, have identified three types of users of English:

1. The *inner* circle consists of countries such as the United States, England, Canada, Australia, and New Zealand where English is the first or dominant language. Though other languages are recognized and spoken, in the public discourse, English is predominant.

2. The *outer* circle comprises countries such as India, Nigeria, Pakistan, South Africa, Singapore, where English has a long history of institutionalized role and functioning as a language of education, governance, literary creativity, and so forth.

3. The *expanding* circle consists of countries in which English has various roles and is widely studied but for more specific purposes than in the outer circle including but not certainly limited to acquiring knowledge for scientific and technical purposes; such countries include Japan, China, Korea, Indonesia (Kachru and Nelson 2001: 13).

Those who use English in 'outer' and 'expanding' circles come from pluri-lingual, pluri-cultural, and pluri-religious contexts, and they are expressively innovative with English in expressing their multi-identities. They move between two worlds or several worlds, and in the process they move freely within a number of languages. Mehrez cites as an example the Moroccan sociologist, novelist, and poet, Abdelkebir khati-bi, for his pluri-lingual upbringing and the way he hierarchizes languages. He speaks the Moroccan dialect at home, classical Arabic at Koranic schools, and French, the language of the colonizer, at the French *lycée* (Mehrez 1992: 121). This could be equally true of persons from Asia as well. For instance, an Indian in his or her daily transaction moves with ease from his or her mother tongue to regional and to national language and to English. Plurilingualism embraced by postcolonials infringes on hegemonic values, redirects indigenous traditions, and reconceptualizes identities.

What modern biblical translation does is to standardize patterns and thereby restrict the variety of local forms of English. The standardized form acts as a mask which hides and suppresses those who are learning to speak and are beginning to use it as a space of resistance. Any translation, and especially any Bible translated into English, goes a long way to neutralize, internationalize, and homogenize English. What neutralized or neutered 'international English' does is to cancel out and invalidate local constructions of English. It streamlines and doctors the varieties of English into a uniform entity, and at the same time it makes the standardized English the norm, internationally acceptable and accessible. Those writers or speakers who use their own vernacularized English across the world have to choose between their provincial riches and the homogenized international norms. The particular concern for biblical translators is how not to lose sight of the richness of indigenized English.

Bible translations are produced by translators who belong to the inner circle of English, but their product is used widely in second and third language contexts. Future biblical translators should be aware of three things about the global spread and diffusion of English: the principal one is that standard English which comes out of the inner circle does not act as a gatekeeper nor does it impose meaning and norm upon other forms of English. The second is somewhat linked to the first one: biblical translators have to accept the inevitable 'pluri-centricity' of English rather than carrying on with the tradition that there can only be a duo-centricity, namely, the British or American. The third point is that biblical translators have to contextualize the English language translations of the Bible, acknowledge multi-identities and multi-uses of it, and try to encompass other usages. To restate these points succinctly: translation as a culturally and linguistically homogenizing process is somewhat over. The ultimate dream of all translators is to produce a Bible for all. This will remain a distant dream.

In the postcolonial context, the role of translation is to subvert meanings, grammatical arrangements, and linguistic practices. Its function is more than critiquing. Often, these two terms, subversion and critique, are employed as if they meant the same. Talal Asad has brought out a useful distinction between them. Notwithstanding the fact that both these terms are transposable, for Asad, critique 'refers to the process of rational appraisal and judgement' whereas subversion 'is a matter of overturning, undermining and destroying'. In his reckoning, 'critique has pretensions to shared standards of reasoning and justice, subversion assumes a state of war and a determination to eliminate the enemy—or at least his power. For purposes of subversion, anything goes. The instruments available to criticism are more narrowly defined' (Asad 1996: 328). Although what Asad says comes out of the perspective of secular translation studies, it has relevance to biblical translation as well. I would end by reiterating his words that 'translation can play an important part in subverting values, practices, modes of life quite independent of critique'(Asad 1996: 328).

NOTES

1. In a letter to Augustine, Jerome complained that he was not told what mistranslation he had made which caused the bishop to lose his pastorate, thereby robbing Jerome of a chance to defend himself. Jerome's guess was that Augustine meant 'ivy' for 'gourd' in Jonah 4: 6. Jerome's defence was that he used ivy to agree with other translators like Aquila, a Greek proselyte who made a literal translation of the Hebrew Scripture into Greek (*Saint Augustine Letters*, trans. W. Parsons (Washington, DC: The Catholic University of America Press, 1981), 367).

2. My thanks to Alison Mukherjee for drawing my attention to this. The Bible Society published romanized Bengali version from 1838 to 1921, but they were commercially unsuccessful. The initial idea of attracting the native intelligentsia did not materialize either. Later, the Bible Society hoped that a larger number of illiterates would benefit from the Roman script version.

3. A. Sivasubramaniyan, 'Fatted Calf and Fatted Lamb', *Kanaiyazhi*, Jan. 2000, 53–5.

4. For examples of political interference, see Ward Allen (ed. and trans), *Translating for King James: Notes Made by a Translator of King James's Bible* (paperback edn.) (Nashville: Vanderbilt University Press, 1993).

5. I owe this point to John Bowden, see his *Jesus: The Unanswered Questions* (London: SCM Press, 1988), 137. Subsequent revision of the NEB omit these phrases.

6. I rely here on the manuscript form of Ian Ritchie's article 'Bodily Ways of Knowing in the Hebrew Bible: Implications for Biblical Studies'. Although this article has been accepted for publication, I have been unsuccessful in getting the bibliographical details. My apologies to Ritchie.

7. Martin Bright, 'Foreign Tongues Spread the English Word', *The Observer*, 29 Oct. 2000, 1.

8. Terry Eagleton, 'The Centre cannot hold', *The Guardian Saturday Review*, 23 June 2000, 8.

7

HERMENEUTICS IN TRANSIT: DIASPORA AND INTERPRETATION

All I desired was to walk upon such an earth that had no maps.

(*The English Patient*, Ondaatje 1993: 261)

I think we should start looking for a h-o-m-e'.

(*Chorus of Mushrooms*, Goto 1997: 4)

Home is where my books are.

(Ryszard Kapuściński[1])

Consider the following scene in the film, *Keeping the Faith*, which half-seriously and half-humorously captures the mood of the diasporic condition. Brian Finn, a Catholic priest, played by Edward Norton, despite his vow of chastity falls in love. But the girl of his dreams is having an affair with his best friend, a Jewish rabbi, Jake Schramm. Finn, after an all-night drinking binge, confesses his passion to an Asian bartender of a New York Irish theme pub and bemoans that his heart is broken. Complicated you might think, but listen to what the Asian bartender has to say. 'Oh, God,' he says. 'What do I know? I'm a half Punjabi Sikh, one quarter Tamil-separatist. My sister married a Jewish doctor from New Jersey and our grandmother was an Irish nun, who left me this bar—which is a very long story.' Finn was disconcerted. 'You're a Sikh Catholic Muslim with Jewish in-laws?' he asks. 'Yes, yes, it gets very complicated. I am reading Dianetics.'[2]

In recent years the problems and possibilities of crossing borders, transgressing boundaries, exile, return, immigration and migrancy, deter-ritorialization, inhabiting in-between spaces, have become increasingly a preoccupation in a wide variety of fields, coming under the rubric of 'diaspora.'

Defining diaspora

Diaspora is a secular term with religious roots, and in the initial stages it was confined to Jewish and Christian circles. The usage of the term has so radically shifted from its original Jewish-Christian frame that it has led Martin Baumann to say that 'most scholars in Jewish and Christian theo-logical studies have not even noticed the popularity and usage of the term outside their disciplines' (Baumann 1997: 386).

Even within Jewish and Christian thinking, the term 'diaspora' has gone through a number of continuously shifting and contested definitions. Robin Cohen, in trying to trace the origin of the term, has suggested moving its location from the biblical to the Greek context. He postulates that before the term came to be linked with biblical usage, it meant 'migra-tion and colonization' among Greeks in the Archaic period (800–600 BCE), describing the colonization of Asia Minor and the Mediterranean region. Notwithstanding the poverty, displacement, and war that dispersion caused, the dominant features of diaspora were seen as 'an expansion through plunder, military conquest, colonization and migration' (Cohen 1999: 2). However, Cohen's claim has been disputed. The verb 'diaspora' gained wide currency in the fifth century BCE among philosophers and Hellenist writers for whom it implied a 'process of dispersion and decom-position, a dissolution into various parts without any further relation to each other' (Baumann 1997: 393).

The term 'diaspora' gained connotations such as displacement, hard-ship, and suffering, when it came to be used within the theologies and histories of Jews and Christians, thus acquiring a new overall emphasis—victimhood. The term was used generally to denote Jews who lived outside 'the promised land' (Palestine), and carried with it three meanings which were interlocked—the act of dispersion, the land across which one was dispersed, and the people who were dispersed. The originating event which established the victim imagery was the deportation that happened to Jews in 597 BCE. Contrary to popular belief that there was one single deportation, there were three. In a sense, the dispersal of the Jewish community started in 722 BCE with the Assyrian invasion, which resulted in the deportation of the population of the people of the Northen Kingdom to Mesopotamia (2 Kgs. 15: 29). The second one, the one which really caught the popular imagination, was around 597 BCE, when Nebuchadnezzar, the king of Babylon, took captive the Jewish king of the time, Jehoiakim, and a large group of government officials. But ten years later there was a stronger rebellion this time under Zedekiah. Unlike the leniency showed earlier, Nebuchadnezzar showed no mercy and took the Judean king captive and forced the upper classes to resettle in Babylon, and looted everything from the land, gold, silver, and bronze to the pots and vessels used in the temple. People were forced to flee from the promised land: 'So Judah was taken into exile out of its land' (2 Kgs. 25: 21 and also Jer. 52: 12–14). But not all were deported. In fact, a sizeable number was left behind, including the poorest inhabitants of the land such as vinedressers, ploughmen, and artisans. The third deportation took place in 582 BCE. But it was the Babylonian invasion and destruction of Israel which began earlier which became the defining and constitutive moment in the history of the dispersal of Israel. Jerusalem became the symbolic centre for Jews, to which they looked for direction and eventual return. Their loneliness and sadness at their displaced state are memorably captured in Psalm 137:

By the waters of Babylon, there we sat down and wept, when we remembered Zion. On the willows there we hung up our lyres. For there our captors required of us songs, and our tormentors mirth, saying, 'Sing us one of the songs of Zion!' How shall we sing the Lord's song in a foreign land? (1–4)

The description of diaspora as deportation and dispersal associated with the Assyrian and Babylonian conquests soon changed, and also the pain and harsh treatment that went with it. The colonial endeavours of the 'heirs of Alexander the Great' resulted in the intermingling of various people in the Roman empire. This, in Karl Ludwig Schmidt's view, contributed to the extension of the meaning of diaspora, which in addition to deportation now included 'voluntary emigration' (Schmidt 1964: 100). Along with the tone of lamentation, the prophetic indictment of the dispersal of God's people as divine judgement and curse also disappeared (Isa. 35: 8; Jer. 23:24; Ezek. 22: 15), and 'diaspora' came to be tempered with

'Hellenistic optimism' (Schmidt 1964: 100). In the Septuagint, the term is used to 'veil the stark severity of Hebrew expressions which pitilessly describe the judgement of scattering which God executed on Israel' (Schmidt 1964: 100). While the earlier description of the term indicated geographical uprootment and alienation, the new definition included political, social, and religious dimensions of the Jewish population living beyond Palestine. Karl Schmidt notes:

> As later more and more Jews came to live in the diaspora, this was bound to affect Israel's consciousness of its alien status, on the one side by enhancing it, on the other by diminishing it. Whereas eschatological and apocalyptic Judaism, followed by primitive Christianity, brought the dispersion into connection with recollection of the Babylonian captivity and therefore directly with the land of Palestine, Hellenistic Judaism went its own way and increasingly weakened the historical bond.   (Schmidt and Schmidt 1967: 848)

The notion of diaspora underwent another change when, in the first century CE, Christians mobilized it, and reworked it to suit the theological demands of the time, determined by Christian eschatological thinking. The opening sentence of the Letter of James—'to the twelve tribes in dispersion'—is an indication that the Christian Church is taking on the mantle of the new people of God. Without going into detail on the complicated question as to whether the Christian churches mentioned in James and Peter consisted of Jews or Gentiles, or singling out one of these as diasporan, what is important to acknowledge is that the term in Christian usage acquires a religious sense. Now the Christian community which sees itself as the fulfilment of the earlier promises of God, modifies the term to describe their new status as temporary residents. The Christian Church is seen as a wandering pilgrim and a dispersed community, in the sense that they are instruments to fulfil God's eschatological purpose. The home they are striving for is not an earthly home but a home which is above and yet to come: 'But our commonwealth is in heaven, and from it we await a Saviour, the Lord Jesus Christ' (Phil. 3: 20; see also Heb. 13: 14: 'For here we have no lasting city, but we seek the city which is to come'). On earth, Christians living in dispersion would function as the seed in disseminating the message of Jesus. The term that Christians used to describe themselves was *paroikoi*—'resident aliens' (1 Peter 2: 11)—at home everywhere but fully at home nowhere. John Elliott, in his study of 1 Peter, is of the view that the addressees in the letter were not exiles in the modern sense of the term though, as the provincial poor with few of the rights of citizens, not much better than exiles (Elliott 1981: 46). Because of their acceptance of Christ, however, 1 Peter transmutes their need for a second home by reference to eschatological destiny and purpose. They knew that they were living in a distinctive way which had wider global and salvational significance. There was something catholic and something universal about the life they shared with others across the Empire. After acquiring institutional status, however, the early Christian movement slowly forgot this notion of a sojourning, wandering people of God with transnational inclinations. Christians were still called *paroikoi* -'resident aliens', but the term took on a new meaning in that it came to denote their newly established status as residents and parishioners. Alan Kreider draws attention to the altered condition:

It [resident alien] now meant resident, parishioners, people whose distinctiveness was not that they were unlike their neighbours, but they were unlike people in other countries whose rulers espoused some other faith. Where everyone was a Christian, their primary allegiance was no longer to the transnational family of God; it rather was to people with whom they shared a common race and place. So the internationalism of early Christianity withered, and God came to be associated primarily with one's own country. (Kreider 1994: 29)

Once a marginal community and seen as a perfect paradigm for provisional sojourning spirit, the Christian community had gradually lost its subalternity, now moving into the centre.

Postcolonialism and diaspora

Diaspora, the term once used to describe Greek and Jewish dispersion, has now been widened to include other, parallel experiences, based on the transnational migrations which have been a major consequence of the colonial project. The first application of the term in this sense was to the movement of African slaves across the Atlantic. The first to advocate such a usage was George Shepperson, who saw historical correspondences between the expatriation of Jews and the dispersion of sub-Saharan Africans through the colonial slave trade. This was seen as compulsory eviction, with those who were deported yearning for home (Shepperson 1968: 152–76). Since then there have been many diasporas, Irish, Tamil, Armenian, to name a few. Historically, as we have seen, the concept of diaspora refers to the dispersion of the Jews as a scripturally narrativized spiritual experience. Postcolonial usage, alluding to these more recent dispersals, differs from the Jewish-Christian usage. In recent discussions, there has been a tendency to move beyond its original Jewish religious background and place it on a secular, metaphorical plane. In postcolonial discourse, diaspora has become a key word. The entry on diaspora in *Key Concepts of Post-colonial Studies* begins with the lexical origins of the word and then goes on to speak about the diasporas caused by colonialism, first by the slave trade and after the abolition of slavery, by the introduction of indentured labour, which resulted in three million Indians being shipped about the world to meet the shortage of labour in the plantations (Ashcroft, Griffiths, and Tiffin 1998: 68–70). Postcolonial discourse, which is intensely secular in its orientation and inclination, bypasses the original Jewish-Christian milieu and locates the concept in the colonial context, thus further endorsing the secular status of the term.

Though the Greek word 'diaspora' is translated into English as dispersion, in postcolonial writings it has a more precise connotation. It is about the ambivalences and contradictions of being at home in many places, and among many peoples and many experiences much written about in poetry and fiction. It challenges the territorially confined notion of national culture through the fact of wide-ranging movements of people. In postcolonial terms, diaspora signifies the formation of identities based on diversity and difference and is not necessarily seen in terms of reconnecting with a reverential notion of homeland. It is a narrative about journeys from homelands to new places, trying to forge a shared memory and history while at the same time acknowledging that not all diasporas are the same. The shared common story they try to construe is a highly contentious one; it reflects profoundly different cultures, histories, oral accounts, religions, rituals, literatures, philosophies, and socio-economic backgrounds. Importantly, these patterns of transnational migration have not in fact resulted in the severance of the relationship between culture and territorial belonging. If anything, dispersed peoples have often tended to experience an intensified longing for, and a clarified image of 'home'. The concept of home is sharply divided between the homeland that one left behind and the hostland in which one is trying to set up a new 'home'. Essentially, what the new diaspora does is to challenge the old Kiplingesque paradigm of East is East and West is West, with no possibility of the two meeting, no possibility of weaving the religious and cultural traditions from home into the complex and varied cultures of the host country. The literature produced by diasporic writers such as V. S. Naipaul, Buchi Emecheta, Hanif Kureishi, Caryl Phillips, and Benjamin Zephaniah in England, Bharati Mukherjee, Jhumpa Lahiri, Amy Tan, and Chang-Rae Lee in the United States, and M. G. Vassanji in Canada, and Adib Khan in Australia, to name a few, demonstrates how successfully these writers have been able to explore their memories of home, their in-betweenness, and their marginal status, to resist the forces of uniformity and challenge conventional ideas of belonging and fixity.[3]

Uprootings of text and persons: Diaspora and biblical interpretation

Unlike the literary field, where diasporic literature is attracting critical attention, diasporic biblical interpretation is still in its infancy. Only a handful of biblical scholars have been engaged in the task, and it is too early to make any critical assessment of their work.[4] Although there is, as we have noted, a move to include African-Americans as part of the diasporic discourse, the current African-American hermeneutics is more interested in recovering black presence and identity in the Bible than in addressing issues of diaspora. However, going through what has so far emerged in the way of disaporic interpretation, one can see at least three kinds of engagement. The first entails an attempt to theorize the diasporic experience. The person who is single-handedly engaged in this task is Fernando Segovia, the Cuban-American. He proposes a 'hermeneutic of diaspora—a Hispanic-American hermeneutics of otherness and engagement' and advocates a reading strategy which includes: (a) acknowledgement and analysis of text as culture-specific; (b) readers as not universal, but flesh and blood, situated socially, and historically-conditioned; (c) critical analysis of both text and readers; and (d) decolonization of biblical studies and eliminating its Eurocentric leanings, thus making it a global discourse in which all interpreters have an equal voice and speak from their own social locations and otherness (Segovia 1995: 58–9). What Segovia proposes should be the aim of all biblical interpretation, and it is unclear what is so special about its diasporic nature or content. Since Segovia has yet to work out exegetical examples based on his theoretical suppositions, his proposal remains an ideal, though it was a timely and important intervention.

The second task is to uncover comparable experiences in the Bible to authorize and validate the current uprootedness. The experiences of biblical Jews, for example, escape, flight, and arrival in a Promised Land, are seen as analogous to and replicated in the lives of diasporic communities. Jung Yong Lee, one of the earliest of the current crop of interpreters to arrive in the United States, recalls his experience of coming to America from the war-torn Korea of the 1950s as being similar to that of the Jewish wanderings in the past: 'Like the Hebrews, I too experienced the wilderness, not for forty years but for four, during which I roamed from one place to another without shelter and sustenance. It was a miracle, or by the grace of God, that I survived starvation and physical torture. My coming to the United States is like the Israelites' arrival in the Promised Land' (Lee 1999: 39). Similarly, the Japanese-American David Paul Nagano invokes the Exodus experience as an apt paradigm for the indignity of internment which he and other Japanese-Americans faced during the Second World War (Nagano 1999: 77).

Eleazar Fernandez, a Filipino-American, also uses the Exodus narrative, but reads it differently. He does not mine the themes which often accompany the narrative such as 'release', 'liberation', 'conquest', and 'election', but sees it as a release from poverty and fatalism such as were prevalent in Canaan (= Philippines), and as an exodus towards Egypt (= America) the land of wealth and opportunity. Unlike the traditional narrative which begins with, and moves out of, Egypt, in Fernandez's hermeneutical scheme the Exodus narrative starts with Canaan/Philippines, and ends up in Egypt/America. In this revised framework, the story begins not with the exploits of Moses in Egypt, but with Jacob and his descendants in the book of Genesis, especially with Joseph and the events which led him to Egypt. His Moses, therefore does not lead people out of Egypt but leads them to Egypt. Unlike the biblical Israelites, Filipino-Americans have no intention of leaving Egypt/America, but have decided to throw in their lot with the new land and have started to have their dreams there, some unfinished, some nightmarish. For Fernandez, what the narrative indicates is immigration and settlement. He writes:

I want to emphasize that the narrative also takes into account the process of settlement in the new country, the experience of immigration in the United States. Emigration (exodus) and immigration (settlement) should be seen, therefore, as two facets of the one exodus-toward-Egypt narrative. Such a view of the exodus is consistent with that standing interpretation of it not as a one-time event led by the breakthrough figure of Moses but as a continuing struggle for liberation. (Fernandez 2001: 169–70)

In the case of Ada María Isasi-Díaz, a Cuban-American, it was the Psalms, and especially Psalm 137, which, as we saw earlier, defined her sense of alienation and humiliation in an alien country. In it, she saw the parallel circumstances of those who sang it originally and herself as a Cuban exile in the United States (Isasi-Díaz 1995: 149–63).

Going beyond historical events, other diasporic interpreters seek value in biblical characters, especially those who have gained access to royal courts, like Esther and Joseph, as authorizing their own uprooted experience. Esther is seen as an appropriate model among Asian Americans because she not only succeeded as an outsider in an alien world, concealing her Jewishness but also recovered her identity, and at the risk of her own life was able to overturn the decree that went against her people (Sano 1979: 258–64; Kuan 2000: 161–73).

The other biblical figure who has provided inspiration is Joseph, whose diasporic existence in Egypt is seen as a story of expulsion, estrangement, treachery, torment, and eventual achievement and ascendency to power and authority. The Cuban-American, Francisco Gracía-Treto, who has used the story of Joseph to bolster the image of the dislocated Cuban, writes:

Like Jerusalem's diaspora in Babylon, like Latin America's diaspora in the United States, Joseph found himself in Egypt as a result of an unwilled uprooting, ripped away from the centre that had nurtured his childhood and youth by the action of his own brothers, and placed (in his case as a foreign slave and as a prisoner) in the most peripheral of positions in a new society. At the same time, as for many members of the diasporas of the ancient Jerusalem or of contemporary Havana, Joseph's experience in the land of his exile is one

of settlement, assimilation and success far surpassing mere survival. (García-
Treto 2000: 136)

García-Treto goes on to say that the elevation of Joseph from utter powerlessness to unlimited power, placing him at the centre of Egyptian society,
described in Genesis 39–41, was the turning point in the diasporic story of
Joseph. García-Treto claims that he finds these chapters 'illuminated in a
special way' when he approaches them 'from the point of view of a member of the Cuban diaspora in the United States' (García-Treto 2000: 136).
The struggles of immigrants and the harsh realities of an alien land are
typologically compared with the experience of Joseph, God's elect exile.
The reason for the popularity of Esther and Joseph is that they are suggest-
ive of the American dream. Both biblical characters have all the hallmarks
of an outsider, rejected and humiliated and finally making it big in a
foreign world.

Though these studies draw hermeneutical sustenance from such biblical
personalities, they pay no attention to the ambivalent nature of these characters in the rest of the narratives, nor do they problematize their role.
Their complexity and variety are flattened. Both Esther and Joseph seek
assimilation to bolster their socio-economic status. In Esther's case, the
colonial backdrop of the story is treated obliquely. A closer reading will
reveal that the narrative promotes a survivalist agenda rather than an
emancipatory one. It advocates incorporation and assimilation. Utilizing
these strategies, Esther is eventually received into the royal household, and
Mordecai gets an appointment in the colonial administration. A strategy of
assimilation encourages conformity to the values and expectations of the
host society, which are assumed to be good for all. The appropriation of
the Joseph story is also problematic. He, too, was assimilated, and given a
royal appointment. But as we saw in the previous chapter, when his turn
came, Joseph made use of his privileged status to impose greater hardships
upon the ordinary people who needed his help. García-Treto overlooks
Genesis 47, where Joseph's exploitative nature is evident. As we have seen,
Joseph's success eventually led to the enslavement of his people. These
initial attempts at diasporic interpretation fall prey to the temptation
to which all those in the business of interpretation often succumb, of
latching on to one specific angle and then massively over-projecting it as
the biblical view. The facile approval and benevolent treatment of biblical

characters are indications that diasporic hermeneutics is yet to confront its own hermeneutical presuppositions and offer its own critique.

The third engagement with the Bible in the diasporic context comes not from the field of biblical studies but from the world of literature. It comes from a novel, *The Joy Luck Club* by Amy Tan. In this novel, the Bible, is regarded as a provider of meaning, and at the same time its overawing power and presence are punctured. This comes out very clearly in an incident in the novel (Tan 1990: 116–30). The novel is about five Chinese families settled in the United States. The story is seen from both the perspective of the older generation of Chinese mothers and the new generation of their daughters. While the former long for the past, the latter try to come to terms with their dual identity as Chinese and Americans. One of the mothers who had become a Baptist, loses her son, Bing, in a beach accident. She is a woman of *nengken*, meaning an ability to do anything once she puts her mind to it, and is further strengthened by the Baptist faith which taught her that when everything else fails, faith will make things happen. But the dead son does not come back. She no longer sees value in such a faith. So she puts the leatherette Bible which she used to carry with her on the floor to prop up one of the legs of the kitchen table. However, the daughter notices that her mother keeps on dusting the Bible every night after dinner, and the Bible was 'still clean white' (Tan 1990: 116). By putting the Bible on the floor, under the table, the mother simultaneously demystifies her past and relinquishes her innocence. Whenever any one asks what the Bible is doing there, her reply is 'Oh! this, I forgot' (Tan 1990: 116). Like any other household icon, however, she keeps dusting it. The Bible, as an icon, provides cohesion and continuity in a strange country. In an alien environment, holding on to a meaningful life includes embracing icons, for they mediate power and provide powerful resources for connection and continuity. As an icon, the Chinese mother is not overawed by the Scripture's mysterious power. She realizes the need for the past and seeks to hold on to it. But at the same time, she will not let her romantic attachment to the past determine the demands of the present dislocated life. What the mother's action indicates is that she and other diasporans like her will have to create a new critical memory of the past and the present, move away from their victim status, give up their nostalgia, relinquish their innocence, and work out a hermeneutics of wisdom that will sustain them in their often inhospitable, often hostile environment. The constant dusting of the Bible becomes part of that exercise, as the new context generates both new anxieties and new opportunities.[5] What is important is to embody, live, and work with these disjunctures and ambivalences.

Diasporic hermeneutics: some markers

Diasporic existence and current globalization have demonstrated that people are no longer one thing or another. All identities are intrinsically coalitional and multi-layered in that they seek to establish a ground of affinity. As one of the characters in Hanif Kureishi's novel, *Black Album*, put it, 'There was no fixed self; surely our several selves melted and mutated daily? There had to be innumerable ways of being in the world' (Kureishi 1996: 274). While identities are important, it is not enough simply to overemphasize them. The task is to demonstrate what constitutes them, what purpose they serve and what elements go on to compose them.

One of the basic assumptions of biblical hermeneutics has been to engage in interpretative activity as though people lived settled lives, and as though those lives could be conceptualized in terms of a cultural totality of shared values and meanings. The major part of biblical interpretation, and for that matter most theologies from Asia, Africa, Latin America, the Caribbean, and the Pacific, carry out their task with an assumption of rooted, localized, integrated, and self-contained communities leading settled lives. Vernacular hermeneutics became a cause for celebration when people led a settled life and thought in terms of cultural wholes. Now, when peoples' lives are being rearranged by globalization, and when there is a constant movement of people for political conflicts and natural disasters, or in some cases for professional reasons, finding cultural-specific analogues may be an increasingly difficult task. The connection between the vernacular and the global is now so deep that it is becoming increasingly difficult to determine what is native and what is non-native. Alternatively, of course, diasporic hermeneutics with its new multi-vision may throw up its own hitherto undiscovered parallels. At a time when there is intermixing of cultures both at popular and elitist levels, and when local/global and vernacular/metropolitan divides are shrinking, diasporic hermeneutics is more about mobility than about roots.

Diasporic hermeneutics, then, is called upon to address the state of 'homelessness'. It is an attempt to find a home for those people who have been made homeless because of political or professional circumstances, or due to natural disasters, and a home also for their histories, languages, religions, and the texts that they carry with them. It is finding a home in a world without fixities.

Rather than dreaming about home and a time which no longer exists, and striving to reclaim a past which is becoming more and more contestable, the future of diasporic hermeneutics would seem to lie in its ability to evolve a hybridized style of interpretation. Its relevance will be measured not by its ability to invoke lost authenticities of ancient cultures or to superintend the purity of the gospel, but by its ability to ensure critical distance, and create an allegory of theological hybridity. Its success will depend on the willingness to undergo an enormous reassessment, give up its claim to be the sole conveyor of truth, and renegotiate its role built on differences. It is essential to acknowledge that there is no stable epistemological point of view, nor a homogeneous unique truth.

The postcolonial notion of hybridity is not about the dissolution of differences but about renegotiating the structure of power built on differences. It is not synonymous with assimilation. Assimilation is something that the colonialists, and later the nativists advocated. Hybridity is a two-way process in which both parties are interactive so that something new is created. Living in multiple contexts means reforming the Christian identity. In this way it will be accepted as complementary to other religious discourses and as a companion in the search for truth and religious harmony.

Though diasporic hermeneutics already has some profound things to say about hyphenated and hybridized forms of identity and how these operate within individuals and communities, it has yet to work out a hybridized form of textual interpretation as an interpretative strategy in biblical studies. Third World biblical hermeneutics is still in the grip of the warning of missionaries against syncretism, overtly Christocentric in its outlook and reluctant to let go its Christian moorings. Though syncretism and hybridity are kindred terms, hybridity alone has positive connotations attributed to it. In the conceptual world of missionary thinking, definite cultural and theological borders were essential for maintaining and legitimizing the Christian gospel and Christian identity. In this world-view, any proposal for coalescing or interchange was seen as adulteration and dis-integration of the gospel. Hybridity not only indicates a more dynamic view of cultural exchange but also draws attention to the stark history of colonial domination and the present inequalities experienced in the wake of colonialism.

One person who exemplified and to an extent worked out a hybridized form of hermeneutics is Mahatma Gandhi. Firmly grounded in his Hindu faith fluid as it was, Gandhi's hermeneutics was informed and enriched by creative borrowing from various textual traditions, Buddhist, Jain, and Islamic as well as from oral traditions.[6] His eclecticism included borrowing from both elitist Sanskrit and non-elitist traditions. Thus, in addressing a group of missionaries in Calcutta, Gandhi quoted from a mediaeval devotional poet from the Sudra caste to summarize the essentials of various religious texts. In his memoirs, *An Autobiography or the Story of My Experiment with Truth*, Gandhi gives a clue to his own thinking:

But the New Testament produced a different impression, especially the Sermon on the Mount which went to straight to my heart. I compared it with the *Gita*. The verses, 'But I say unto you that ye resist not evil: but whoever shall smite thee on thy right cheek, turn to him the other also. And if any man take away thy coat let him have thy cloak too,' delighted me beyond measure and put me in mind of Shamal Bhatt's 'For a bowl of water give a goodly meal' etc. My young mind tried to unify the teaching of the *Gita*, the *Light of Asia*,[7] and the Sermon on the Mount.   (Gandhi 1927: 51)

Gandhi's hermeneutics was built on two presuppositions. First, he saw various religions as ultimately derived from one and the same source. All religions are both equal and imperfect: 'All faiths constitute a revelation of Truth, but all are imperfect and liable to error. Reverence for other faiths need not blind us to their faults.' The other is that all religious traditions are interdependent and no one religion contains all the truth: 'The world, and therefore we, can no more do without the teachings of Jesus than we can without that of Mohammed or the Upanishads. I hold all these to be complementary of one another, in no case exclusive. Their true meanings, their interdependence and interrelation have still to be revealed to us' (Ellsberg 1991: 40).

Gandhi's incorporation and reinterpretation of ideas from various religious traditions are very evident in two of his beliefs—*satyagraha* and the unity of all religions. One of the important concepts which governed Gandhi's thought, *satyagraha*, which is often rendered as non-violence but means struggle for truth, is an amalgam of various religious traditions. The framework for *satyagraha* came from several texts, both religious and secular. It was influenced by Jain and Buddhist notions of *ahimsa* (non-violence). It contained things Gandhi had gleaned from his reading of the Sermon on the Mount, especially the saying of Jesus 'Love your enemies, bless them that persecute you' (Matt. 5: 44). The idea of disinterested service, which is crucial to the concept, is drawn from the *Bhagvadgita*'s notion of *nishkama karma*. The Russian novelist, Leo Tolstoy's concept of absolute pacifism, too, was woven into it. Similarly, Gandhi's understanding of truth as many-sided was influenced by the Jain concept of *anekantavada* which connotes the partial, sketchy, and fragmentary nature of our understanding of reality. Gandhi was not simply absorbing these various writers and texts but was critically interweaving them to make hermeneutical sense, and to use them for political purposes. Certainly he was spurred on by their ideas but he rearranged them to suit his own hermeneutical needs.

Gandhi's method was simple and straightforward, and would horrify scholars raised in the historical-critical tradition. He selected texts at the redacted level which he thought would be useful in his hermeneutical task, namely to reread the message 'in terms of what is happening around us' (Ellsberg 1991: 41). He did not unduly worry about cumbersome questions such as the historical background of the narratives, the philological origins of words, or even who wrote them. In one of his many talks with missionaries, Gandhi told them that many things in the texts have to be 'interpreted in the light of discoveries—not of modern science, but in the spiritual world in the shape of direct experiences common to all faiths' (Ellsberg 1991: 41). In Gandhi's hermeneutics one finds the marks of diasporic receptivity—rootedness and openness. Rooted in the ancient heritage of his native Hinduism, he was nevertheless open to the spiritual inheritance of various religious traditions. Gandhi's advice to the missionaries is equally relevant to present-day hermeneuts: 'If you have come to give rich treasures of experiences, open your hearts out to receive the treasures of this land, and you will not be disappointed, neither will you have misread the message of the Bible' (Ellsberg 1991: 41). Hybrid texts emphatically contravene inherited Christian concepts and received interpretations. They challenge and resist the false notion of immaculate textual purity and authenticity.

Like any other theological proposition, hybridity can become a powerful ideology in the current hermeneutical warfare. In the face of more coercive discourses which insist on a single truth, single world-view, and single history, the postcolonial mode of hybridization can be seen as more pliable, accommodating, and willing to incorporate dissenting voices. On the other hand, this hybridization can in its turn become a demon and effectively take possession of and try to control the interpretative agenda. The case remains strong at present, however for adaptive rather than coercive discourses. At a time of virulent nationalism and communalism, hybridization with its insistence on critical integration not only deflates particularisms but also facilitates redefinitions of identities.

Rey Chow has been warning that a critiquing of 'nativism does not mean a happy endorsement of hybridity' as postulated by postmodernist thinking. Hybridity in the postmodern lexicon is defined as possessing emancipatory potential and an antidote to the virulent form of nativist thinking. While nativism seeks to eradicate any form of impurity in the indigenous culture, postmodern notions of hybridity tend to sweep under the carpet the cultural and political impact of colonialism. Such a notion of hybridity is oblivious to the economic hardship, helplessness, and marginalization which are ongoing realities (Chow 1998a: 155).

Not all border crossings generate hybridity. Some of the Third World cosmopolitan elites can easily assimilate and celebrate their hybridity, while other migrant workers, refugees and asylum seekers stowed away in the lorries, do not have the luxury of articulating their experiences. Yet another cadre, especially those who work for international corporations, move effortlessly across cultures and countries without any need to hybridize.

What hybridity, as a discursive practice, does is to shift the conceptualization of identity. Rather than seeing identity as a stable reference point, it switches to a different 'epistemological paradigm in which it is liminality, instability, impurity, movement and fluidity that inform the formation of identities' (Chow 1998b: 166). Multiculturalism implies the juxtaposition of fixed cultures, whereas hybridity is concerned with the fluid and shifting base of cultures and their interaction. It is perfectly possible for a society to exist as a multicultural society and be segregated.

In one sense, the hybridized state is not new. One of those earlier theologians who took seriously the hybridized form as a mode of doing theology was a Bengali, Brahmabhandhav Upadhyay (1861–1907). He captured the essence of the hybridized state, when he wrote in *Sophia*:

By birth we are Hindus and shall remain Hindu till death. But as *dvija* (twice-born) by virtue of our sacramental rebirth, we are Catholic, we are members of the indefectible communion embracing all ages and climes. In customs and manners, in observing caste and social distinctions, in eating and drinking, in our life and living we are genuine Hindus: but in our faith we are neither Hindu, nor European, nor American, nor Chinese, but all-inclusive. Our faith fills the whole world and is not confined to any country or race, our faith is universal and consequently includes all truths.   (Upadhyay 1898: 25)

There are three aspects of the earlier forms of hybridity that one should pay attention to. First, it was seen as a validating exercise to strengthen the self-identity of Indian Christians. The very survival of Indian Christian theology, or for that matter the Indian Church, depended on its capacity to respond to a society at times tolerant, but often sceptical of a minority community committed to a religion with foreign origins and linked and conflated with recent colonialism. Fusing the indigenous culture with the gospel demonstrated that Indian Christians were part of Indian culture. Second, the previous attempts still worked on the assumption of the superiority of the Christian gospel. It was the gospel which provided the yardstick against which other religious traditions were analysed and explained. Third, Upadhyay's proposal contests the notion that postcolonialism as a critical practice started after the lowering of the flags of empire. The writings of Upadhyay and countless others during the colonial period indicate that whenever a native writer put pen to paper to reconfigure his or her identity in the face of colonial assault, the project of postcolonialism was under way.

Some concluding remarks

The task of the disaporic interpreter is to be, to use Homi Bhabha's phrase, a 'vernacular cosmopolitan'. In Bhabha's view, a vernacular cosmopolitan translates between cultures, renegotiates traditions from a position where 'locality' insists on its own terms, while entering into larger national and societal conversations. This is not a cosmopolitanism of the elite variety inspired by universalist patterns of humanist thought that run gloriously across cultures, establishing an enlightened unity. Vernacular cosmopolitans are compelled to make a tryst with cultural translation as an act of survival. Their specific and local histories, often threatened and repressed, are inserted 'between the lines' of dominant cultural practices.   (Bhabha 2000: 139)

Those who are on the margins have no option but to occupy in-between spaces as a survival strategy. From this interstitial space any claim to cultural purity, stability, or autonomy are less important than the hybridized diasporic conditions of perpetual intercultural exchange, juxtaposition, interrogation, and transgression. Vernacular cosmopolitanism is about the ambiguity of being a wanderer and a transitional. It reflects something of a migratory world.

Edward Said sees much potential in the marginal position of displaced persons, immigrants, and minorities. For him such people have the power to offer a crucial perspective which can challenge and resist the forces of hierarchy, uniformity, and hegemony:

Yet it is no exaggeration to say that liberation as an intellectual mission, born in the resistance and opposition to the confinements and ravages of imperialism, has now shifted from the settled, established, and domesticated dynamics of culture to its unhoused, decentred, and exilic energies, energies whose incarnation today is the migrant, and whose consciousness is that of the intellectual and artist in exile, the political figure between domains, between forms, between homes, and between languages.   (Said 1993: 403)

While diasporans have an advantage in working out a new hermeneutics, there are temptations too. One is to dramatize their status as exiles and immigrants for the benefit of the majority or mainstream audience, and the other is to produce exotic images of the home countries they have left behind. But diasporans could play a positive role in challenging the stereotypical and homogenizing images that the host-country media and politicians tend to circulate in the public domain. Since these images are used in deciding the way the immigrant community is going to be treated, they will have their effect on the everyday life of the diaspora subjects, and on the way asylum seekers are treated. It is important to continue to question these images, and construct alternatives which will rectify these negative portrayals without idealizing or romanticizing them.

The mournful story of expulsion, flight, and exile tells only half the story of the diaspora concept. Migrancy and marginality are nowadays much more talked about in academic circles than by refugees tucked away in lorries and asylum seekers languishing in dilapidated inner-city housing estates. For these refugees, hybridity and mobility are not agents of emancipation. Mobility and migration across borders are often prompted by poverty and violence. A diasporic hermeneutics which celebrates hybridity but fails to take up the cause of refugees and asylum seekers has failed in its task. The strength of a hermeneutical enterprise is at its best measured by the causes it serves and the protection it offers to people who are at the receiving end of the system. The way it extends its scope to address the crucial issues people face acts as the test for the rightness of its goals.

Postcoloniality is perhaps the sign of an increased realization that it is not feasible to deduct a civilization, a custom, a narrative history, a literature, from the wider influences and trends of the increasingly shrinking globalized world. In other words, it is not always feasible to recover one's authentic 'roots' or even to go back to the real 'home' again. At a time when societies are becoming more multicultural, where traditions, histories, and texts commingle, and interlace, a quest for unalloyed pure native roots could prove to be not only elusive but also dangerous. It could cause complications for the everyday business of living with neighbours of diverse cultures, religions, and languages. This means finding oneself subject to an ever wider and more complex web of cultural negotiation and interaction. What diasporic interpretation indicates is that we take for granted more-or-less fractured, hyphenated, double, or in some cases multiple identities.

The Third World as a whole is marked by diversity rather than homogeneity. But now the question is: what is the value system that links umbilically the commuter in Brazil, the paddy grower in Burma, the urban dweller in a Nairobi flat, the computer engineer in Silicon Valley, the countless peasants trying to eke out an existence in different Asian, African, and Latin American countries, and the asylum seekers languishing in Western detention camps. Important frameworks of life and sources of identification should be sought in the cultural sites which have emerged in the interstices of the local and global condition. We need to direct our attention to the interrelationship of moving and dwelling in a whole world of global interconnections. What is needed is a hermeneutical space that will take into account the flow of people across continents and cultures. One of the potential spaces is the hybridized space. This inclusive space could be a comparatively effective way of avoiding the kind of clannish outlook which irrupts into religious, national, and ethnic jingoism.

We conclude with a quotation from Edward Said. In fact it comes from a twelfth-century monk, Hugo of St Victor. Said concludes his *Culture and Imperialism* with the words of the medieval priest: 'The person who finds his homeland sweet is still a tender beginner; he to whom every soil is as his native one is already strong' (Said 1993: 407). In a way these words sum up the task of the diasporic interpreter. The interpreter, whether diasporic or indigenous, achieves originality and autonomy not by jettisoning native impulses or by uncritically embracing metropolitan values, but, as the monk might have said, by working through them.

NOTES

1. In an interview with Tim Adams, 'Ryszard as the Lion Heart' in the *Observer Review*, 20 May 2001, 3.

2. *The Guardian*, G2, 21 Sept. 2000, 19.

3. Diasporic literature is too extensive to list here. The following anthologies provide a useful entry into the subject: R. Rustomji Kerns (ed.), *Living in America: Poetry and Fiction by South Asian American Writers* (Boulder, Colo.: Westview Press, 1995); *Our Feet Walk the Sky: Women of South Asian Diaspora*, ed. The Women of South Asian Descent Collective (San Francisco: Aunt Lute Books, 1993); John Riley and Briar Wood (eds.), *Leave to Stay: Stories of Exile and Belonging* (London: Virago, 1996). For a survey and critique, King-Kok Cheung (ed.), *An Interethnic Companion to Asian American Literature* (Cambridge: Cambridge University Press, 1997). For interviews and views of various diasporic writers, see Chelva Kanaganayakam (ed.), *Configurations of Exile: South Asian Writers and their World* (Toronto: TSAR Publications, 1995).

4. For example, see the essays in Fernando F. Segovia (ed.), *Interpreting Beyond Borders: The Bible and Postcolonialism 3* (Sheffield: Sheffield Academic Press, 2000); Peter C. Phan and Jung Young Lee, *Journeys at the Margins: Towards an Autobiographical Theology in American-Asian Perspective* (Collegeville, Minn.: The Liturgical Press, 1999); and also Ada María Isasi-Díaz, ' "By the Rivers of Babylon": Exile as the Way of Life', in F. F. Segovia and M. A. Tolbert (eds.), *Reading from This Place*, i. *Social Location and Biblical Interpretation in the United States* (Minneapolis: Fortress Press, 1995), 149–63.

5. I have benefited from but move beyond Rita Nakashima Brock's reading of the same narrative. See her 'Dusting the Bible on the Floor: The Loss of Innocence and the Power of Wisdom in Asian American Women's Writing', *In God's Image*, 2/3 (1992), 3–10.

6. For an incisive introduction to the influence of different religious traditions on Gandhi, see Margaret Chatterji, *Gandhi's Religious Thought* (London: Macmillan, 1983).

7. *The Light of Asia* is a poetic re-telling of the life and teaching of Gautama the Buddha by Sir Edwin Arnold.

AFTERWORD

The hermeneutical landscape in recent years has changed dramatically. This is a time when one is expected and even encouraged to be ethnic and tribal. Everyone seems to be abandoning the centre and rushing to the margin. What is paramount is that one has an accent, personal passions, subjective priorities, and commitments. One has to have ethnic or sexual particularities to prove one's authenticity. Hermeneutical engagement is seen as having to do with language, identity, representation, sexuality. Once it was about detachment and dealing with raw historical facts, but now it is about narratives and telling stories. These autobiographical stories have become an acceptable currency. Those on the margin write about themselves, so that now we have come to know a lot more about them than the texts they are supposed to unravel. The 'other' is installed and endowed with an authoritative voice. Writing from the margin also produces an illusion of intimacy. The margin is not an attractive place nor pleasant to be in but it is where a lot of people want to be. It has now become so crowded that it has prompted Terry Eagleton to say that 'there is now standing room only'.[1] The fragmentation of biblical criticism into marginal interests—feminist, liberationist, subalternist—has freed scholarly approaches from their enslavement to value-free and scientific exegesis. The multiplication of perspectives has virtues as well as potential drawbacks. The positive aspect of these readings is that they have helped to unearth counter interpretations which had been hitherto overlooked or suppressed by mainstream scholarship. For the countless minorities who have been written out or sidelined by the dominant scholarship, to find an interpretative voice is not a luxury nor a claim to academic fame and credibility, but part of the proof of their existence and presence, and a warning that they are not going to go away. To have one's voice recognized and one's interpretation acknowledged after long years of neglect and repression is a great achievement. But the negative aspect of identity hermeneutics is that it has helped to create ghettos. Further, it has created an inability to empathize with anyone who is outside the circle. Among these various groups there is no attempt to relate to one another in recognition of shared marginalization and shared goals, nor an attempt to address the complexities of their experiences and differences. Overall what these readings have accomplished is to enable biblical scholarship, which has been long neglected, to see links between life and work, and to facilitate a dialogue with the world whilst discouraging an insular and universalist mode of reading, writing, and theorizing.

Those who are engaged in the project of uplifting and representing subaltern voices are often asked: how do we, who hold on to teaching positions in Western universities, have the credentials to represent subalterns, and how do we make discourses which are purported to speak about them, easily accessible to the very subalterns we write about. But the whole point of postcolonial criticism is that it does not claim to represent anyone. The function of the postcolonial critic is to enable academia and disciplines to which we belong to understand the implications of the content of the knowledge and the type of the curriculum we impart, as well as draw attention to the absent, distorted, and suppressed voices in the courses we teach and the reading lists we produce. The key function of postcolonial criticism is to register 'how the knowledge we construct and impart as academics is structured by the absence, difficulty or impossibility of representation of the subaltern. This is to recognize, however, the fundamental inadequacy of that knowledge and of the institutions that contain it, and therefore the need for a radical change in the direction of a more democratic and non-hierarchical social order' (Beverley 1999: 40). There are a number of ways a postcolonial critic can function. We can subvert the comfortable 'academic' certainties and hegemonic tendencies which would like to keep the subaltern concerns out. We can also disarm any attempt to perpetuate an untruthful misinterpretation of subaltern histories and causes. We can constantly intervene in discussions and debates and ask why questions are framed in the way they are, and analyse the data which distort the picture. We can advocate an integrated approach rather than treating the theological output of the Third World as an interesting extra. We can resist the tendency to construct a unitary and recognizable India, Africa, etc. There is a compulsion to essentialize Asia, Africa, Latin America, the Caribbean and the Pacific through an evocation of local colour or accent. Certain exotic and 'unreal' versions of the cultures of these regions are much in demand to meet classroom demands. We can challenge the standardization of culture in academic output, highlighting the diversity of the Indian subcontinent, Africa and Latin America which have been slowly but surely substituted by a sort of monocultural vision aided and abetted by globalizing tendencies.

On the accessibility of the materials to subalterns, Elsa Tamez's words are worth bearing in mind. In her essay about the indigenous religions of the Americas, she is clear about the purpose of her enterprise: 'These reflections are not directed to the indigenous people who maintain their native religions, but to white and *mestizo* Christians who live out their faith under rigidly set boundaries and who undervalue other living expressions of faith which are not of their own. Perhaps for those indigenous people who are politically aware (*conscientes*) of their reality this contribution will say nothing new and will be of no consequence' (Tamez 1993*b*: 33). What the marginalized need is not stories about themselves which, as Tamez points out, they already know. What is of critical importance to them are stories about the powerful and about how the state, the institutionalized Church, media, and global corporations wield power, control their lives, and stifle their progress.

It would be naive to think that biblical hermeneutics can offer solutions to oppression or that it can deal with the problems of political, economic, and sexual discrimination in the pages of *Biblical Interpretation* or *New Testament Studies*. As José Cárdenas Pallares queried, 'what biblical periodical has ever fallen under any suspicion of being subversive? Biblical specialists have curiously little to suffer from the Neros and Domitians of our time. But neither do their studies instill light and strength in Christians persecuted by the lords of this world' (Pallares 1986: 2). At the most what biblical interpretation can do is to clarify and rectify some misrepresentations of these issues, based on biblical teachings, while pointing out that, in activating passages from the Bible, an allowance ought to be made for the cultural differences between the book, which had its origins in a wide variety of ancient cultures, and our time. All we can do is to underline the unsafe nature of the book and the perils of transferring or transposing its teachings to our postcolonial context without first thoroughly scrutinizing it. Admirable as it is to take up causes in the wider world, we need to look closer to home. Biblical interpretation as a specific discipline in the academy has its own structural problem, and to ignore this problem in favour of representing the oppressed leads us into what the editor of the *Third Text* calls 'sentimental solidarity' (Araeen 2000: 20). Biblical studies as a discipline has its own notable vices—self-reproducing expert culture, ritualizing our methods, and turning concepts which were once thought of as being liberatory into clichés through endless repetition. There is so much investment in our own rhetoric that we have forgotten how to relate or think beyond our subdiscipline enclaves. No one will quarrel with creative intellectual work but what concerns is the overt intellectualism. Our heavily footnoted essays not only stifle arguments but also keep the uninitiated away. Our job is not simply to critique the prevailing systems outside our little biblical world but to critique the very world we inhabit and function in. It is one thing to promote values like liberation, justice, and equality in the outside world, but it is of no value unless we work to promote these same values within the disciplines and institutions in which we work.

There are two kinds of reading: instinctual and institutional. The instinctual reading is about the desire to read spontaneously without any restrictions or without conforming to any protocol or pressures whatsoever. This type of reading is misleadingly espoused by many as the ultimate form of reading. But reading is not a free-ranging activity. There is no reading which starts in a vacuum. All readings draw on an infinite combination of conventions, symbols, or codes which influence our reading and interpretative practices. However, even this process of drawing on these conventions is not a completely free-ranging activity. Which conventions people draw upon is determined by their experiences, ethnic identities, and their affiliations to particular political or religious groups. It is also partly determined by the pressure to conform to the prestigious conventions set by the groups they belong to, and to position themselves favourably in the eyes of these groups. At the other end of this position is the reading undertaken by institutions. These institutionalized discourses offer to read on our behalf, and their reading is preconstructed to suit institutional and denominational ideologies or theological positions and to enforce discipline and order. Since texts have potential for multiple meanings, it is difficult for institutions to enforce their desired meaning or thought. Ultimately reading is produced not by completely deserting spontaneity and originality nor by conforming to readings permitted by institutions but by negotiating these polarities. Interpretation is a struggle between instinctive, untutored, untheorized modes of appropriation and institutional conventions, codes, practices, and doctrinal manipulation. One has to work against dominant meanings to produce new knowledge or to deepen or indeed to problematize well-established positions. Reading, in the final analysis, has to be dissenting and liberatory.

The Bible, as David Jasper once remarked, 'simply swarms us'. Western culture and literature are saturated with its language and imageries. It has invaded colonies and has intruded into the political and social and cultural life of peoples who were not necessarily part of the biblical heritage which is infused with Semitic and Greek and Hellenistic imageries and concepts. The overwhelming presence of the Bible was the result of modernity. The impetus for the current production of the Bible and its dissemination in many vernacular languages, was provided by the invention of the printing machine and the emergence of marketing techniques which were part of the modernist agenda. But like most things about modernism, the Bible, too, is now facing a crisis. Armed with modernist traits of confidence, compulsion, and authority, the Bible asserted its credibility. But the way it dominated the cultural and religious sphere is now increasingly coming under attack, and as a result of which its power and presence are in retreat. The dislocation of the Bible as the premier text has come about through the challenge presented by both secular and sacred texts of other faith traditions. We live at a time when these texts are increasingly challenging the claim that the Bible is the only true story, the only right way, and those who refuse to accept its authority are in the dark, entrenched in their own ungodliness. The answers to human despair and hope, faith and disbelief, suffering and redemption—which were once proudly paraded as the Bible's unique contribution—are now seen as available and textualized in other religious and secular texts as well. Such a recognition, and a dent in its authority, has not only impoverished the role of the Bible but it has also imposed restrictions upon the way we read the Bible.

One way to avoid any kind of sectarian essentializing leading to religious fanaticism is to read these texts in comparative and inclusive ways. It is not the comparative and inclusive method advocated by the earlier generation of comparativists. For them, the sacred texts of other people were containers of natural religion and as such they had to be scrutinized in relation to the special revelation deposited in the Bible. Or they were to be used as an evidence to corroborate historical events in the Bible, or to posit the Bible as the ultimate mark of textual Darwinism outwitting other texts and culminating in the present venerable form. The comparative and inclusive attitude I have in mind is not a superficial tolerance of religions, nor is it aimed at defusing religious conflicts. Rather, it is an attitude of having encountered the reality and being able to comprehend the analogous encounters of others, and to recognize and revere them. It is characterized by the Indian attitude, *sarvadharmasambhava* (acceptance of all religious experience):

The attitude of *sarvadharmasambhava* has a deeper root: it is the result of one's own experience of the ultimate through which he or she is able to understand a similar experience of the other and respect it. From the experience of the ultimacy and universality within the realm of one's own religious faith, what results is not the affirmation of its uniqueness over against others; what results rather is the capacity to understand the faith of the other in its ultimacy and universality. (Soares-Prabhu 1994: 187)

From such an experience of ultimacy within the sphere of one's own religious texts, what follows is not the assertion of the Bible's unparalleled nature or its claim over other texts but the ability to understand the spiritual and religious imagination embodied in religious texts of other faiths in their ultimacy and universality. The *sarvadharmasambhava* way of thinking allows one to accept other sacred texts as complementary disclosures. Such an attitude perceives other texts as complementary and not as competing for truth-claims. It prompts us to read the Bible not exclusively for its dogmatic claims, nor to read it with the intention of evangelising the other because of spiritual and theological defects in their texts and teachings.

Ideally one should be able to read the Bible without any recourse to a recent commentary, or, even better, read it without employing one of the latest theories in order to appreciate its contents and its potential. But one realizes that like all simple ideas, it is not easy to put into practice. The Bible is instantly accessible and at the same time deceptively difficult to read. This is due to the fact that the Bible is neither a coherent nor a unified book. It is riddled with inherent contradictions and gaps and textual ambivalences which permit multiple readings, none of which can be conclusive or exhaustive.

Those who are impatient and tired of endless convoluted theories— pastors, Sunday school teachers, adult group leaders, and even some academics—often ask: does being critical spoil the pleasure of reading? Can't one read just for pleasure? The underlying aspiration is: why can't we just read the Bible for pleasure. Perhaps it would have been possible in the pre-Saidian state of innocence? Ever since Said introduced Orientalism as a handy descriptor for managing texts, echoing the Foucaultian notion of the link between knowledge and power, both texts and readers have lost their innocence. To paraphrase Fanon, reading is not a pleasurable act but a political one. No reading of the text can neglect its contextuality, form, structure, intentions, however imperfectly these may be constructed and discerned. Pointing at a text's historical and political provenance and ideological bias may not increase the pleasure of reading. The most it can do is give a clue to distinguish between different levels of meanings in the text, and who is managing the text, and against whom these texts are used.

Finally, postcolonial biblical criticism should go beyond the Protestant preoccupation with words and texts and scriptures. The sense of the scripture has to be discerned beyond words, parables, and paradoxes, even quite independently of the scriptures themselves. Rewriting the Bible, as suggested in some circles, will only serve to reinforce its textual power and its hold on readers. It may sound blasphemous, but the interpreter's task is not confined to bringing out the meaning of texts, or occasionally protecting them from 'wayward' 'misreadings', but, when the moment comes, he or she should be prepared to give up the very texts themselves. Biblical stories were told not necessarily to record what actually happened but to encourage us in the present and to furnish a vision of an open future. What is important is not the texts but the meanings they convey, the interpretation they provide and the vision they forge. The relationship between text and meaning is poignantly brought out by the Turkish novelist, Orhan Pamuk, in his novel, *My Name is Red*, a philosophical thriller in the same league as Umberto Eco's *Name of the Rose*. What Eco did for medieval Catholicism, Pamuk has done for medieval Islam. Set in the world of miniaturists and illuminators in the Ottoman empire, the novel is constructed around the debate between medieval Western and Islamic art concerning true artistic meaning. A conversation between a European master and great miniaturist of the Orient goes like this. The European master tells the other, 'If you depicted one of the trees in this forest, a man who looked upon the painting could come here, and if he so desired, correctly select that tree from among others.' On hearing this, the tree with Ottoman roots objects: 'I do not want to be a tree. I want to be its meaning' (Pamuk 2001: 51). The hermeneutical implication is that texts are not crucial but the meanings they convey are. Texts are seen not as an immediate access to truth but as a medium. Their paramount function is to be a guide and companion in the search. As in the Buddhist parable, scriptures are like a raft to cross the ocean, and once the shore is reached there is no need to carry further. Scriptures are only pointers and not an end in themselves. Texts, dogmas, and creeds are not the only access to reality. I end with a quotation from a text which advocates both embracement and eventual abandonment, attachment and detachment from text. It comes from an ancient Indian text, *The Upanishads*. It contains this apparently sacrilegious thought: 'Read, study and ceaselessly ponder the Scriptures; but once the light has shined within you, throw them away as you discard a brand which you have used to light your fire' (*Amritanada Upanishad* 1).

NOTES

1. Terry Eagleton, 'The Centre cannot hold', *The Guardian Saturday Review*, 23 June 2001, 8.

REFERENCES

Ahmed Khan, S. (1873; 2000). *The Causes of the Indian Revolt* (Oxford in Asia, Historical Reprints). Karachi: Oxford University Press.

Ahn, Byung Mu (1995). 'Jesus and the Minjung in the Gospel of Mark', in R. S. Sugirtharajah (ed.), *Voices from the Margin: Interpreting the Bible in the Third World* (new edn.). Maryknoll, NY: Orbis Books, 85–104.

Allen, Ward (ed. and trans.) (1993). *Translating for King James: Notes Made by a Translator of King James's Bible* (paperback). Nashville: Vanderbilt University Press.

Althaus-Reid, Marcella (1998). 'The Hermeneutics of Transgression', in G. De Schrijver (ed.), *Liberation Theologies on Shifting Grounds: A Clash of Socio-Economic and Cultural Paradigms*. Leuven: University Press, 251–71.

Anderson, Christopher (1845). *The Annals of the English Bible* i. London: William Pickering.

Appadurai, Arjun (1990). 'Disjuncture and Difference in the Global Cultural Economy'. *Public Culture*, 2/2: 1–24.

Appasamy, A. J. (1992). 'My Theological Quest', in T. D. Francis (ed.), *The Christian Bhakti of A. J. Appasamy*. Madras: The Christian Literature Society, 134–65.

Appasamy Pillai, A. S. (1924). *Fifty Years' Pilgrimage of a Convert*. London: Church Missionary Society.

Araeen, Rasheed (2000). 'A New Beginning: Beyond Postcolonial Cultural Theory and Identity Politics'. *Third Text: Critical Perspectives on Contemporary Art & Culture*, 50: 3–20.

Arasanayagam, Jean (2000). *In the Garden Secretly and Other Stories*. New Delhi: Penguin Books.

Arias, Esther, and Arias, Moritmer (1980). *The Cry of My People: Out of Captivity in Latin America*. New York: Friendship Press.

Armstrong, Karen (1999). *The Epistle of Paul the Apostle to the Hebrews with an Introduction*. Edinburgh: Canongate Books.

Arul Raja, M. (1996). 'Towards A Dalit Reading of the Bible: Some Hermeneutical Reflections'. *Jeevadhara: A Journal of Christian Interpretation*, 26/151: 28–34.

—— (1997). 'Assertion of Periphery: Some Biblical Paradigms'. *Jeevadhara: A Journal of Christian Interpretation*, 27/157: 25–35.

—— (1999). 'A Dialogue between Dalits and Bible: Certain Indicators for Interpretation'. *Journal of Dharma*, 24/1: 40–50.

Asad, Talal (1996). 'A Comment on Translation, Critique, and Subversion', in

A. Dingwaney and C. Maier (eds.), *Between Languages and Cultures: Translation and Cross-Cultural Texts*. Delhi: Oxford University Press, 325–32.

Ashcroft, Bill (2001). *Post-Colonial Transformation*. London: Routledge.

—— Griffiths, Gareth, and Tiffin, Helen (1989). *The Empire Writes Back: Theory and Practice in Post-Colonial Literatures*. London: Routledge.

—— —— —— (1995). *The Post-Colonial Studies Reader*. London: Routledge.

—— —— —— (1998). *Key Concepts in Post-Colonial Studies*. London: Routledge.

Ateek, Naim S. (1995). 'Biblical Perspectives on the Land', in R. S. Sugirtharajah (ed.), *Voices from the Margin: Interpreting the Bible in the Third World* (new edn.). Maryknoll, NY: Orbis Books, 267–76.

Avalos, Hector (1996). '*The Gospel of Lucan Gavilán* as Postcolonial Biblical Exegesis'. *Semeia: An Experimental Journal for Biblical Criticism*, 75: 87–105.

Avotri, Solomon K. (2000). 'The Vernacularization of the Scripture and African Beliefs: The Story of the Gerasene Demoniac among the Ewe of West Africa', in G. O. West and M. W. Dube (eds.), *The Bible in Africa: Transactions, Trajectories and Trends*. Leiden: Brill, 311–25.

Baago, Kaj (1969). *Pioneers of Indigenous Christianity* (Confessing the Faith in India Series, no. 4). Bangalore: The Christian Institute for the Study of Religion and Society.

Baikie, James (1928). *The English Bible and Its Story: Its Growth, Its Translators and Their Adventures*. London: Seeley, Service & Co. Limited.

Baird, Mary M. (1920). 'The Gadarene Demoniac'. *Expository Times*, 31/4: 189.

Balch, David L. (1988). 'Household Codes', in D. E. Aune (ed.), *Greco-Roman Literature and the New Testament: Selected Forms and Genres*. Atlanta: Scholars Press, 25–50.

Barclay, William (1968). *The New Testament: A New Translation*, i. *The Gospels and the Acts of the Apostles*. London: Collins.

Bateson, Bernard L. (1947). *The British Empire in the Light of Prophecy*. London: Covenant Publishing Company.

Bauman, Zygmunt (1995). *Life in Fragments: Essays in Postmodern Morality*. Oxford: Blackwell.

Baumann, Martin (1997). 'Shangri-la in Exile: Portraying Tibetan Diaspora Studies and Reconsidering Diaspora(s)'. *Diaspora*, 6/3: 377–404.

Beverley, John (1999). *Subalternity and Representation: Arguments in Cultural Theory*. Durham: Durham University Press.

Bhabha, Homi K. (1994). *The Location of Culture*. London: Routledge.

—— (2000). 'The Vernacular Cosmopolitan', in F. Dennis and N. Khan (eds.), *Voices of the Crossing: The Impact of Britain on Writers from Asia, the Caribbean and Africa*. London: Serpent's Tail, 133–42.

Boff, Clodovis (1991). 'Hermeneutics: Constitution of Theological Pertinency', in R. S. Sugirtharajah (ed.), *Voices from the Margin: Interpreting the Bible in the Third World*. London: SPCK, 9–35.

Boff, L. (1980). 'Christ's Liberation via Oppression: An Attempt at Theological Construction from the Standpoint of Latin America', in R. Gibellini (ed.), *Frontiers of Theology in Latin America*. Maryknoll, NY: Orbis Books, 100–34.

The Book and the Sword: A Popular Illustrated Report of the British and Foreign Bible Society for the Year 1914–1915 (1915). London: The Bible House.

Bowden, John (1988). *Jesus: The Unanswered Questions*. London: SCM Press.

Bray, Gerald (ed.) (1994a). 'The Second Henrician Injunctions 1538', in *Documents of the English Reformation*. Cambridge: James Clark & Co. Ltd, 179–83.

—— (ed.) (1994b). 'The Preface to the Geneva Bible 1560', in *Documents of the English Reformation*. Cambridge: James Clark & Co. Ltd, 355–63.

A Brief Narrative of the Operations of the Jaffna Auxiliary Bible Society in the Preparation of a Version of the Tamil Scriptures (1868). Jaffna: Strong and Asbury Printers.

Bruce, F. F. (1970). *The English Bible: A History of Translations from the Earliest English Versions to the New English Bible* (new and revised edn.). London: Lutterworth Press.

Cadorette, Curt, et al. (1992). *Liberation Theology: Introductory Reader*. Maryknoll, NY: Orbis Books.

Cannon, Garland (1990). *The Life and Mind of Oriental Jones: Sir William Jones, the Father of Modern Linguistics*. Cambridge: Cambridge University Press.

Canton, William (1914). *The Bible and the Anglo-Saxon People*. London: J. M. Dent & Sons Ltd.

Cardenal, Erneto (ed.) (1982). *The Gospel in Solentiname*, trans. D. D. Walsh, vols. 1–4. Maryknoll, NY: Orbis Books.

Carroll, Robert and Prickett, Stephen (1998a). 'Introduction', in R. Carroll and S. Prickett (eds.), *The Bible: Authorized King James Version with Apocrypha* (paperback; Oxford World Classics). Oxford: Oxford University Press, pp. xi–xlvi.

—— —— (1998b). 'The Translators to the Reader', in R. Carroll and S. Prickett (eds.), *The Bible: Authorized King James Version with Apocrypha* (paperback; Oxford World Classics). Oxford: Oxford University Press, pp. liii–lxxii.

Chandran, J. R. (1953). 'Christianity and Social Planning'. *Bulletin of the Christian Institute for the Study of Society*, 1/1: 49–56.

Chari, V. K. (1990). *Sanskrit Criticism*. Delhi: Motilal Banarsidass Publishers.

Chatterji, Margaret (1983). *Gandhi's Religious Thought*. London: Macmillan.

Chatterji, S. K. (1967). 'Towards a Revolutionary Transformation of Society'. *Religion and Society*, 14/4: 15–25.

Cheung, King-Kok (ed.) (1997). *An Interethnic Companion to Asian American Literature*. Cambridge: Cambridge University Press.

Childs, Peter, and Williams, Patrick (1997). *An Introduction to Post-Colonial Theory*. London: Prentice-Hall.

Chingota, F. L. (1996). 'The Use of the Bible in Social Transformation', in Kenneth R. Ross (ed.), *God, People and Power in Malawi: Democratization in Theological Perspective*. Blantyre: Christian Literature Association in Malawi, 41–62.

Chow, Rey (1998a). *Ethics After Idealism: Theory-Culture-Ethnicity-Reading*. Bloomington: Indiana University Press.

—— (1998b). 'The Postcolonial Difference: Lessons in Cultural Legitimation'. *Postcolonial Studies*, 1/2: 161–9.

Christian, Barbara (1995). 'The Race for Theory', in B. Ashcroft, G. Griffiths, and H. Tiffin (eds.), *The Post-Colonial Studies Reader*. London: Routledge, 457–60.

Clévenot, Michel (1985). *Materialist Approaches to the Bible*, trans. W. J. Nottingham. Maryknoll, NY: Orbis Books.

Clifford, Anne M. (2001). *Introducing Feminist Theology*. Maryknoll, NY: Orbis Books.

Clutton-Brock, A. (1938). 'The English Bible', in V. F. Storr (ed.), *The English Bible: Essays by Various Authors*. London: Methuen & Co Ltd, 68–79.

Cohen, Jeffrey Jerome (ed.) (2000). *The Postcolonial Middle Ages*. Basingstoke: Macmillan Press.

Cohen, Robin (1999). *Global Diasporas: An Introduction*. London: UCL Press.

Colenso, John W. (1861). *St. Paul's Epistle to the Romans: Newly Translated and Explained from a Missionary Point of View*. Cambridge: Macmillan and Co.

—— (1862). *The Pentateuch and Book of Joshua Critically Examined*. London: Longman, Green, Longman, Roberts, & Green.

—— (1879). 'What doth the Lord require of us? A sermon preached in the cathedral church of St. Peter's, Maritzberg, on Wednesday, March 12, 1879'. Reprinted in *Natalia*, 6 (1976): 15–23.

Colley, Linda (2000). 'Britain and Islam: 1600–1800: Different Perspectives on Difference', *Yale Review*, 88/4: 1–20.

Cook, Albert S. (1909). 'The Authorized Version and its Influence', in A. Ward and A. Waller (eds.), *The Cambridge History of English Literature*, iv. Cambridge: Cambridge University Press, 26–50.

Cook, Scott B. (1996). *Colonial Encounters in the Age of High Imperialism*. New York: Longman.

Coomaraswamy, Ananda K. (1909). *Essays in National Idealism*. Madras: G. A. Natesan.

—— (1983). 'The Religious Basis of the Forms of Indian Society'. *Studies in Comparative Religion*, 15/1–2: 9–29.

The Common Bond (1935). London: The British and Foreign Bible Society.

Cooppan, Vilashini (2000). 'W(h)ither Post-colonial Studies? Towards the Transnational Study of Race and Nation', in L. Chrisman and B. Parry (eds.), *Postcolonial Theory and Criticism*. Suffolk: D. S. Brewer, 1–35.

Coote, Robert T. (2000). 'Finger on the Pulse: Fifty Years of Missionary Research'. *International Bulletin of Missionary Research*, 24/3: 98–105.

Daiches, David (1941). *The King James Version of the English Bible: An Account of the Development and Sources of the English Bible of 1611 with Special Reference to the Hebrew Tradition*. Chicago: University of Chicago Press.

—— (1967). *Literary Essays*. Chicago: University of Chicago Press.

Daniell, David (2001). *William Tyndale: A Biography*. New Haven: Yale University Press.

Deissmann, A. (1910). *Light from the Ancient East*. London: Hodder and Stoughton.

Derrett, J. and Duncan, M. (1979). 'Contributions to the Study of the Gerasene Demoniac'. *Journal for the Study of the New Testament*, 3: 2–17.

Devasahayam, V. (1992). *Outside the Camp: Bible Studies in Dalit Perspective*. Madras: Gurukul Lutheran Theological College and Research Institute.

—— (1997). *Doing Dalit Theology in Biblical Key*. Madras: Gurukul Lutheran Theological College and Research Institute.

Dixon, W. Macneile (1938). 'The English Bible', in V. F. Storr (ed.), *The English Bible: Essays by Various Authors*. London: Methuen & Co. Ltd, 43–67.

Donaldson, Laura E. (1996). 'Postcolonialism and Biblical Reading: Introduction'. *Semeia: An Experimental Journal for Biblical Criticism*, 75: 1–14.

—— (1999). 'The Sign of Orpah: Reading Ruth through Native Eyes', in R. S. Sugirtharajah (ed.), *Vernacular Hermeneutics*. Sheffield: Sheffield Academic Press, 20–36.

Drury, John (2000). *Painting the Word: Christian Pictures and Their Meanings* (second printing). New Haven: Yale University Press.

Dube, Musa W. (2000). *Postcolonial Feminist Interpretation of the Bible*. St Louis: Chalice Press.

Dubois, Abbé J. A. (1823; 1982). *Letters on the State of Christianity in India*. New Delhi: Associated Publishing House.

Elliott, John H. (1981). *A Home for the Homeless: A Sociological Exegesis of 1 Peter: Its Situation and Strategy*. London: SCM Press.

Elliott-Binns, L. E. (1952). *The Development of English Theology in the Later Nineteenth Century.* London: Longmans, Green and Co.

Ellsberg, Robert (ed.) (1991). *Gandhi on Christianity.* Maryknoll, NY: Orbis Books.

Equiano, Olaudah (1995). *The Interesting Narrative and Other Writings.* London: Penguin.

Fabella, Virginia, and Sugirtharajah, R. S. (2000). 'Introduction', in V. Fabella and R. S. Sugirtharajah (eds.), *Dictionary of Third World Theologies.* Maryknoll, NY: Orbis Books), pp. xxi–xxiii.

Fanon, Frantz (1970). *A Dying Colonialism,* trans. H. Chevalier. Harmondsworth: Penguin Books.

—— (1986). *Black Skin, White Masks,* trans. C. L. Markmann. London: Pluto Press.

—— (1990). *The Wretched of the Earth,* trans. C. Farrington. London: Penguin Books.

Farred, Grant (ed.)(1996). *Rethinking C. L. R. James.* Oxford: Blackwell Publishers.

Fernandez, Eleazar S. (2001). 'Exodus-toward-Egypt: Filipino-Americans' Struggle to Realize the Promised Land in America', in E. S. Fernandez and F. F. Segovia (eds.), *A Dream Unfinished: Theological Reflections on America from the Margins.* Maryknoll, NY: Orbis Books, 167–81.

For the Healing of the Nations (1916): *A Popular Report of the British and Foreign Bible Society 1915–1916.* London: The Bible House.

Francis, Dayanandan T. (1989). *The Relevance of Hindu Ethos for Christian Presence: A Tamil Perspective.* Madras: The Christian Literature Society.

Francis, M. (1998). *Why the Innocent Suffer: Job and Harichandra: Biblical and Puranic Expression.* Hyderabad: St John Regional Seminary.

Freyne, Sean (2000). *Galilee and Gospel: Collected Essays.* Tübingen: Mohr Siebeck.

Gallagher, Susan VanZanten (1994). *Postcolonial Literature and the biblical call for Justice.* Jackson: University Press of Mississippi.

Gandhi, Leela (1998). *Postcolonial Theory: A Critical Introduction.* Edinburgh: Edinburgh University Press.

Gandhi, M. K. (1927). *An Autobiography or The Story of My Experiments with Truth.* Ahmedabad: Navajivan Publishing House.

—— (1944; 1977). *India of My Dreams.* Ahmedabad: Navjivan Publishing House.

Gnanavaram, M. (1993). 'Dalit Theology and the Parable of the Good Samaritan'. *Journal for the Study of the New Testament,* 50: 59–83.

Gordon, Lewis R., Sharpley-Whiting, T. D., and White, Renée T. (eds.) (1996). *Fanon: A Critical Reader.* Oxford: Blackwell Publishers.

Goto, Hiromi (1997). *Chorus of Mushrooms.* London: The Women Press Ltd.

Gracía-Treto, Francisco (2000). 'Hyphenating Joseph: A View of Genesis 39–41 from the Cuban Diaspora', in F. F. Segovia (ed.), *Interpreting Beyond Borders: The Bible and Postcolonialism 3*. Sheffield: Sheffield Academic Press, 134–45.

Greaves, Richard L. (1976). 'Traditionalism and the Seeds of Revolution in the Social Principles of the Geneva Bible'. *Seventeenth Century Journal*, 7/1: 94–109.

Green, J. R. (1903). *A Short History of the English People*, iii. (illustrated edn.). London: Macmillan.

Guha, Ranajit (1988). 'On Some Aspects of the Historiography of Colonial India', in R. Guha and G. C. Spivak (eds.), *Selected Subaltern Studies*. New York: Oxford University Press, 37–44.

Gutiérrez, Gustavo (1973). *A Theology of Liberation: History, Politics, and Salvation*, trans. C. Inda and J. Eagleson. Marynoll, NY: Orbis Books.

—— (1987). *On Job: God-Talk and the Suffering of the Innocent*. Maryknoll, NY: Orbis Books.

—— (1988). *A Theology of Liberation: History, Politics, and Salvation*, trans. C. Inda and J. Eagleson. Maryknoll, NY: Orbis Books.

—— (1993). *Las Casas: In Search of the Poor of Jesus Christ*, trans. R. Barr. Maryknoll, NY: Orbis Books.

Hall, Stuart (1973). *Encoding and Decoding in the Television Discourse*. Birmingham: Centre for Cultural Studies University of Birmingham.

Hammond, Gerald (1982). *The Making of the English Bible*. Manchester: Carcanet New Press.

Hanke, Lewis (1974). *All Mankind is One: A Study of the Disputation between Bartolome de Las Casas and Juan Gine de Sepulveda in 1550 on the Intellectual and Religious Capacity of the American Indians*. DeKalb, Ill.: Northern Illinois University Press.

Hargreaves, Cecil (1972). *Asian Christian Thinking: Studies in a Metaphor and Its Message*. Delhi: ISPCK.

Harrison, Robert C., Jr (1997). 'Qoheleth among the Sociologists'. *Biblical Interpretation: A Journal of Contemporary Approaches*, 160–80.

Hau'ofa, Epeli (1983; 1994). *Tales of the Tikongs*. Honolulu: University of Hawaii Press.

Have Ye Never Read? (1913). *A Popular Illustrated Report of the British and Foreign Bible Society*. London: The Bible House.

Hawley, Susan (1996). 'Does God Speak Miskitu? The Bible and Ethnic Identity among Miskitu of Nicaragua', in M. G. Brett (ed.), *Ethnicity and the Bible*. Leiden: E J Brill, 315–42.

Healy, Joseph, and Sybertz, Donald (1996). *Towards an African Narrative Theology*. Maryknoll, NY: Orbis Books.

Henson, Herbert Hensley (1938). 'Introductory Essay', in V. F. Storr (ed.), *The English Bible: Essays by Various Authors*. London: Methuen & Co. Ltd, 1–15.

Hill, Christopher (1993). *The English Bible and the Seventeenth-Century Revolution.* London: The Penguin Press.

Hipsley, H. (n.d). *The Bible in the School: A Question for India.* London: Alfred W. Bennett.

Hoare, H. W. (1901). *The Evolution of the English Bible: Historical Sketch of the Successive Versions.* London: John Murray.

Hogg, W. Richey (1984). 'The Scriptures in the Christian World Mission: Three Historical Considerations'. *Missiology: An International Review,* 12/4: 389–404.

Horsley, Richard A. (1998). 'Submerged Biblical Histories and Imperial Biblical Studies', in R. S. Sugirtharajah (ed.), *The Postcolonial Bible.* Sheffield: Sheffield Academic Press, 152–73.

Huber, Friedrich (1980). 'Toward an Applicablity-Aimed Exegesis', *Indian Journal of Theology,* 29: 133–48.

In the Mother Tongue (1930). London: The British and Foreign Bible Society.

In the Vulgar Tongue (1914). *A Popular Illustrative Report of the British and Foreign Bible Society 1913–1914.* London: The Bible House.

Isasi-Díaz, Ada María (1995). ' "By the Rivers of Babylon": Exile as the Way of Life', in F. F. Segovia and M. A. Tolbert (eds.), *Reading from This Place,* i. *Social Location and Biblical Interpretation in the United States.* Minneapolis: Fortress Press, 149–63.

James, P. D. (1998). 'Canons of Authorship', *Times Literary Supplement,* 25 Dec. 21.

Kachru, Braj. B. and Nelson, Cecil L. (2001). 'World Englishes', in A. Burns and C. Coffin (eds.), *Analysing English in a Global Context: A Reader.* London: Routledge, 11–25.

Kanaganayakam, Chelva (ed.) (1995). *Configurations of Exile: South Asian Writers and Their World.* Toronto: TSAR Publications.

Kaplan, Amy, and Pease, Donald E. (eds.) (1993). *Cultures of United States Imperialism.* Durham: Duke University Press.

Kapoor, Kapil (1998). *Literary Theory: Indian Conceptual Framework.* New Delhi: Affiliated East–West Press Private Limited.

Kilgour, R. (1939). *The Bible Throughout the World: A Survey of Scripture Translations.* London: World Dominion Press.

King, Bruce (1996). *New National and Post-Colonial Literatures: An Introduction.* Oxford: Clarendon Press.

King, C. Richard (2000). 'Introduction: Dislocating Postcoloniality, Relocating American Empire', in C. Richard King (ed.), *Post-Colonial America.* Urbana: University of Illinois Press, 1–17.

Kinukawa, Hisako (1994). *Women and Jesus in Mark: A Japanese Feminist Perspective.* Maryknoll, NY: Orbis Books.

Klein, Naomi (2001). 'Reclaiming the Commons'. *New Left Review*, 7: 81–9.

Koonthanam, George (1982). 'An Indian Understanding of Prophet Amos Today'. *Jeevadhara: A Journal of Christian Interpretation*, 12/68: 111–28.

Kreider, Alan (1994). 'Worship and Evangelism in Pre-Christendom'. The Laing Lecture 1994. *Vox Evangelica*, 24: 7–38.

Krishnan, Mini (2000). 'Project and Series Editor's Note', in Bama, *Karukku*. Chennai: Macmillan.

Kuan, Jeffrey Kah-jin (2000). 'Diasporic Reading of a Diasporic Text: Identity Politics and Race Relations and the Book of Esther', in F. F Segovia (ed.), *Interpreting Beyond Borders: The Bible and Postcolonialism 3*. Sheffield: Sheffield Academic Press, 161–73.

Kureishi, Hanif (1996). *The Black Album*. London: Faber and Faber.

Kuribayashi, Teruo (1995). 'Theology of Crowned with Thorns', in D. Carr (ed.), *God, Christ & God's People in Asia*. Hong Kong: CCA Theological Concerns, 93–114.

Landry, Donna and Maclean, Gerald (1996). *The Spivak Reader*. New York: Routledge.

Las Casas, Bartolomé de (1992*a*). *The Only Way*, (ed.) H. R. Parish, trans. F. P. Sullivan. New York: Paulist Press.

—— (1992*b*). *In Defense of the Indians*, trans. S. Poole. DeKalb: Northern Illinois University Press.

Lawton, D. (1990). *Faith, Text and History: The Bible in English*. Charlottesville: University Press of Virginia.

Lee, Jung Young (1999). 'A Life In-between: A Korean-American Journey', in P. C. Phan and J. Y. Lee (eds.), *Journeys at the Margin: Towards an Autobiographical Theology in American-Asian Perspective*. Collegeville, Minn. The Liturgical Press, 23–39.

Leech, Kenneth (1999). 'From Chaplaincy towards Prophecy: Racism and Christian Theology over Four Decades'. *Race and Class*, 41/1–2: 131–42.

Leñero, Vicente (1991). *The Gospel of Lucas Gavilan*, trans. R. Mowry. Lanham, Md: University Press of America.

Levi, Peter (1974). *The English Bible 1534–1859*. Grand Rapids, Mich.: William B. Eerdmans Publishing Company.

Long, James (1874). *Bible Teaching and Preaching for the Million by Emblems and Proverbs*. n.p.

Loomba, Ania (1998). *Colonialism/Postcolonialism*. London: Routledge.

Losada, Angel (1971). 'The Controversy between Sepúlveda and Las Casas in the Junta of Valladolid', in J. Friede and B. Keen (eds.), *Bartolomé de Las Casas in History: Toward an Understanding of the Man and his Work*. DeKalb: Northern Illinois University Press, 279–307.

Lovett, R. (1909). *The Printed Bible 1525–1885*. London: The Religious Tract Society.

McLeod, John (2000). *Beginning Postcolonialism*. Manchester: Manchester University Press.

Madsen, Deborah L. (1999). 'Beyond the Commonwealth: Post-Colonialism and American Literature', in Deborah L. Madsen (ed.), *Post-Colonial Literatures: Expanding the Canon*. London: Pluto Press, 1–14.

Manikkam, T. (1982). 'Toward an Indian Hermeneutics of the Bible'. *Jeevadhara: A Journal of Christian Interpretation*, 12/68: 94–104.

Martin, Clarice J. (1989). 'A Chamberlain's Journey and the Challenge of Interpretation for Liberation'. *Semeia: An Experimental Journal for Biblical Criticism*, 47: 105–35.

Masoga, M. A. (1995). 'Exploring Belief in *Boloi* (Witchcraft) in the Light of Mark 5. 1–20'. *Journal of Black Theology*, 9/2: 53–69.

Mehrez, Samia (1992). 'Translation and the Postcolonial Experience: The Francophone North African Text', in L. Venuti (ed.), *Rethinking Translation: Discourse, Subjectivity, Ideology*. London: Routledge, 120–38.

Memmi, Albert (1990).*The Colonizer and the Colonized*, trans. H. Greenfeld. London: Earthscan Publications.

Metzger, Bruce M. (1989). 'To the Reader', in *The Holy Bible Containing Old and New Testaments with the Apocryphal/Deuterocanonical Books: New Revised Standard Version*, 1–4 Glasgow: Collins Publishers.

Micklem, Nathaniel (1920). *The Galilean: The Permanent Element in Religion*. London: James Clarke & Co. Ltd.

Miguez-Bonino, José (1995). 'Marxist Critical Tools: Are They Helpful in Breaking the Stranglehold of Idealist Hermeneutics?', in R. S. Sugirtharajah (ed.), *Voices from the Margin: Interpreting the Bible in the Third World* (new edn.). Maryknoll, NY: Orbis Books, 58–68.

Mongia, Padmini. (ed.) (1996). *Contemporary Postcolonial Theory: A Reader*. London: Arnold.

More Golden Than Gold (1912). *A Popular Illustrated Report of the British and Foreign Bible Society 1911–1912*. London: The Bible House.

Morrison, Blake (1998). *The Gospel According to John with an Introduction*. Edinburgh: Canongate Books.

Mosala, Itumeleng J. (1992). 'The Implications of the Text of Esther for African Women's Struggle for Liberation in South Africa'. *Semeia: An Experimental Journal for Biblical Criticism*, 59: 129–37.

Mozley, J. F. (1955). 'The English Bible before the Authorized Version', in *The Bible Today: Historical, Social, and Literary Aspects of the Old and New Testaments*. London: Eyre & Spottiswoode, 127–31.

Mukherjee, Sujit (1994). *Translation as Discovery and Other Essays on Indian Literature in English Translation.* Hyderabad: Orient Longman.

Mwikisa, Peter Wamulungwe (2000). 'The Limits of Difference: Ngũgĩ wa Thiong'o's Redeployment of Biblical Signifiers in *A Grain of Wheat* and *I will marry when I want*', in G. O. West and M. W. Dube (eds.), *The Bible in Africa: Transactions, Trajectories, Trends.* Leiden: Brill, 163–83.

Nagano, Paul M. (1999). 'A Japanese-American Pilgrimage: Theological Reflections', in P. C. Phan and J. Y. Lee (eds.), *Journeys at the Margin: Towards an Autobiographical Theology in American-Asian Perspective.* Collegeville, Minn.: The Liturgical Press, 63–79.

Nakashima Brock, Rita (1992). 'Dusting the Bible on the Floor: The Loss of Innocence and the Power of Wisdom in Asian American Women's Writing'. In *God's Image*, 2/3: 3–10.

Narayan, R. K. (1990). *A Story-Teller's World: Stories, Essays, Sketches.* New Delhi: Penguin Books.

Neill, Stephen (1964). *A History of Christian Missions.* Harmondsworth: Penguin Books.

Njoroge, N. J. (2000). *Kiama Kia Ngo: An African Christian Feminist Ethic of Resistance and Transformation.* Accra: Asempa Publishers.

Nkrumah, Kwame (1965). *Neo-Colonialism: The Last Stage of Imperialism.* London: Thomas Nelson and Sons.

Norton, David (1993). *A History of the Bible as Literature*, i. *From Antiquity to 1700.* Cambridge: Cambridge University Press.

Nyabongo, Akiki K. (1936). *Africa Answers Back.* London: George Routledge & Sons Ltd.

Oddie, Geoffrey (1999). *Missionaries, Rebellion and Proto-nationalism: James Long of Bengal 1814–87.* Richmond: Curzon Press.

Ondaatje, Michael (1993). *The English Patient.* London: Picador.

Our Feet Walk the Sky: Women of South Asian Diaspora (1993). The Women of South Asian Descent Collective (ed.). San Francisco: Aunt Lute Books.

Our Heritage (1934). London: The British and Foreign Bible Society.

Pallares, José Cárdenas (1986). *A Poor Man Called Jesus: Reflections on the Gospel of Mark*, trans. R. R. Barr. Maryknoll, NY: Orbis Books.

Pamuk, Orhan (2001). *My Name is Red*, trans. E. Goknar, trans. London: Faber and Faber.

Partridge, A. C. (1973). *English Biblical Translation.* London: Andre Deutsch.

Pattel-Gray, Anne (1995). 'Dreaming: An Aboriginal Interpretation of the Bible', in D. Smith-Christopher (ed.), *Text & Experience: Towards A Cultural Exegesis of the Bible.* Sheffield: Sheffield Academic Press, 247–59.

Phan, Peter C. (1999). 'Betwixt and Between: Doing Theology with Memory and Imagination', in P. C. Phan and J. Y. Lee (eds.), *Journeys at the Margin: Towards an Autobiographical Theology in American-Asian Perspective*. Collegeville, Minn.: The Liturgical Press, 113–33.

—— (2001). 'A Common Journey, Different Paths, the Same Destination: Method in Liberation Theologies', in E. S. Fernandez and F. F. Segovia (eds.), *A Dream Unfinished: Theological Reflections on America from the Margins*. Maryknoll, NY: Orbis Books, 129–51.

—— and Lee, Jung Young (1999). *Journeys at the Margins: Towards an Autobiographical Theology in American-Asian Perspective*. Collegeville: The Liturgical Press.

Phillips, Godfrey E. (1942). *The Old Testament in the World Church: With Special Reference to the Younger Churches*. London: Lutterworth Press.

Pieris, Aloysius (1988). *An Asian Theology of Liberation*. Edinburgh: T & T Clark.

Piper, Karen (1999). 'Post-Colonialism in the United States: Diversity or Hybridity', in D. L. Madsen (ed.), *Post-Colonial Literatures: Expanding the Canon*. London: Pluto Press, 14–28.

Pollard, Alfred W. (ed.) (1911). *Records of the English Bible: The Documents Relating to the Translation and Publication of the Bible in English, 1525–1611*. Oxford: Oxford University Press.

Prasad, G. J. V. (1999). 'Writing Translation: The Strange Case of the Indian English Novel', in S. Bassnett and H. Trivedi (eds.), *Post-Colonial Translation: Theory and Practice*. London: Routledge, 41–57.

Prickett, Stephen (1996). *Origins of Narrative: The Romantic Appropriation of the Bible*. Cambridge: Cambridge University Press.

Quayson, Ato (2000). *Postcolonialism: Theory, Practice or Process?* Cambridge: Polity Press.

Rafael, Vicente L. (1993). *Contracting Colonialism: Translation and Christian Conversion in Tagalog Society under Early Spanish Rule*. Durham, NC: Duke University Press.

Ramanujan, A. K. (1991). 'Three Hundred Rāmāyaṇas: Five Examples and Three Thoughts on Translation', in P. Richman (ed.), *Many Rāmāyaṇas:: The Diversity of a Narrative Tradition in South Asia*. Berkeley: University of California Press, 22–49.

Raychaudhuri, Tapan (1999). *Perceptions, Emotions, Sensibilities: Essays on India's Colonial and Post-Colonial Experiences*. New Delhi: Oxford University Press.

Renan, Ernest (1897). *Life of Jesus*, trans. W. G. Hutchison. London: The Walter Scott Publishing Company.

Rex, Richard (1993). *Henry VIII and the English Reformation*. London: Macmillan Press Ltd.

Richard, Pablo (1990). '1492: The Violence of God and the Future of Christianity'. *Concilium*, 6: 59–67.

—— (1995) 'Indigenous Biblical Hermeneutics: God's Revelation in Native Religions and the Bible (After 500 Years of Domination)', in D. Smith-Christopher (ed.), *Text & Experience: Towards a Cultural Exegesis of the Bible.* Sheffield: Sheffield Academic Press, 260–75.

Riley, John, and Wood, Briar (eds.) (1996). *Leave to Stay: Stories of Exile and Belonging.* London: Virago.

Ritchie, Ian D. (2000). 'The Nose Knows: Bodily Knowing in Isaiah 11:3'. *Journal for the Study of the New Testament*, 87: 59–70.

Roberts, John H. (2000). *Thinking Theologically in Aotearoa New Zealand.* Tui Gr Paihia: Colcom Press.

Rodney, Walter (1972). *How Europe Underdeveloped Africa.* Harare: Zimbabwe Publishing House.

Romero, Oscar (1982). 'The Political Dimension of Faith in Option for the Poor'. *Latinamerica Press*, 18 Mar.: 3–5.

Rustomji-Kerns, R. (ed.) (1995). *Living in America: Poetry and Fiction by South Asian American Writers.* Boulder, Colo.: Westview Press.

Sahgal, Nayantara (1992). 'The Schizophrenic Imagination', in A. Rutherford (ed.), *From Commonwealth to Post-Colonial.* Sydney: Dangroo Press, 30–6.

Sahi, Jyoti (1997). 'Reflections on the Image of the Prodigal Son'. *Indian Theological Studies*, 34/1–3: 169–84.

Said, Edward W. (1985). *Orientalism.* London: Penguin Books.

—— (1991). *The World, the Text, and the Critic.* London: Vintage.

—— (1993). *Culture and Imperialism.* London: Chatto & Windus.

Saint Augustine Letters (1981). W. Parsons (trans.) Washington: The Catholic University of America Press.

Sanders, E. P. (1993). *The Historical Figure of Jesus.* London: Allan Lane.

Sano, R. I. (1979) 'Ethnic Liberation Theology: Neo-Orthodoxy Reshaped or Replaced', in G. H. Anderson and T. F. Stransky (eds.), *Mission Trends 4: Liberation Theologies.* New York: Paulist Press, 258–64.

Satchidanandan, K. (1999). *Indian Literature: Positions and Propositions.* Delhi: Pencraft International.

Sathler, Josué A., and Nascimento, Amós (1997). 'Black Masks on White Faces: Liberation Theology and the Quest for Syncretism in the Brazilian Context', in D. Bastone, E. Mendieta, L. Ann Lorentzen, and D. N. Hopkins (eds.), *Liberation Theologies, Postmodernity, and the Americas.* London: Routledge, 95–122.

Scharper, Philip, and Scharper, Sally (1980). *The Gospel in Art by the Peasants of Solentiname.* Maryknoll, NY: Orbis Books.

Schmidt, Karl Ludwig (1964). 'Diaspora', in G. Friedrich (ed.) and G. W. Bromiley (trans.), *Theological Dictionary of the New Testament II*. Grand Rapids, Mich.: Wm. B. Eerdmans Publishing Company, 98–104.

—— and Schmidt, M. A. (1967). 'Paroikos', in G. Friedrich (ed.) and G. W. Bromiley (trans.), *Theological Dictionary of the New Testament V*, Grand Rapids, Mich.: Wm. B. Eerdmans Publishing Company, 841–53.

Schueller, Malini Johar (1998). *U.S. Orientalisms: Race, Nation, and Gender in Literature, 1790–1890*. Ann Arbor: University of Michigan Press.

Schwarz, Henry, and Ray, Sangeetha (eds.) (2000). *A Companion to Postcolonial Studies*. Oxford: Blackwell Publishers.

Segovia, Fernando F. (1995). 'Towards a Hermeneutics of the Diaspora: A Hermeneutics of Otherness and Engagement', in F. F. Segovia and M. A. Tolbert (eds.), *Reading from This Place*, i. *Social Location and Biblical Interpretation in the United States*. Minneapolis: Fortress Press, 57–73.

—— (ed.) (2000). *Interpreting Beyond Borders: The Bible and Postcolonialism 3*. Sheffield: Sheffield Academic Press.

Segundo, Juan Luis (1976). *The Liberation of Theology*, trans. J. Drury. Maryknoll, NY: Orbis Books.

Sharpe, Jenny (2000). 'Is the United States Postcolonial? Transnationalism, Immigration, and Race', in R. C. King (ed.), *Post-Colonial America*. Urbana: University of Illinois Press, 103–21.

Shepperson, George (1968). 'The African Abroad or the African Diaspora', in T. O. Ranger (ed.), *Emerging Themes of African History*. Nairobi: East Africa Publishing House, 152–76.

Slemon, Stephen (1994). 'The Scramble for Post-Colonialism', in C. Tiffin and A. Lawson (eds.), *De-Scribing Empire: Post-Colonialism and Textuality*. London: Routledge, 15–32.

Smith, Wilfred Cantwell (1993). *What is Scripture?: A Comparative Approach*. Minneapolis: Fortress Press.

Smith, Zadie (2000). *White Teeth*. London: Hamish Hamilton.

Soares-Prabhu, George (1991). 'Class in the Bible: The Biblical Poor a Social Class?', in R. S. Sugirtharajah (ed.), *Voices from the Margin: Interpreting the Bible in the Third World*. London: SPCK, 147–71.

—— (1994). 'The Indian Church Challenged by Pluralism and Dialogue'. *Sedos Bulletin*, 26/6–7: 183–93.

Special Correspondent of *The Times* (1955). 'The Geneva Bible', in *The Bible Today: Historical, Social, Literary Aspects of the Old and the New Testaments*. London: Eyre & Spottiswoode, 132–48.

Spivak, Gayatri Chakravorty (1993). 'Can the Subaltern Speak?' in P. Williams and

L. Chrisman (eds.), *Colonial Discourse and Postcolonial Theory*. New York: Harvester Wheatsheaf, 66–111.

Spurr, David (1993). *The Rhetoric of Empire: Colonial Discourse in Journalism, Travel Writing, and Imperial Administration*. Durham, NC: Duke University Press.

Steiner, George (1976). *After Babel: Aspects of Language and Translation*. Oxford: Oxford University Press.

Stout, Harry S. (1982). 'Word and Order in Colonial New England', in N. O. Hatch and M. A. Noll (eds.), *The Bible in America: Essays in Cultural History*. New York: Oxford University Press, 19–38.

Stratton, Jon (2000). 'The Beast of the Apocalypse: The Postcolonial Experience of the United States', in C. R. King (ed.), *Post-Colonial America*. Urbana: University of Illinois Press, 21–64.

Strauss, D. F. (1879). *A New Life of Jesus*. London: Williams and Norgate.

Sugirtharajah, R. S. (ed.) (1998). *The Postcolonial Bible*. Sheffield: Sheffield Academic Press.

—— (1999). *Asian Biblical Hermeneutics and Postcolonialism: Contesting the Interpretations*. Sheffield: Sheffield Academic Press.

—— (2001). *The Bible and the Third World: Precolonial, Colonial and Postcolonial Encounters*. Cambridge: Cambridge University Press.

Sunder Rajan, Rajeswari, and Park, You-me (2000). 'Post Colonial Feminism/Post Colonialism and Feminism', in H. Schwarz and S. Ray (eds.), *A Companion to Post Colonial Studies*. Oxford: Blackwell Publishers, 53–71.

Sykes, Norman (1955). 'The Authorized Version of 1611', in *The Bible Today: Historical, Social, and Literary Aspects of the Old and New Testaments*. London: Eyre & Spottiswoode, 140–8.

Takenaka, Masao, and O'Grady, Ron (1991). *The Bible through Asian Eyes*. Auckland: ACCA and Pace Publishing.

Tamez, Elsa (1993*a*). *The Amnesty of Grace: Justification by Faith from a Latin American Perspective*, trans. S. H. Ringe. Nashville: Abingdon Press.

—— (1993*b*). 'Reliving our Histories: Racial and Cultural Revelations of God', in D. Batstone (ed.), *New Visions for the Americas: Religious Engagement and Social Transformation*. Minneapolis: Fortress Press, 33–56.

—— (2000). *When the Horizons Close: Rereading Ecclesiastes*, trans. M. Wilde. Maryknoll, NY: Orbis Books.

Tan, Amy (1990). *The Joy Luck Club*. London: Minerva.

Thanzauva, and Hnuni, R. L. (1996). 'Ethnicity, Identity and Hermeneutics: An Indian Tribal Perspective', in M. G. Brett (ed.), *Ethnicity and the Bible*. Leiden: E. J. Brill, 343–57.

Thapar, Romila (1972). 'The Tradition of Historical Writing in Early India', *Indian Church History Review*, 6/1: 1–22.

—— (1992). *Interpreting Early India*. Delhi: Oxford University Press.

—— (2000). *Narratives and the Making of History: Two Lectures*. Delhi: Oxford University Press.

The Thirty-Fifth Report of the British and Foreign Bible Society (1939). London: Oliphant and Co.

Thomas, Alan (1999). 'Modernisation Versus the Environment? Shifting Objectives of Progress', in T. Skelton and T. Allen (eds.), *Culture and Global Change*. London: Routledge, 45–57.

Thomas, M. M. (1959). 'Indian Nationalism: A Christian Interpretation'. *Religion and Society*, 6/2: 4–26.

Thuesen, Peter J. (1999). *In Discordance with the Scriptures: American Protestant Battles over Translating the Bible*. New York: Oxford University Press.

Tillich, Paul (1954). *Love, Power and Justice: Ontological Analyses and Ethical Applications*. London: Oxford University Press.

Todorov, Tzvetan (1992). *The Conquest of America: The Question of the Other*, trans. R. Howard. New York: Harper Perennial.

Tutu, Desmond (1972). 'Some African Insights and the Old Testament'. *Journal of Theology for Southern Africa*, 1 (Dec.): 16–22.

Upadhyay, Brahmabandhab (1898). *The Writings of Brahmabandhab Upadhyay including a Resumé of his Life and Thought*, i. ed. J. Lipner and G. Gispert-Sauch. Bangalore: The United Theological College.

Vidales, R. (1980). 'Methodological Issues in Liberation Theology', in R. Gibellini (ed.), *Frontiers of Theology in Latin America*. London: SCM Press, 34–57.

Vincent, John J. (1991). 'An Inner City Bible', in Dan Cohn-Sherbok (ed.), *Using the Bible Today: Contemporary Interpretations of Scripture*. London: Bellew Publishing, 121–33.

Visram, Rozina. (1986). *Ayahs, Lascars, and Princes: Indians in Britain 1700–1947*. London: Pluto Press.

Viswanathan, Gauri (1989). *Masks of Conquest: Literary Study and British Rule in India*. New York: Columbia University Press.

Waetjen, Herman C. (1989). *A Reordering of Power: A Socio-Political Reading of Mark's Gospel*. Minneapolis: Fortress Press.

Walker, D. F. (1912). *The Call of the Dark Continent: A Study in Missionary Progress. Opportunity and Urgency*. London: The Wesleyan Missionary Society.

Walker, T. (1910). *The Acts of the Apostles*. London: SPCK.

—— (1911). *Missionary Ideals: Missionary Studies in the Acts of the Apostles*. (London: Church Missionary Society.

Walls, Andrew F. (1996). *The Missionary Movement in Christian History: Studies in the Transformation of Faith*. Maryknoll, NY: Orbis Books.

Warren, M. A. C. (1955). *Caesar: The Beloved Enemy: Three Studies in the Relation of Church and State*. The Reinecker Lectures at the Virginia Theological Seminary, Alexandria, Virginia, February 1955. London: SCM Press Ltd.

Watson, J. R. (1993). 'The Bible in English Literature: Review article'. *Expository Times*, 105/1: 15–16.

Watts, Michael (2001). 'Black Acts'. *New Left Review*, 9: 125–40.

West, Gerald O. (1999). 'Local is Lekker, but Ubuntu is Best: Indigenous Reading Resources from a South African Perspective', in R. S. Sugirtharajah (ed.), *Vernacular Hermeneutics* Sheffield: Sheffield Academic Press, 37–51.

—— and Dube, M. W. (2000). *The Bible in Africa: Transactions, Trajectories and Trends*. Leiden: Brill.

Westcott, Brooke Foss (1868). *A General View of the History of the English Bible*. London: Macmillan and Co.

White, Carolinne (ed.) (1990). *The Correspondence (394–419) between Jerome and Augustine of Hippo*. Studies in Bible and Early Christianity, vol. 23. Lewiston: The Edwin Mellen Press.

Wickham Legg, L. E. (1932). 'The Coronation Service', in W. K. L. Clarke and Charles Harris (eds.), *Liturgy and Worship: A Companion to the Prayer Book*. London: SPCK, 690–702.

Wilde, Margaret D. (1989). 'Faith and Endurance in Eastern Nicaragua'. *Christian Century*, 1/Nov.: 973–4.

Wilson, A. N. (1998). *The Gospel according to Matthew with an Introduction*. Edinburgh: Canongate Books.

Xaxa, Virginius (1999). 'Tribes as Indigenous People of India'. *Economic and Political Weekly*, 18/Dec.: 3589–95.

Young, Robert J. C. (2001). *Postcolonialism: An Historical Introduction*. Oxford: Blackwell Publishers.

INDEX OF BIBLICAL REFERENCES

Acts   153n
2:44, 143
4:12, 98
4:42, 143
5:4, 143
9:32–12:24, 98
11:20, 168
12:25–16:5, 98
13:22, 138
16:6–19, 98
19:21–28:31, 98
21:39, 76

Amos   78
5:12, 167

Colossians
3:17, 52
3:18–4:1, 82

1 Corinthians   153n
11:17–22, 64
13:5, 47
15:11, 164

2 Corinthians   153n
2:17, 166

Daniel   76
3:25, 57
11:23, 88

Deuteronomy
15:17, 170

Ecclesiastes   153n
2:4–8, 80
3:12, 81
4:1–3, 81
4:5, 73n
5:12, 81
10:20, 81
10:19, 81

Ecclesiasticus
34:18–22, 46

Ephesians
5:21–6:9, 82

Esther   81, 153n

Ezekiel
22:15, 181

Exodus   153, 153n
1:19, 143
14:13, 143
14:14, 143
21:1–11, 101, 119
22:1, 90

Genesis   153, 153n
2:15–3:13, 68
8:2, 167
13:15, 170
28:14, 1
39–41, 188
47, 188
47:21–2, 101

Hebrews
13:14, 182

Isaiah   171
7:1, 165
11:3, 167
35: 8, 181
40:1, 136
51: 12–15, 152
53:7, 166
55:11, 138
61:1, 169
65:3, 167

James   140, 153, 182
2:1–13, 64
5:1–6, 64

Jeremiah
23:24, 181
52:12–14, 181

Job   77, 153, 153n
28: 13, 166
34:4, 68

John
1:47, 99
4:12, 99
4:46–54, 99
9:1–39, 99
13, 99
13:5, 47
13:36, 99
14, 99
14:6, 98,99
14:8, 99
17:1, 57
19:38, 99
20:30, 98

1John   140

Joshua
24: 26, 135

Jonah
4:6, 155, 178n

Jubilees
21: 13–14, 167

Jude   140

1Kings
1–2, 80
2:46, 80

2Kings
15:29, 181
25:21, 181

Leviticus
19–25, 64
26:31, 167

Luke
3:13, 89
3:13–14, 89
7:1–10, 59
7:25, 88
9:8, 89
9:17, 132
10:25–37, 82
10:29–37, 83
10:38–42, 96
11:17, 88
12:33–4, 88
12:58–9, 89
13:32, 90
13:34, 91
14:31, 88
16:13, 88
16:19–31, 107
18:7–8, 171
19:1–9, 90
19:8, 89
20:20–6, 89
20:22, 89
22:24–7, 87
23:2, 89

Mark
3: 23–5, 88
5:1–20, 92
7:24–30, 59
9:1, 164
9:7, 73n
10: 42–5, 87
11:12–22, 120
11:22–4, 120
12:13–17, 89
12:14, 91
12: 28–34, 82
12:28, 83
12:41–4, 120
12:44, 120
15: 1–32, 91

Matthew
2:16, 96
3:4, 88
5:3, 169
5:5, 169
5:13, 166
5:44, 193
6: 19–21, 88
7:12, 73n
11:8, 88
11:29, 47
12:25, 88
13:12, 107
15:22, 169
16:18, 164
17:15, 169
20:20–8, 87
22:15–22, 89
22:34–40, 82
22:36, 83
22:40, 47
26:53, 92

Numbers
5:5–7, 90
27:1–11, 84
27:7–8, 84
36, 84

1Peter   140, 183
2:11, 182
2:14, 27

2Peter   140
1:17, 55

Philemon   53

Philippians
3:20, 182

Proverbs
1:1, 73n
18: 2, 77
31: 8–9, 115

Psalms   50, 144, 153n, 171
2:1–3, 73n
19: 1–4, 59
23, 135
27:13, 166
34:19, 143
52: 5, 166
137:1–4, 181

Revelation   153,
153n

Romans   153n
1:1–3:20, 59
1:17, 171
1:18–32, 49
4:17, 59
7:18, 59
8:37, 110
8:38–9, 110
12, 59
13:1, 73

Ruth   153n, 171

1Samuel   153n
1:22, 170

2Samuel   153n
8:17, 80
9–20, 80
20:23–6, 80
20:25, 80

Song of Solomon   153

1Thessalonians
3: 12, 55

1Timothy
2:1, 138
2:5, 98

Titus
3:1–3, 73n

INDEX OF NAMES AND SUBJECTS

Abhishiktananda (Swami) 77

Achebe, Chinua 18

Africa Answers Back 18

African-American hermeneutics 185

African biblical hermeneutics 58

Ahmed Khan, Syed 30, 53, 54
  use of the Bible 54–55

Allen, Ward 178n

Althaus-Reid, Marcella 119

Anderson, Christopher 127, 146

Apess, William 53

Appadurai, Arjun 31

Appasamy, A. J. 62

Appasamy Pillai A. S. 56–7, 61–2
  and visual hermeneutics 58

Aquinas, Thomas 101

Araeen, Rasheed 202

Arasanayagam, Jean 11

Arias, Esther 65, 72n

Arias, Mortimer 65, 72n

Armstrong, Karen 145

Arnold, Matthew 154n

Arul Raja, M. 72n

Asad, Talal 177, 178

Ashcroft, Bill 23, 33, 40n, 41n, 184

Asylum seekers 194, 196–7

Ateek, Naim S. 170

Augustine 48, 155, 164–5

Austen, Jane 21, 39

Avolos, Hector 41n

Avotri, Solomon K. 92

Baikie, James 136–8, 140, 143

Baird, Mary 92

Balch, David L. 82

Banda, Hastings 68

Banerjea, K. M. 56

Barclay, William 169–70

Barth, Karl 116

Bates, Ernest Sutherland 154n

Bateson, Bernard 1

Bauman, Zygmunt 31

Baumann, Martin 180

Beverley, John 201

Bhabha, Homi 13, 16, 22, 152, 195–6

Bhagavadgita, the 151, 192–3

Bible, the
  African presence of 58–9
  appropriation by women 68
  as book of the empire 5
  in colonies 146–7, 149
  as a cultural weapon 53, 63
  dislocation of 204
  as an Eastern book 50
  as English book 127–8
  English vernacular 134, 148
  as Englishman's book 19–20, 152–3
  French 136
  German 136
  as an icon 148, 189
  as national epic of the English 128, 166
  as an oriental book 50
  rewriting of 206
  Tamil versions 162
  in the Valladolid debate 46; see also King James Version

biblical studies 25–6, 43, 74

Bishops' Bible 132

Boff, Clodovis 78, 111

Boff, Leonardo 116

Bono 144, 153n

Bowden, John 178n

Bray, Gerald 121, 131, 135, 141

Bright, Martin 178n

British and Foreign Bible Society 51, 57, 128, 145, 149–50, 157–9

Bruce, F. F. 132, 140–2, 154n

burakumin 23, 68, 72n, 105, 121

Byung Mu, Ahn 67

Cabral, Amilcar 16

Cadorette, Curt 123n

Caesar the Beloved Enemy 27

Calmmette, Jean 56

Cannon, Garland 151

Canton, William 152

Cantwell Smith, Wilfred 74

Cardenal, Ernesto 73n, 102n, 123n

Carroll, Robert 130, 131, 134

Causes of the Indian Revolt 53

Césaire, Aimé 16

Chandran, J. R. 63–4, 168

Chari, V. K. 40n, 77

Chatterji, Margaret 199n

Chatterji, Partha 7n

Chatterji, Saral 64

Cheung, King-Kok 198n

Childs, Peter 40n

Chingota, F. L. 68–9, 73n

Chow, Rey 194

Christian, Barbara 14

Church Missionary Society (CMS) 49, 158–9

Churchill, Winston 36

Clévenot, Michel 80

Clutton-Brock, A. 128

Cohen, Jeffrey Jerome 2

Cohen, Robin 180

Colenso, John W. 49–52, 71n

Colley, Linda 38

colonialism 24, 28, 44
  British 130
  different forms of 3
  and English theology
    26–28
  European 4, 12
  Spanish 45
Conrad, Joseph 21, 39
Coomaraswamy, Ananda
  4, 16, 17, 18, 43
Cooppan, Vilashini 16
Cook, Albert S. 128
Cook, Scott B. 44
Coote, Robert T. 28
Counter-reformation 25, 74
Coverdale, Miles 132, 137–8,
  154n
Cromwell, Thomas 131, 138

Daiches, David 135–6, 154n
Dalai Lama 153n
Dalits 23, 72n, 100, 105, 119,
  121
  definition of 72n
Daniell, David 133
Davies, Mike 36, 42n
de Bernières, Louis 153n
Deissmann A. 50
de Rhodes, Alexandre 56
Derrett, J. 92–3
Derrida, Jacques 21
Devasahayam, V. 72n
Dhmmapada, the
diaspora
  Africa 23
  and biblical
    interpretation 185–9
  definitions of 180–183
  postcolonial usage 184
  and postcolonialism 183
diasporic hermeneutics
  190, 197
Dixon, W. Macneile 136,
  165–6
Dodd, C. H. 164
Donaldson, Laura 42n, 86,
  118
Drury, John 96
Dube, Musa W. 41n, 71n,
  102n
Dubois, Abbé 162–3

Du Bois, W. E. B. 16

Eagleton, Terry 175, 178n,
  200, 207n
Eco, Umberto 206
Ecumenical Association of
  Third World
  Theologians
  (EATWOT) 35
Elliott, John H. 182–3
Elliott-Binns, L. E. 76
Ellsberg, Robert 193
Emecheta, Buchi 185
empire 24, 36
  American 42n
  British 37, 97
  Iberian 44
  Roman 24, 86, 89, 93, 97
Empire Writes Back 23, 40n
Enlightenment 11, 25, 44,
  70, 101, 114, 157, 167
  as missionizing project 31
Equiano, Olaudah 53

Fabella, Virginia 3
Fanon, Frantz 16–18, 38,
  41n, 93–4, 206
feminism 28
  and postcolonialism
    28–30
Fernandez, Eleazar 123n,
  186–7
Filipino-Americans 186
Forster, E. M. 39
Foucault, Michel 21
Francis, Dayanandan 162
Francis, M. 61–2, 78
Frazer, James George 154n
Freyne, Sean 79, 88, 91,
  102n

Gandhi, Leela 40n
Gandhi, M. K. 37, 129, 192
  and hermeneutics
    192–4
Geneva Bible 133–4, 138–9
  as the Bible of the
    people 139
  its innovations 139–140
  marginal comments
    142–3

globalization 30
  élite 32
  grassroots 32
Gnanavaram, M. 72n
Goto, Hiromi 179
Gracía-Treto, Francisco
  187–8
Griffiths, Gareth 23, 33,
  40n, 41n, 185
Great Bible, the 132, 138,
  141, 154n
Greaves, Richard 142
Green, R. J. 128, 136
Grossman, David 153n
Guha, Ranajit 22
Gutiérrez Gustavo 66,
  71n, 104
  on Job 108–10

Hall, Stuart 5, 79
Hammond, Gerald 143
Hanke, Lewis 71n
Hargreaves, Cecil 169
Harrison, Robert C. 102n
Hau'ofa, Epeli 41n
Hawley, Susan 73n
hegemonic code 79–81
Henson, Herbert Hensley
  128, 133
hermeneutical circle 106
hermeneutics:
  visual 58, 96
hermeneutics of suspicion
  106
Hill, Christopher 142
Hipsley, H. 146
historical-critical method
  67, 76, 96, 114, 193
Hnuni, R. L. 72n
Hoare, H. W. 129–30, 137
Hogg, Richey 172
Horsley, Richard A. 91
Hsu, R. L. 41n
Huber, Friedrich 76–7
Huxley, Thomas 128, 166
hybridity 22–3, 191–2, 194
  as in-between space 22,
    175

imperialism 24, 74
  European 30

Interesting Narrative 53
Isasi-Díaz, Ada María 187,
198n

James, C. L. R. 16, 18, 40n
James, P. D. 144, 153n
Jasper, David 204
Jerome 155–6, 178n
Jeremias, Joachim 106–7
Jones, William 151

Kachru, Braj B. 176
Kanganayakam, Chelva
198n
Kaplan, Amy 42n
Kapoor, Kapil 14, 77
Kapuściński, Ryszard 179
Khan, Adib 185
Kilgour, R. 48
King, Bruce 41n
King, C. Richard 36, 42n
King James Version
(Authorized Version)
53, 128–9, 131, 141, 164,
165, 173
and colonization 146
as literary phenomenon
147–8; see also English
Bible
Kinukawa, Hisako 78
Klein, Naomi 32
Koonthanam, George 78
Kreider, Alan 183
Kuan, Jeffrey Kah-jin 187
Kureishi, Hanif 185, 190
Kuribayashi, Teru 72n

Lacan, Jacques 21
Lahiri, Jhumpa 185
Las Casas, Bartolomé de
44–5, 51
richness of the Bible 48
role of the Bible 45, 47
Lawton, David 130
Lee, Chang-Rae 185
Lee, Yung Yong 186, 198n
Leech, Kenneth 41n
Leñero, Vicente 41n
Lessing, Doris 154n
Levi, Peter 128, 134, 139
liberation 39, 65–6

liberation hermeneutics
67, 71, 103–4, 112–13
dependence on
modernism and
postmodernism 113
employment of critical
tools 114
hallmarks of 104–6
and poor 120–1
and postcolonialism
117–20
reading of Exodus 118
and theology of
religions 115–16
liberation theology 104–5
reconstruction of Jesus
113
Long, James 49–52
López, Eleazar 115
Loomba, Ania 40n
Losada, Angel 71n
Lovett, R. 173

McLeod, John 15, 21, 40n,
41n
Madsen, Deborah 34–5
Manikkam, T. 77
marginality 197
Marti, José 16
Martin, Clarice 98
Marx, Karl 41n, 116
Masoga, M. A. 92
Matthew's Bible 154
Mbatha, Azariah 100
Mehrez, Samia 174–6
Memmi, Albert 11, 16
Metzger, Bruce M. 168, 172
Micklem, Nathaniel 87
migrancy 197
Miguez-Bonino, José 106–7
Mill, W. H. 56
Minjung 66–7
missionaries 6, 145, 149, 191,
193
translators 157–61
Mongia, Padmini 40n
Mosala, Itumeleng 103
Morrison, Blake 145
Moulton, H. G 154n
Moxnes, Halvor 79
Mozley, J. F. 130

Mukherjee, Bharati 185
Mukherjee, Sujit 166
Mwikisa, P. W. 41n

Nagano, Paul 186
Naipaul, V. S. 18, 22, 185
Nakashima Brock, Rita 198n
Narayan, R. K. 175
Nascimento, Amós 116
Native Americans 53, 118
negotiated code 79, 82–3
Neill, Stephen 45
Nelson, Cecil L. 176
neo-colonialism 3, 24–5, 36
New Revised Standard
Version (NRSV) 6
imperialistic
renditions 169–171
Ngũgĩ wa Thiong'o 17–18,
41n
Njoroge, N. J. 157
Nkrumah, Kwame 24–5, 37
Norton, David 133
Nyabongo, Akiki 4, 18–21

Oddie, Geoffrey 51
O'Grady, Ron 102n
Ondaatje, Michael 179
Orientalism 15, 21
orientalism 206
marks of 75–9
orientalists 56, 151

Pallares, José Cárdenas 74,
120–1, 202
Pamuk, Orhan 206
Park, You-me 30
Partridge, A. C. 132, 135
patriarchy 29
Pattel-Gray, Anne 72n
peasants of Solentiname
96, 105
Pease, E. Donald 42n
Phan, Peter 60–1, 123n,
198n
Phillips, Caryl 185
Phillips, Godfrey 76
Pieris, Aloysius 116, 120
Piper, Karen 34, 42n
Pollard, Alfred 131–2,
139–40, 142

poor, the   23, 46, 65–6, 71,
    81, 83, 88–9, 103, 106–8,
    110, 169
    romanticization of   120
postcolonial
    meaning of   2
    status of United States of
        America   4, 33–6
postcolonial biblical
    criticism   25, 71, 95, 97,
        99, 101, 206
postcolonial critic   201
postcolonial criticism
    39–40, 75, 85
    and biblical studies   25
postcolonialism
    arrival of   15
    as creative practice   11
    and feminism   28
    as methodological
        category   11–12
    as male-centred   29
    and minority discourse
        15
    and postmodernism   12,
        13, 117
    as a style of enquiry
        13–14
postmodernism   1, 71, 113,
    194
Prasad, G. J. V.   175
Prickett, Stephen   127, 130–1,
    134, 166
professional code   79, 81–82
protest/oppositional code
    79, 84–5

Quayson, Ato   40n

Rafael, Vicente L.   156
Ramanujan, A. K.   174
Ramayana, the   173–4
Ray, Sangeetha   40n
Raychaudhuri, Tapan   37
readings:
    dissentient   67–70
    dissident   44–52
    heritagist   55–62
    instinctual   203
    institutional   203
    liberationist   65–7

Maori   72n
    nationalistic   63–4
    resistant   52–5
Reformation   25, 74
refugees   197
Renan, Ernest   75–6
Rendell, Ruth   153n
'reverse Exodus'   118
Rex, Richard   148–9
Ricci, Matteo   56
Richard, Pablo   114–17
Rig Veda, the   56
Riley, John   198n
Ritchie, Ian D.   167, 178n
Roberts, John H.   72n
Rodney, Walter   41n
Rogers, John   137, 154n
Romero, Oscar   65–6
Rose, Steve   153n
Ross, Kenneth R.   73n
Rustomji-Kerns, Roshni
    198n

Sahgal, Nayantara   38
Sahi, Jyoti   60
Said, Edward E.   14–6, 21, 24,
    26, 75, 196, 198
Sanders, E. P.   79
Sandinistas   69
Sano, R. I.   187
sarvadharmasambhva   205
Satchidanandan, K.   40n
    152–3
Sathler, Josué   116
satyagraha   192–3
Scharper, Philip   73n,
    102n, 123n
Scharper, Sally   73n,
    102n, 123n
Schmidt, Karl Ludwig
    181–2
Schmidt, M. A.   182
Schueller, Malini Johar
    33–4
Schwarz, Henry   40n
Segovia, Fernando F.
    102n, 123n, 185–6,
    198n
Segundo, Juan Luis   106
Self, Will   153n
Selwyn, Edward   27

Sepúlveda, Juan Ginés
    45–8
Shakespeare, William
    19, 128, 130, 147, 148, 153
Shalev, Meir   153n
Sharpe, Jenny   15, 35–6
Shepperson, George   183–4
Sivasubramaniyan, A.   178n
Slemon, Stephen   12
Smith, Zadie   155
Soares-Prabhu, George   83,
    205
Society for the Propagation of
    the Gospel (SPG)   49
Somoza, Anastasio   69–70,
    96–7, 105
Soyinka, Wole   18
Spivak, Gayatri
    Chakravorty   16, 22
Spurr, David   151
Steiner, George   129, 155
Stout, Harry S.   142
Stratton, Jon   42n
Strauss, David Frierich   78
Sugirtharajah, R. S.   3, 71n,
    83, 86, 102n, 154n
Sunder Rajan, Rajeswari   30
Sykes, Norman   173

Takenaka, Masao   102n
Tamez, Elsa   59, 62, 102n,
    104, 107, 202
    on Paul   110–12,
Tan, Amy   185, 189
Thanzauva   72n
Thapar Romila   78
Theology of Struggle   66
Third World   3, 14, 23, 25,
    29, 35, 65, 71, 78, 122, 194,
    197, 201
    definition of   3
    feminist hermeneutics
        72n
    feminist scholars   29, 41n
    globalization   32,
    and theorizing   14
Thomas, Alan   42n
Thomas, M. M.   41n
Thuesen, Peter J.   165, 172
Tiffin, Helen   23, 33, 40n,
    41n, 184

Tillich, Paul   28, 34, 42n
Todorov, Tzvetan   37, 41n
Tolbert, Mary Ann   198n
Tolstoy, Leo   193
translation
   as a colonial project   156,
      Indian   166
   and missionaries   160–1
   postcolonial   171–2, 177
   role of colonialists   157
Trevelyan, C. E.   159–160
Tribals   68, 70
   discussion on the term
      72n
Trollope, Joanna   153n
Tutu, Desmond   58
Tyndale, William   131–3, 137,
   164

Upadhyay,
   Brahmabhandhav   195
Upanishads, the   77, 153, 192,
   207

Vadales, Raul   114
VanZanten Gallagher,
   Susan   41n
Vassanji, M. G.   185
Vedas, the   57
'vernacular cosmopolitan'
   195
vernacular hermeneutics
   190
'Victorian Holocaust'   36
Vincent, John   121
Viswanathan, Gauri   147–8,
   154n

Waetjen, Herman C.   93
Walker, D. F.   150
Walker, T.   76, 97–8
Walls, Andrew F.   71n
Warren, M. A. C.   26–28, 37
Warrior, Robert Allen
   118
Watson, R. J.   144
Weldon, Fay   153n

West, Gerald O.   41n, 71n,
   100
Westcott, Brooke Foss
   137–8, 173
White, Carolinne   155–6,
   164–5
Whittingham, William
   139–40
Wickham Legg, L. E.   138
Wilde, Margaret D.   73n
Williams, Patrick   40n
Wilson, A. N.   145
Wood, Briar   198n
'writing back'   23
Wycliffe, John   129, 134

Xaxa, Virginus   72n

Young, Robert J. C.   40n

Zephaniah, Benjamin   185
Zulus   49, 51
   and their culture   100